Global Software and IT

Global Software and IT
A Guide to Distributed Development, Projects, and Outsourcing

Christof Ebert

A John Wiley & Sons, Inc., Publication

Published by John Wiley & Sons, Inc., Hoboken, New Jersey.
Published simultaneously in Canada.

For general information on our other products and services or for technical support, please contact our Customer Care Department within the United States at (800) 762-2974, outside the United States at (317) 572-3993 or fax (317) 572-4002.

Wiley also publishes its books in a variety of electronic formats. Some content that appears in print may not be available in electronic formats. For more information about Wiley products, visit our web site at www.wiley.com.

Library of Congress Cataloging-in-Publication Data:
ISBN: 9780470636190

oBook ISBN: 9781118135105
ePDF ISBN: 9781118135075
ePub ISBN: 9781118135099
eMobi ISBN: 9781118135082

10 9 8 7 6 5 4 3 2 1

Contents

Part V Advancing Your Own Business

Appendices

Foreword

Ongoing economic challenges are affecting and impacting business and society in nearly every industry and geographical region. Taking decisive action to reprioritize the way we are doing business is a key focus for companies. Around the world, companies are taking the necessary measures that will enable us to adjust to today's reality and to future challenges. In adjusting and refocusing we need to stay on course to ensure that short-term challenges won't distract us from planning for longer-term opportunities to achieve sustainable growth. Information technology is part of the solution if handled in a truly global scale.

With decades of experience in making companies globally successful, I believe that we are faced with a unique opportunity to nurture global economic prosperity. Global software engineering, IT outsourcing, and rightshoring are all pieces toward readjusting the software and IT business. The prestigious journal *Harvard Business Manager* recently stated that outsourcing with global IT services and software development ranks as one of the top business ideas of the past 100 years. This certainly makes sense, because software and IT industries are today truly global. Be it offshoring or outsourcing, component or service integration, managing global software engineering has rapidly become a key competence for successful engineers and managers. The diversity of suppliers, cultures, and products requires dedicated techniques, tools, and practices to overcome challenges.

This book, *Global Software and IT*, written by my colleague and friend Christof Ebert, summarizes experiences and provides guidance, processes, and approaches for successfully handling global software development and outsourcing. It offers tons of practical hints and concrete explanations of "how to do it better." Readers will get an opportunity to explore the current state of practice in this area as well as new thoughts and trends that will shape the future.

Global Software and IT provides a framework for mastering global software and IT, and also summarizes experiences from companies around the globe. The book is very readable and provides a wealth of knowledge for both practitioners and researchers. With its many practical insights, this book will be a useful desktop reference for industry practitioners and managers within the software engineering and IT communities.

Global IT and software development, service, and provisioning imply a great organizational and industrial shift in structure. Let's rise to the challenge and, in doing so, raise the quality of life and our economic prosperity for generations to come. Now is the time to grow and improve global software and IT and thus empower all of the world's citizens to participate in the human network.

New York   MICHAEL CORBETT
July 2011

About the Author

Christof Ebert is managing director at Vector Consulting Services. A trusted advisor for companies around the world, he supports clients to improve product development and product strategy and to manage organizational changes. Dr. Ebert sits on a number of advisory and industry bodies. Over the years he has set up several offshoring sites, performed due diligence assessments, and supported numerous companies in improving their global software engineering and IT outsourcing programs. He serves on the executive board of the IEEE International Conference on Global Software Engineering (www.ICGSE.org) series and teaches at the University of Stuttgart.

He can be contacted at christof.ebert@ vector.com.

Introduction

Things do not change; we change.
—*Henry David Thoreau*

Software and IT have gone global at a fast pace. Be it IT outsourcing, global software engineering, or business process outsourcing, growth rates are more than 20% per year [IAOP09, USA07]. While the cost advantage and skill pool of global development and outsourcing may appear to be advantageous, they bear a set of risks that come on top of the regular project risks. Not knowing these risks and not mitigating against them means that your project may soon belong to the growing share of failed global endeavors.

Global Software and IT provides guidance and examples of experiences, as well as processes and approache,s to successfully handle global software development and outsourcing. It offers many practical hints and concrete explanations of "how to do it better."

Global Software and IT addresses practitioners, namely:

- Developers and engineers workingin global development projects to make their collaborations more effective, through
  - captive sourcing within a company
  - provision of outsourcing services to clients, or
  - engaging in open source development.
- Software and IT managers on all levels from the individual working in a distributed team to the senior manager who decides where to open a new site and what it means to be successful.
- Project managers and project teams who want to succeed with distributed activities.
- Product managers and R&D managers taking advantage of globalization.
- Procurement teams interested in making sourcing of development partners more effective.
- Suppliers trying to understand the practices and needs that drive their clients.

Global Software and IT: A Guide to Distributed Development, Projects, and Outsourcing,
First Edition. Christof Ebert.
© 2012 the Institute of Electrical and Electronics Engineers, Inc. Published 2012 by
John Wiley & Sons, Inc.

Global Software and IT provides a framework for global development, covering topics such as management of people in distributed sites, management of projects across multiple locations, mitigation of the risks of offshoring, processes for global development, practical outsourcing guidelines, and use of collaboration and communication to achieve goals. It summarizes experiences from companies of different sizes and organizational layouts as well as information about industries around the globe. This book shares the best practices from various professional projects, including ones that involve locations in different continents and a variety of cultures. Perhaps most relevant, the book explains the means and strategies needed to survive in a globally dispersed work environment.

This book helps each reader to improve his global software activities by providing examples of:

- Hands-on experiences, including opportunities, lessons learned, and risks
- Management education and training in companies
- Self-learning for students in business and software
- Hands-on practical insights for industry practitioners and managers, and
- A course layout for university or professional training.

When writing the book we decided for readability purposes to only use the male form of pronouns. We are well aware that software and especially global projects is one of the few engineering fields where we find today almost the same number of women as men. We thank you for your understanding.

Global Software and IT provides practitioners with practical guidance as well as examples of experiences from companies and projects from across the globe and different application domains. Hands-on examples are shown in shaded boxes. Practical guidelines and take-away tips are also prominently displayed. Some topics, such as cultural differences, play a role in all global projects, while others depend on the size and organizational styles of individual companies and projects. We provide an explanation for why something is done in a certain way as well as which risk is addressed by which method. We recommend "translating" these concepts to your own environment, rather than taking a specific solution as the one and only possible.

I want to thank IEEE and John Wiley & Sons for supporting this book and asking me to write this second edition. A book about such a quickly evolving topic would be impossible to write without the continuous feedback of my colleagues and clients. Special thanks go to Alberto Avritzer, Suttamally Bala, Werner Burger, Daniela Damian, Filippo Lanubile, Audris Mockus, Daniel Paulish, S. Sadagopan, Bikram Sengupta, Andree Zahir, and everyone else who has for provided insight from their own in global software and IT experiences. Additionally, Filippo Lanubile, Rafael Prikladnicki, and Aurora Vizcaino deserve thanks for contributing to tools topics. Finally, I would like to thank Dave Gustafson and Dan Paulish for being good and long-time companions while going global.

The IEEE conference series ICGSE (International Conference on Global Software Engineering) has helped to build a strong research and industry community of smart people who drive knowledge and competence evolution in this quickly growing field. I am honored to serve on its executive committee and look forward to the evolution of this discipline.

Global software and IT is not for free. Often people argue that we are going global because of cheaper labor rates. But software and IT business based solely on cost is almost certainly doomed to fail. Successful global software businesses, on the other hand, are driven by global innovation, talent, and markets. Salaries adjust over time; innovation keeps moving.

Global software and IT necessitates a shift in culture. This cultural adjustment is often underestimated, but in order to be successful we need to change. We need to reinvent business models and working paradigms, we need to learn new formats of collaboration and communication. This book will show what it means and how to succeed.

There are two challenges with going global: to get started and to keep going. With the many rewards from your business combined with guidance from this book, you will translate risks to chances and opportunities, which is what they should be. I wish you, the reader of this book, the best of success in this endeavor!

Berlin   CHRISTOF EBERT
August 2011

Part I
Strategy

Chapter 1

Different Business Models

Summary: Globalized software development and various formats of information technology outsourcing (ITO) are as natural for the software and IT business as project management or requirement engineering. Going global with software and IT is a great way to distribute work effectively as well as appropriately assign tasks to employees who are most qualified for the task at hand. To attain the greatest success in the fields of software and IT we must take advantage of opportunities for continuous collaboration around the globe. This chapter looks at different business models in software and IT.

The annual volume of global IT outsourcing and software development in 2010 was approximately $100 billion. Considering the field's growth rate of 5 to 10 percent per year, the industry is clearly rife with portential [BCG09, McKinsey08]. When one examines the facts about the software business, it becomes readily evident that it has become a truly global venture. Examples are manifold:

- Offshoring is growing at double-digit rates across Europe and the United States throughout many different industries and all major business functions.
- Offshoring is no longer just about cost reduction, low-end manufacturing, IT, and back office work; it has become a major driver for entire business processes.
- 50% annual growth in the offshoring of core innovation activities (i.e., R&D, product design, engineering).

As early as 1962, EDS began offering IT on spare capacity, also known as time-shared computing as an external service (today this is called application service provisioning). In 1976 EDS started deploying global IT services, such as financial accounting. Entrepreneurs in India realized early on that this form of business could help the country leapfrog into current technologies, therefore becoming a major business partner to the Western world. Indian institutes of technology were formed in the 1960s. They featured strong computer science curricula which laid the

Global Software and IT: A Guide to Distributed Development, Projects, and Outsourcing, First Edition. Christof Ebert.

foundtions for India's current success in the IT domain. The first e-mail sent from China to a foreign country was on September 20, 1987 to the University of Karlsruhe. The text was short, yet powerful: "Across the Great Wall we can reach every corner in the world." It was the vision of an increasingly connected world in which all citizens and enterprises would have the ability to do business with one another. The world was getting smaller. The notion of "across the wall" is about bridging gaps. It demonstrates that being connected does not necessarily mean sharing the same values with one another, nor does it make countries and continents borderless and integrated.

Today, practically all new business plans contain offshoring as a key element for containing cost and creating flexibility in order to cope with changing demands on skills and numbers of engineers. Different business models are applied in the global context.

First, there is a distinction made between outsourcing and offshoring:

- **Offshoring**—is a business activity beyond sales and marketing which takes place outside the home country of an enterprise. Enterprises typically either have local branches in low-cost countries or they ask specialized companies abroad to perform a service for them.—Offshoring performed within the company is called captive offshoring.

- **Outsourcing**—is a business's lasting and result-oriented relationship with a supplier who executes business activities for an enterprise which were traditionally executed inside the enterprise. Outsourcing is site-independent. The supplier can reside in direct neighborhood of the enterprise or offshore.

Offshoring and outsourcing are two dimensions in the scope of globalized software development and IT. They do not depend on each other and can be implemented individually.

For sourcing, a distinction is made based on the type of service being sourced from an external supplier:

- **Business Process Outsourcing (BPO)**—where a business process (or business function) is contracted to a third-party service provider.

- **Information Technology Outsourcing (ITO)**—where software and It related services are outsourced to a third-party service provider. ITO is a form of Business Process Outsourcing (BPO) for software and information technology activities.

- **Application service provisioning (ASP)**—where computer-based services are sourced from a third-party service provider. ASP is a form of Information Technology Outsourcing (ITO) for operationally provisioning software and IT functionality.

- **Software sourcing**—where software components are sourced from an external supplier. Sourcing is a business process that summarizes all procurement practices. It includes finding, evaluating, contractually engaging, and managing suppliers of goods and services.

- **Open source**—where, considering restrictions such as IPR, software is sourced from a supplier (often unknown) and a community of developers in different parts of the world. Global software and IT do not depend on having legal entities as suppliers. The open source movement has shown that big global software projects can also be conducted by enthusiastic individuals.

The time and relationship perspective of the outsourcing demands a third distinction:

- **Tactical Outsourcing**—is a form of outsourcing with short-term ("just in time") focus. Suppliers are selected on a case-by-case basis for activities within projects. Those suppliers who are best suitable for the concrete task at hand are selected . Tactical outsourcing, which is similar to subcontract management, is used to improve operational efficiency.

- **Strategic outsourcing**— is a form of outsourcing with long-term and sustainable focus. A business process is moved to an external supplier in order to focus resources on the core business. Within engineering projects this can be a process (e.g., maintenance, test) or a system (e.g., legacy product). Strategic outsourcing changes the entire value chain.

Outsourcing and offshoring allow more flexibility in managing operational expenses because resources are allocated to places and regions that are most suited to flexible needs and ever-changing business models. Figure 1.1 summarizes the reasons for outsourcing and offshoring [Ebert07a, BCG09, IAOP09, IDC07, Hussey08, Rivard08][1].

Figure 1.2 shows the penetration of enterprises with different types of global development and IT activities [IAOP09, Aspray06]. The horizontal axis provides the share of

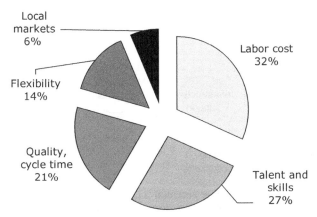

Figure 1.1   Reasons for outsourcing and offshoring.

---

[1] There are many such studies elaborating on reasons for global development. Exact percentages are not relevant here. It is the rank order that is important. Further studies are mentioned in the ACM Job Migration report [Aspray06].

offshoring (as a proxy for the degree of global software engineering and IT in an enterprise for an activity) and the vertical axis provides a view on the penetration of enterprises for a specific activity. For instance, maintenance projects already penetrate more than half of all software activities worldwide (position on vertical axis) and it is typically done in an offshore environment rather than a single place in a highly paid country (right position on horizontal axis). Some activities, such as new applications and OEM product development, are clearly not yet where they could be.

The share of offshoring or globalization depends on the underlying IT needs and on what software is being developed. While for mere IT applications or internet services global development is fairly easy, embedded software still presents major challenges to distributed development. A 2010 study by embedded.com found that only 30% of all embedded software is developed in a global or distributed context, while the vast majority is collocated. Similarly, the amount of quality deficiencies and call-backs across industries has increased in parallel to growing global development and sourcing.

 Business risks increase with global software, IT development, and sourcing. Not all software engineering tasks and projects benefit from outsourcing and offshoring.

The journey has begun, but it is far from being clear what the end result will be. Some countries will come to saturation because global development essentially means that all countries and sites have their fair chance to become players and to

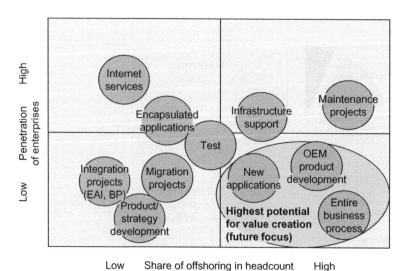

Figure 1.2   Impacts of IT and software offshoring.

compete based on skills, labor cost, innovativeness, and quality. Software engineering is based upon a friction-free economy in which any labor is moved to the site (or engineering team) that is best suitable amongst a set of constraints. No customer is in a position to judge whether a piece of software from one specific site is better or worse when compared to the same software being produced somewhere else in the world. In essence, the old economy labels of "made in country x" has become a type of thinking that does not relate to software industries. What counts are business impacts and performance such as resource availability, productivity, innovativeness, quality of work performed, cost, flexibility, skills, and the like.

BUSINESS PROCESS OUTSOURCING

Business Process Outsourcing (BPO) is the form of outsourcing where a business process (or business function) is contracted to a third-party service provider. BPO involves outsourcing of operations and responsibilities of that process or function. For example, one could use BPO for business processes such as supply chain, maintenance, welcome desk, financial services, or human resources. Historically, Coca Cola was the first company to use BPO for outsourcing parts of their supply chain. In the software industry, EDS was the first supplier for outsourced services.

Today, business process outsourcing is a key element in most R&D and IT-driven industries. The reasons for this are manifold, and saturation has not yet been reached. In fact, outsourcing arrives at different speed in different industries. Figure 1.3 shows the offshore outsourcing penetration of different business processes across industries ranging from automotive and manufacturing, to finance, consumer, ICT, and health [Duke07].

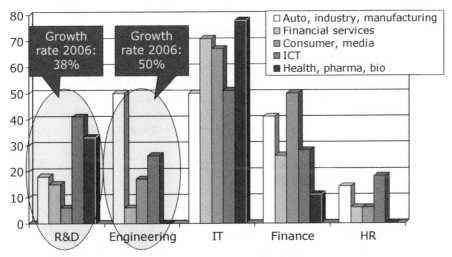

Figure 1.3   The penetration of business process outsourcing (BPO).

IT functions have the highest degree of outsourcing capacity across the five sectors, however, the core of these sectors, namely R&D and engineering functions, are at the steepest growth rate. No longer are support functions and services outsourced as we were once used to. Today's emphasis is on globally utilizing research and engineering to develop products. Global software engineering and IT are at the crossing point of both the IT sector and the engineering function which naturally builds the spearhead of this radical business change. IT outsourcing has reached 50% and more of all expenses for IT services occur across industries. But R&D and engineering is not yet saturated. They will continue to grow at rates way above 20% per year. This means that global software development as well as IT service outsourcing will further grow during this decade.

INFORMATION TECHNOLOGY OUTSOURCING

Information Technology Outsourcing (ITO) is the form of outsourcing in which software and IT related services are outsourced to a third-party service provider. ITO is a form of Business Process Outsourcing (BPO) for software and information technology activities. Historically, EDS was the first ITO supplier. Examples of ITO are outsourcing of software maintenance or IT provisioning services.

ITO is either driven by the need to reduce capital costs or by business process outsourcing. There is hardly any strategic component in ITO despite the fact that many companies claim otherwise. Essentially, companies that are in need of capital in the short term sell their IT assets and resources while immediately sourcing it back to maintain services. As shown in recent years by the cases of Xerox, J.P. Morgan, Swiss Bank, and Delta Airlines, when a company claims strategic reasoning in the sale of IT assets, in reality, the ITO has actually failed to deliver the expected long-term benefits. [Lacity09]. Realizing any strategic goals with ITO is difficult and demands a high degree of managerial attention.

GLOBAL SOFTWARE ENGINEERING

Global software engineering (GSE) is software development and maintenance in globally distributed sites. Different business models and work breakdown schemes, such as outsourcing, offshoring, and rightshoring, are used. Thus, GSE is not correlated with outsourcing and can coexist, for instance, by means of captive development centers within the boundaries of an enterprise or distributed project teams.

NETSOURCING AND APPLICATION SERVICE PROVISIONING

Netsourcing or Application service provisioning (ASP) is the form of sourcing in which computer-based services are outsourced to a third-party service provider. The application service provider (also ASP) provides these services to customers over a network. Therefore, increasingly, the term "Netsourcing" is used for this business model. ASP is a form of Information Technology Outsourcing (ITO) for operationally provisioning software and IT functionality. Software offered using an ASP model is called on-demand software or software as a service (SaaS). Examples of this are customer relationship management and sales (e.g., salesforce.com), as well as, increasingly, desktop applications. ASP is limited and is also a risk (to performance, security, and availability) because access to a particular application program takes place through a standard protocol such as HTTP. The market is divided as follows: Functional ASP delivers a single application, such as timesheet services; a vertical ASP delivers a solution for a specific customer type, such as a chimney sweepers; and an enterprise ASP delivers broad solutions, such as finance solutions.

SOFTWARE SOURCING

Software sourcing is the form of sourcing in which software components are sourced by an external supplier. Sourcing is a business process that summarizes all procurement practices. It includes finding, evaluating, contractually engaging, and managing suppliers of goods and services. Sourcing includes different types of goods and components and, therefore, license models. This starts with commercial off the shelf (COTS), includes a variety of tailored components and solutions, and ends with the different community, open source distribution, and access models. Software component sourcing is also a type of distributed development. Today, distributed development is mostly a global business and, as a result, is part of global software development.

OPEN SOURCE SOFTWARE

One key driver in new value networks is free and open source software. Worldwide companies of various industries are investing in open source. They effectively use it as a viable ecosystem for access to skills, as well as for creating new markets. Today, a variety of global business models around open source are exploited The risks are known, but mitigating solutions exist. Specific communities have been created with suppliers and their customers using open source processes and mechanisms to provide faster access to hardware drivers, software updates, or specific features. New value networks are enhancing traditional approaches. Suppliers are teaming up to share their software basis and to offer tailored services to single user segments. Independent software vendors (ISV) distribute popular solutions and components, or integrate them, thus helping to accelerate integration efforts.

Chapter 2

The Bright Side: Benefits

Summary: Going global makes sense because we have access to talent, markets, and the flexibility to adjust according to our own business needs. On the other hand , we all know that software development demands teamwork and collaboration. First we will look into the motivation for global development. We will then analyze challenges and provide solutions for those of you who are embarking on global software and IT or questioning which format most suits your specific demands.

Cost reduction is still the major trigger for globalization although its relevance has been decreasing in the past years. The reasoning for cost reduction is simple yet effective, so effective, in fact, that you can find it in any newspaper. Labor cost varies across the globe. In different parts of the world, you pay different amounts of money per working hour or per person per year for similar skills and output. An examination of labor costs for comparable skills of educated IT engineers shows that several Asian countries offer a rate of 10%-40% of the expected pay for the same work time in Western Europe or the United States. For instance, in 2008 an "associate engineer" in India earned around US$ 4,400 per year as compared with US$ 55,000 for a new engineer employed in Europe or North America [BCG09]. This reduces R&D labor cost by 40%–60% (not considering hidden costs and additional overheads, which severely reduce this potential).

Specifically, Asian countries offer such a huge amount of skilled and highly motivated engineers that it is impossible not to consider such potential for project planning. The 2006 ACM Job Migration Task Force report on globalization and software offshoring [Aspray06] and the annual World Bank Reports [Worldbank11] both underline that globalization of the software industry will further increase due to both information technology itself (e.g. skills and technology demands as well as market evolutions in emerging economies), government actions (e.g. moving into IT sectors to reduce dependencies on raw materials in places such as China), and, finally, by economic factors (e.g., labor cost differences).

Labor cost will remain a major driver for any type of IT and software outsourcing and offshoring for a long time to come. Figure 2.1 shows the annual wage distribution across the world [McKinsey08, Worldbank11, EconomistIntelligence11].

Global Software and IT: A Guide to Distributed Development, Projects, and Outsourcing,
First Edition. Christof Ebert.
© 2012 the Institute of Electrical and Electronics Engineers, Inc. Published 2012 by
John Wiley & Sons, Inc.

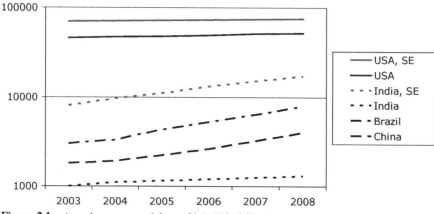

Figure 2.1   Annual wages around the world (in U.S. dollars).

The top two lines are for U.S. software engineers and average, the two dotted lines are India, and the remaining two lines are Brazil and China. The average income of American and Indian software engineers is shown in order to contrast the relationship with the average income across all professions.[1] While the growth rate is clearly bigger in lower income countries such as India or China, the distance will further attract global software development and IT outsourcing.

Other factors, therefore, begin to influence the decision for global software engineering and IT (Fig. 2.2). Increasingly, global software development and offshoring is about proximity to markets, sharing the benefits of resources from different cultures, and flexibility in skill management. IT and R&D managers want access to on-demand specialist knowledge with less forecasting and provisioning. This often contains a great deal of fixed cost which, in today's competitive environment, is not easy to bear. Increasingly, the target is quality improvement and innovation; both are related to blending cultures and thus achieve internal competition and new stimulus for doing better.

For the decade of 2010–2020, we see four major goals fueling the need for outsourcing and offshoring, namely efficiency, presence, talent, and flexibility.

Figure 2.2 provides an overview of these goals, which will be briefly explained here:

1. Presence. Global R&D and software engineering has become part of the growth strategies of many companies. This is because they are closer to the

---

[1] Sources: http://www.glassdoor.com/Salaries, http://globaltechforum.eiu.com

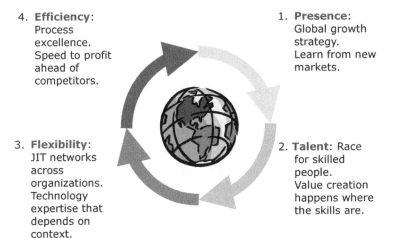

4. **Efficiency**:
   Process
   excellence.
   Speed to profit
   ahead of
   competitors.

1. **Presence**:
   Global growth
   strategy.
   Learn from new
   markets.

3. **Flexibility**:
   JIT networks
   across
   organizations.
   Technology
   expertise that
   depends on
   context.

2. **Talent**: Race
   for skilled
   people.
   Value creation
   happens where
   the skills are.

Figure 2.2   The self-sustaining momentum of globalized software and IT.

companies' markets and they better understand how to cope with regional needs, be it software development or services. Such global growth is a self-sustaining force, as it demands increasing capacities in captive or outsourced software engineering centers.

2. **Talent.** Computer science and engineering skills are scarce. Many countries do not have enough resources locally available to cope with the demand for IT and software products and services. Fueling this trend, many younger people got nervous because of media-driven misrepresentations of the dangers of outsourcing/offshoring for the entire software field. As a result, they decide to pursue careers in completely different fields. The consequence is a global race for excellent software engineers. Outsourcing/offshoring is the instrument to provide such skills and to handle the related supplier-processes.

3. **Flexibility.** Software organizations are driven by fast changing demands on skills and sheer numbers of engineers. With the development of a new and innovative product, many people with broad experiences are needed, while, when arriving in maintenance, these skill needs look different. Additionally, manpower distributions are also changing. Such flexible demands can no longer be handled inside the enterprise. Outsourcing/offshoring is the answer to provide skilled engineers and to allow the building of flexible ecosystems, combining suppliers, customers with engineering, and service providers.

4. **Efficiency.** Software and IT companies need to deliver quickly and reliably because their competition is literally a mouse click away. Hardly any other business has such low entry barriers as IT. These low entry barriers stimulate an endless fight for efficiency along the dimensions of improved cost, quality, and time-to-profit. Outsourcing/offshoring clearly helps in improving efficiency. This is due to labor cost differences across the world, better quality

with many well-trained and process-minded engineers (especially in Asia), and shorter time-to-profit in following the sun and developing and maintaining software in two to three shifts in different time zones.

Many factors cannot be quantified or made tangible initially, but will sooner or later contribute heavily to overall performance. For instance, innovation is a major positive effect that is boosted by going global. Engineers with all types of cultural backgrounds actively participate to continuously improve the product, innovate new products, and to make the processes more effective. Even with the slightly more complex decision making process involved in going global, achievements are substantial if engineers of different educational and cultural backgrounds unite to solve problems. The best practices can be shared, and, sometimes, small changes within the global development community can have big positive effects.

Obviously, not all companies that engage in global software engineering and IT look at each of the four goals (presence, talent, efficiency, and flexibility) with the same levels of motivation. As a matter of fact, we even see a kind of trajectory in which a vast majority of companies start with efficiency needs (i.e., cost savings), and then move on to presence in local markets. Only after these two forces are understood do the companies move on to tackle talent and flexibility. Also, it is clear that these four factors feed themselves. The more energy a company spends on building a regional pool of skilled software engineers, the more it also considers how to best utilize these competencies to, for instance, build a regional market or develop new products for such markets.

Chapter 3

The Dark Side: Challenges

Summary: Working in a global context obviously has advantages but there are also some drawbacks. While the positive side accounts for time-zone effectiveness or reduced cost in various countries, we should not close our eyes to the risks and disadvantages. Practitioners of global software development and IT outsourcing clearly recognize that difficulties exist. In this chapter, we will look at risks and failures in global software and IT projects. Only when we are aware of risks and past failures, do we have a chance of doing better ourselves.

It seems rational to put stakeholders in one place, share the objectives, and execute the project. The need to work in one location is a major lesson to take away from many failed projects; it has even found its way into many practice development methodologies such as agile development. So, what are the strategies and tactics to survive globally dispersed projects?

One-fifth of the executives in a recent survey say that they are dissatisfied with the results of their outsourcing arrangements, while another fifth of the respondents see no real benefits [McKinsey08, BCG09, IDC07]. As a rule of thumb, 20%–25% of all outsourcing relationships fail within two years and 50% fail within five years. This is in line with our own experiences over the past decade. The figures actually did not improve over time [Ebert07a, IDC07, Hussey08, Rivard08].

Working in a globally distributed project means businesses must worry about overheads for planning and managing people, it means there will be both linguistic and cultural barriers, and it creates jealousy between the more expensive engineers who become afraid of losing their jobs while they are forced to train their much cheaper counterparts/possible replacements. In this book, we will try to summarize experiences and to share the best practices from projects of different types and sizes, which involve several locations on different continents and in various cultures.

Global Software and IT: A Guide to Distributed Development, Projects, and Outsourcing,
First Edition. Christof Ebert.
© 2012 the Institute of Electrical and Electronics Engineers, Inc. Published 2012 by
John Wiley & Sons, Inc.

The business reasons for working in a low-cost country are surely not a simple trade-off for the various costs of engineering in different regions. Many companies struggle because they only focus on the perceived differences in labor cost and not on risks and overhead expenses. Twenty percent of all globalization projects are canceled within the first year.

Big savings in global software engineering and IT have only been reported from (business) processes which are well defined and already performed before offshoring begins, and which do not require much control [IAOP09, Hussey08, Rivard08]. This includes maintenance projects (under the condition that the legacy software has some type of description) for which some or all parts can be distributed, technical documentation (i.e., creation, knowledge management, packaging, translation, distribution, and maintenance), or validation activities. Development projects have shown good results in all cases in which tasks have been well separated so that distributed teams would have direction and ownership.

Global development projects fail if tasks are broken down too much. For example, asking a remote engineer to do the verification for software developed concurrently in another site did not work out positively for the company [Carmel01, Grinter99, Herbsleb00, Hussey08, Rivard08]. In this case, distance and lack of direct communication slow down development rather than help it. The single biggest source of difficulties in outsourcing/offshoring is related to communication across sites. Bad communication hinders both coordination and creates insufficient management processes [Cramton05, O'Hara94, Krishna04]

For instance, continuous integration of insufficiently verified and encapsulated software components fails if done separately from parallel ongoing software development. Distributed teams working on exactly the same topic (e.g., the famous follow-the-sun pattern of developing a piece of software in different time zones) posed the highest challenges for coordination and often resulted in severe overheads that would be measurable or tangible only later on (e.g. features misinterpreted, insufficient quality, lack of ownership and responsibility, etc.).

The challenges in global software engineering and IT can be summarized as follows:

- **Lack of strategy and shared values** in parent organization resulting in insufficient collaboration, and unclear work split and ownership. Roadmaps might be fragmented or provide insufficient visibility of business strategy, both of which contribute to insecurity of teams and cause sub-optimal results. A clear sign for lack of strategy would be if the senior manager announced , "We will work in India because it is cheaper," or the engineering lead explaining, "Any work can be done by virtual teams." A major underlying reason for dysfunctional global work is a cultural difference in values as well as underlying societal factors [House04, O'Hara94, Krishna04]. We often superficially label this as "cultural issues" or even worse as "soft factors," claiming that we cannot handle it with our limited management and software education. For instance, time perception in a society has profound impact on many behaviors such as insufficient planning and monitoring which cannot be cured only as symptoms. A culture deeply rooted in the present will always be portrayed as lazy and unfocused by a society rooted in the future that demands accurate planning. The same idea applies to societies that value entrepreneurship and spontaneous (re)actions for events as opposed to those societies that prefer clearly outlined roles and responsibilities. Such differences must be recognized, considered, and dealt with. A shared value system and continuous team building activities will help everyone involved as well as serving to unite employees across these different societies.

- **Insufficient communication** due to distance, time zones and cultural barriers. Note that distance impacts start at around 10–15 meters which is far closer in distance than one would usually assume. People talk and share only if they are close to one another and frequently see each other without in spontaneous situations. Lucent and others did extensive studies on communication in global teams and found that 15% of software development is made up of informal communication [Herbsleb00, Herbsleb03, DeMarco99, Hussey08]. Distributed teams are less effective than a collocated team working on the same task.

- **Dispersed work organization** is the global nature of project and product work which obscures a holistic view of project success factors. More sites add cost due to overhead management, separated and dysfunctional processes, and tools and teams. While Tools help however, they are not enough to build a distributed team. Process immaturity is a key roadblock and cause of inefficiencies and rework. Gartner, BCG, and Standish report that 10% management overhead, that is, one person to synchronize for 10 persons allocated an offshored task [BCG09, Hussey08]. Our own experiences show that having two sites working on the same development project immediately adds 10%–20% cost while reducing visibility and impacts of management. Overall effort overheads are ca. 35% if work is in two places. This is due to interface control, management, replication, frictions, and so on [Jones07, Herbsleb00, Ebert07a, Grinter99, Mockus01, Hussey08].

- **Inadequate global management** results in micromanaged tasks or lack of visibility. Often project managers fear lack of control and establish very small fragmented tasks in order to stay in control. Micromanagement creates a lack of buy-in from the teams as they expect that the manager to interfere and, therefore, they feel that they don't have to pay attention. On the other end of the spectrum is insufficient visibility starting with estimates and continuing with change management and progress tracking. Global team management often suffers from biased attitudes. Functional and regional rivalries exacerbate the tendency to claim credit for success and shift blame for failures. We've experienced, in several such global product lines, that roadmaps and features are overly volatile because of local optimization on regional customer basis. Our experiences show that change rate of requirements will, in consequence, be much higher than industry average (1%–3% per month). Lucent reports 30%–100% delays for multi-site change requests and overall project delays if a project is distributed across sites [Herbsleb00].

- **Isolated learning.** Improvements derived from past experiences are rarely applied beyond the originating organizational silo. We found that, in global software engineering and IT, individual sites have their own individual tools and processes even if they are working on the same product lines. Different countries or regions sometimes launch independent infrastructure optimization in order to differentiate from one another. This is often amplified by dysfunctional regional competition as many companies have established the need to challenge "high-cost" countries with "low-cost" countries. For that reason, the parent organization might hesitate to provide all necessary support due to the fear that work may be taken away. Additional obstacles in sharing experiences arise from insufficient risk mitigation related to intellectual property or third party access to tools and knowledge repositories. SAP reports, "Distributed development is slower and less forgiving in case of mistakes. We need to communicate more but we have less capacity to communicate. Effects of mistakes are not easily apparent and tend to be hidden by regional owners longer than possible in a centralized development" [Zencke04].

- **Less agility compared with colocated teams** is almost certain as soon as an integrated task is done in different sites. Workflow, monitoring, and engineering processes must all be strengthened to assure that different stakeholders collaborate well. This is perceived as overhead by the teams and if they are not well-trained they try to escape which causes major trouble during development [Grinter99, Herbsleb03, Olsson00, Hussey08].

- **Insufficient contract management.** Contracts are absolutely crucial for managing external suppliers. They must include defined and measurable Service Level Agreements (SLAs) to assure appropriate quality levels. For captive offshoring, it may be wise (depending on organization structure) to govern by means of internal contracts and SLAs. SLAs are advantageous because targets and measurements are agreed upfront. This prevents the need for continuous debates with senior management if some delivery is late. Certainly, such internal contracts and SLAs combined with a culture of accountability and clearly assigned responsibilities also help to circumvent the political game of finger pointing and claiming that "the others" did not do their job well.

- **Unknown legal environment** is a major trap for any global activity whether it is sales or engineering. It means you must get very familiar with local laws such as contracts, liability, intellectual property, or human resource management. If you do not yet have enough experience with global development and specific regulations, we strongly recommend using consulting to ramp up your competencies and processes *before* you actually engage in global development. Never rely on the legal support from a supplier in the host country to which you want to expand your engineering teams.

- **Higher employee turnover rate**. Turnover rates are higher in offshore centers than onshore in comparable job positions [Hussey08, Aspray06]]. The reasons for this are manifold, but can be reduced to three factors, namely, different cultures, insufficient management, and reduced motivation. We see different local patterns of employee turnover rates across the world. Some can be explained by cultural clichés such as the ones claiming that Europeans and Chinese people are married to their company while Indians and U.S. Americans are on a continuous job hunt. Low motivation can make engineers search for another job. Often, it is simply job content (e.g. doing only legacy repair, having only scattered assignments with low personal commitment and ownership) and lack of career path within the job which makes engineers move to another company. For instance, India's IT industry is growing so quickly that many engineers are continuously approached by other companies with more interesting job offers. With additional effort and skilled management however, turnover rates can be reduced. We have experienced for ourselves that it is feasible to manage an Indian engineering team that, over a many years, can have turnover rates similar to those in Europe [Ebert08]. It all depends on management, culture, responsibilities, and, ultimately, motivation.

With these challenges, reported cost reduction from global software engineering and IT is much less than the aforementioned potential of 40%-60% savings if the same process is split across the world with changing responsibilities [Hussey08, Rivard08]. Successful companies reported from their global software projects a 10%–15% cost reduction after a two to three year learning curve. Of all outsourcing relationships, 20%–25% fail within two years and half fail within five years [Ebert07a, IDC07, Hussey08, Rivard08], partially because, initially, outsourcing demands up to 20% additional effort.

Figure 3.1 shows the average contribution of this hidden cost to the overall cost of R&D. For mere IT outsourcing, specifically for management, overheads are lower.

 Externalization of insufficient engineering processes creates extra cost and delays driven by the necessary learning curve on both sides. These additional costs can be as much as 20%–40% of regular costs of engineering.

The learning curve for transferring an entire software package to a new team (e.g. location) takes twelve months [Karolak98, Herbsleb00, Hussey08]. Our own experiences [Ebert01a, Ebert01b, Ebert07a, Ebert08], and research [Aspray06, IDC07, Sangwan07, USA07] show that the effectiveness for software design and

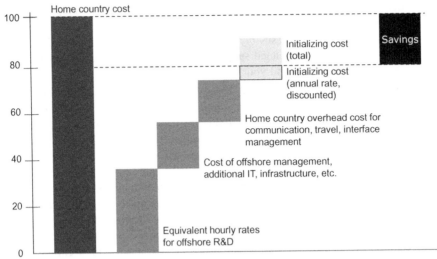

Figure 3.1   Cost comparison, including hidden cost.

coding grows in a learning curve of 50% effectiveness which can be reached after one to three months and 80% after three to five months. However, these percentages obviously depend on process maturity and technology complexity. Each of the following bullets accounts for a 5%–10% increase to regular onshore engineering costs in the home country:

- Supplier and contract management
- Coordination and interface management
- Fragmented and scattered processes
- Project management and progress control
- Training, knowledge management, communication
- IT infrastructure and global tools licenses
- Liability coverage and legal support.

To mitigate these risks of global software development, we found several good practices reported from different global software teams, such as[1]:

GE: After years of no results with reducing software cost, J. Welch concluded that there is a need for a clear and simple policy to split work between locations. If there is no clear policy, no progress will be made . The GE policy demands that 30% of software

---

[1] Own research based upon: Article evaluation in IEEE Software magazine, discussions and reports at the IEEE International Conference on Global Software Engineering and case study books [Zencke04, Ebert07a, Herbsleb00, Herbsleb05, Rivard08, Sangwan08].

must be developed locally in North America while 70% is developed in one of seven offshore development centers.

Ford: Never split projects between too many different areas (i.e. departments and regions). Favor projects with less than three areas involved in design and test.

Alcatel-Lucent: The best results are achieved if coherent tasks are colocated. If resources are scarce, you must colocate functions rather than products or projects. Create a sufficiently large pool of similar resources to ensure flexibility, continuous mentoring and learning, and mobility of resources. Certain independent process steps can be separated from one another and distributed across sites (at the known overhead cost): (1) requirements management/ product management, (2) development, and (3) system and interworking tests. If work is to be distributed, it is better to do it for well-defined contents (i.e., a mobile communication protocol standard), but not for flexible and innovative projects.

Thales: Effective offshoring requires strong and aligned processes and tools.

SAP: Very strong focus on global team management with shared values and excellent collaboration environment.

Bosch: Common language across projects and regions is achieved by using standard processes based on the CMMI.[2]

With the needs, rewards, and mitigation patterns that we have shown here, you can translate risks to chances and opportunities which is exactly how they should be seen to create the best business opportunities.

---

[2] CMMI denotes the Capability Maturity Model for Development (CMMI-DEV) [SEI11]. Since global software engineering is primarily about the development and maintenance processes, CMMI-DEV has the best capture of engineering and management processes. Terminology across the CMMI constellations is aligned, and so is our use of terms. We recommend looking also to CMMI for Acquisition (CMMI-ACQ), CMMI for Services (CMMI-SVC), COBIT and ITIL for additional coverage and good practice guidelines in the sourcing, service and IT domains.

Chapter 4

Deciding the Business Model

Summary: Success with global software and IT starts with selecting the appropriate business model and sourcing strategy. Global software development and ITO are not restricted to a particular stable business model, nor is it limited to working with or without an external supplier. In this chapter we will look at different business models and provide decision support depending upon your specific environment and constraints.

The business model and the decision to work with a supplier and the best way to manage that supplier heavily influence the entire process and management of global software engineering and IT. We will briefly examine the aspects of working with internal development centers or distributed teams in the home company and then contrast this scenario with a single external supplier for global development services. Having several suppliers adds to complexity, but does not change the process. This explains why we can limit our analysis to the two basic models with internal or external global teams.

Figure 4.1 shows how different business models typically evolve. The starting point for most companies is the lower left quadrant which implies that providing localized services typically shows presence, eases installation and support, and boosts local sales. Alternatively, the lower right quadrant demonstrates another possible starting point which translates into work packages being done by an offshore center or by people working in a remote site. Neither model is a stable end point except in that localized services are necessary. However, to fully experience global development creates the potential and provides the perception that it can boost the productivity that is demanded by companies moving to the upper half of the portfolio. A stable end point for many IT and software companies is the upper right quadrant which demonstrates the need to implement a viable and sustainable strategy for work split and collaboration across multiple sites.

Various field studies and empirical research demonstrate that trying to accomplish too much too fast is associated with lower levels of success [Lacity09].

Global Software and IT: A Guide to Distributed Development, Projects, and Outsourcing, First Edition. Christof Ebert.
© 2012 the Institute of Electrical and Electronics Engineers, Inc. Published 2012 by John Wiley & Sons, Inc.

As a rule of thumb, clients that outsourced more than 80% of their IT budgets had success rates of below 30%, while clients who outsourced less than 80% of their IT budgets had success rates of over 80%.

The Australian federal government ITO project provides an interesting case study [Lacity09] from when they experienced poor results both financially and operationally, losing close to US$1 billion, because they clustered too many different IT functions in one step. The intention, of course, was to save money in a short period of time through the economies of scale. However, the increased frictions, overheads, and subsequent management costs across disparate IT functions, severely reduced savings below what was to be expected from a reduced outsourcing scope. The content of what is outsourced or offshored also matters. More savings can be achieved by outsourcing systems operations and ICT than by outsourcing software development, end user support, and systems management.

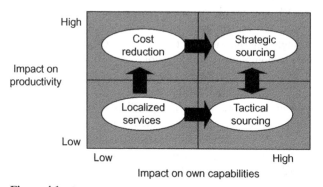

Figure 4.1 Impacts of globalized software and IT on a company's productivity and capabilities.

In case that kind of outsourcing or sourcing is considered, the supplier's capabilities must fit with those of the client. The degree of sourcing depends on this fit in order to mitigate sourcing risks (see Chapter 8). Table 4.1 shows typical scenarios and how they influence decisions on the business model and sourcing strategies. Check the environmental constraints on the left side of the table. For instance, the innovation degree of the product could be high or low. Empty fields indicate that the answer won't matter here. Once you have identified the most appropriate column (and thus scenario), you find some concrete guidance at the bottom part. Note that not all scenarios can be easily applied. For instance, high innovation degree and low client maturity create high outsourcing risks—even if the supplier has high process and domain expertise (right column).

Table 4.1 Sourcing Scenarios Must Match the Client's Needs and Capabilities

Criteria	Typical Scenarios				
Innovation degree of product	Low	High		Low	High
Complexity: Management and interactions	Low		High	Low	
Client's process maturity	High	High	High	Low	Low
Client's technical expertise				High	
Supplier's domain/ environmental expertise	High	High	High		
Decision	Ok	Feasible	Feasible	Feasible	No!
Typical outsourcing model and suggested risk mitigation	Standard outsourcing: You know your business and the supplier the technology.	Continue working as before. The supplier needs to ramp up.	Risk project. Optimize interface mgmt. Tight project management.	Risk project. Improve your processes right away. Tight project management.	Very high risk! A dedicated model might help with close third-party support.

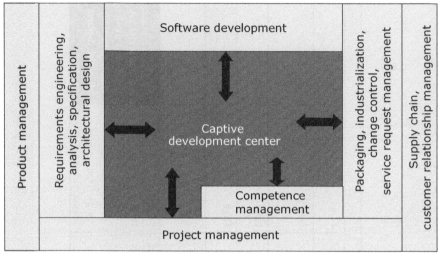

Figure 4.2   Global software engineering with a home-based captive development center (offshoring).

Interface and transaction complexity depend upon the chosen business model and sourcing strategy. The fully internalized global development is shown in Figure 4.2. The relevant functions along the product's life-cycle are put into various boxes with the engineering center at the middle of the diagram. From left to right we see the typical business cycle of product life-cycle management, namely a product manager who owns the business and makes decisions about requirements, business case, roadmap and make vs. reuse vs. buy, and so on. Following the product management, we see requirements engineering, systems analysis, design activities, and architecture design. From here on, global development might come fully or partially into the picture.

Take, for example, the simple scenario of full product development in a globally distributed team (the box called "captive development center"). The center has the responsibility of managing skills and competences (forecasting, provisioning, career development, etc.), team management skills, providing results according to plans and commitments, and so on. The arrows depict major interfaces between this specific global engineering center and the traditional activities around product management, requirements engineering, project management, people/competence management, supplier agreement management, packaging/industrialization, and supply chain management. The small supplier box in the upper right of the figure shows a component supplier as it is frequently used for software components. Such a global engineering center typically evolves from standardized and well-defined services (task-based) towards full product responsibility. It is rarely the case that the center stagnates in a sub-optimal position working only on piecemeal-like tasks. This would reduce the gains expected from a global team dramatically.

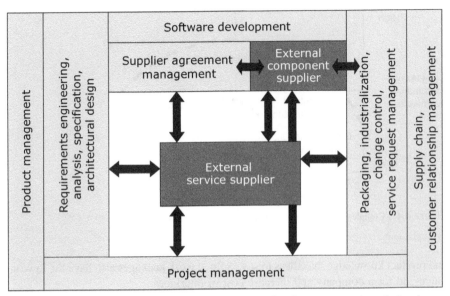

Figure 4.3 Global software engineering with external suppliers for components (sourcing) and services (outsourcing).

Figure 4.3 demonstrates the elements of working with an external supplier that provides the engineering services in an offshore (or nearshore) scenario. The supplier of the (global) engineering services will build strong interfaces to the major functions of the product life-cycle of its client from day one. Again, these interfaces are shown with arrows. Interface management may look like overhead for the client, but it is the clear professional need of the supplier. Frankly, it is overhead, but it is overhead born out of the risk mitigation of the supplier who would otherwise fear that changes would continuously ripple from the client to his organization, thus making it impossible to keep SLAs and delivery commitments. Those interfaces cost an additional 10%–20% (depending on the maturities of both the client and supplier) on top of regular project cost without any value-add as seen by the client. With several other suppliers involved for the sake of component deliveries, such overheads can grow into the 30% range. Needless to say, people management and competence management are handled from within the supplier (not shown for the external component supplier which is even more separated) on the basis of forecasts delivered by means of the contract and regular client stakeholder reviews.

The complexity of global development, and thus the risks of global development, depend on the business model selected for global development. Figure 4.4 shows a qualitative graph relating complexity of handling global development dependent upon the business model (bubbles) and its scope (horizontal axis). A defined work package (e.g., perform inspections) can certainly be handled at any part of the world if it is well defined and not overly demanding regarding domain

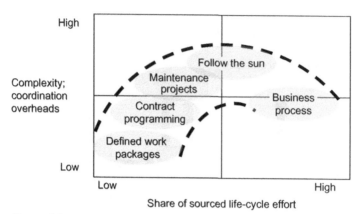

Figure 4.4   Complexity evolves depending on the business model.

and product knowledge. Needless to say, defined work packages also have the lowest value-add for a company and increase cost of interfaces.

Handling complexity increases toward entire tasks (e.g., a feature development or a test team) or projects (e.g., a maintenance or development project) handled in a global context. It improves with a business process managed in a global context, such as the responsibility for a product line. As a rule, the left side of the figure is easier to introduce, while the right side is easier to sustain with a positive business case. Business cases must be explored for all scenarios.

Chapter 5

Preparing the Business Case

Summary: Too often the business case on global software and IT is done primarily by looking at cost per person. In fact, we hardly ever see complete business cases that are periodically evaluated. This chapter provides some insight on setting up a business case. It shows various experiences as well as how to calculate the hidden parameters.

A business case presents a business idea or proposal to a decision maker. Essentially, it should prove that the proposal is sufficiently solid and that it fits economically and technically with the company's strategy. It is part of a more general business plan and emphasizes costs and benefits, how to finance the endeavor, technical needs, feasibility, market situation, environment, and the competition. It is created early in the product life-cycle and serves as the major input before a decision for investment is taken.

Many global projects and products fail simply because the business case was never done or was not done correctly [Ebert07a, IDC07, Hussey08, Rivard08]. The key to a successful business case is that it must connect the value proposition with the technical and marketing concept as well as with the market evolution and the company's potential. A lack of research and forethought on one of these four dimensions invalidates the entire business case.

The business case that is used to decide on a business model for outsourcing/offshoring consists of the following elements:

- Summary.
- Introduction (motivation of the business proposal, market value, relationship to existing products, solutions or services, home business' capabilities and capacity, and different scenarios being evaluated).
- Market analysis (market assumptions, industry trends, target market and customers, volume of the target market, competitors, home business' positioning, and evaluation of these assumptions through strengths, weaknesses, opportunities, and threats, as well as make versus reuse versus buy, and related opportunities and threads).

Global Software and IT: A Guide to Distributed Development, Projects, and Outsourcing,
First Edition. Christof Ebert.

- Marketing plan (marketing contents and sales strategies).

- Business calculation (sales forecasts, profit/loss calculation, cash flow, financing expenses, business risk management, securities, present value of investments, and evaluation of assumptions. Calculation needs to be done for many different scenarios which are then to be compared and evaluated).

- Operations plan (customer interfaces, production planning, supply chain, suppliers, make versus reuse versus buy, platforms and components to be used, service needs, management control, quality objectives and quality management, managing global development, involved sites, training aspects, skill and knowledge management, and intellectual property evaluation and growth).

- Project and release plan (resources, skills, milestones, dependencies, and risk management).

- Organization (type of organization, management structure, reporting lines, and communication).

- Further details of the business case as attachments to above elements.

A business case has to prove that the proposed concept fits both technically and commercially within the enterprise. It is part of the business plan and is created before the launch of the product development segment of the process. Preparing the business case in a global software engineering and IT environment consists of several steps:

1. **Coin a vision and focus**. What is the message you want to get across? What will the proposed product or solution change? Use language that is understood by decision makers and stakeholders be concise and discuss financial and marketing aspects more than technology. Focus on what you are really able to do. For the global development scenario, it is crucial for you to introduce a clear life-cycle vision and not to simply say that several sites in low cost countries will be considered for the purposes of cost reduction.

2. **Analyze the market environment and commercial situation**. How will you sell? How much, to whom, and with what effect? For improvement projects you must identify the symptoms of poor practice and what those will mean for your company (e.g., cost of non-quality, productivity, cycle time, and predictability). Quantify the costs and benefits, the threats and opportunities. For IT projects you should consider that the IT direct cost is only the tip of the iceberg. The true value proposition is in the operational business processes. In a globally distributed development it is helpful to analyze different scenarios and evaluate impacts of each on customer perception, market penetration, speed and efficiency depending on market proximity, competitive evaluation of outsourcing/offshoring, and the necessary localized sales support (starting with requirements elicitation and impact analysis).

3. **Plan the proposed project**. Show how it will be operationally conducted. Describe the resources, organization, skills, and budget you plan to use.

What are the risks and their mitigation? What suppliers will you utilize? Perform a reality check on your project. Does the combined information make sense? Can you deliver the value proposed in step one ? How will you track the earned value? What measurements and dashboard will be utilized? Consider total cost of ownership, not simply the effort and resources that must be used to develop. Plan the impacted engineers, the necessary skills, how to ramp-up sites and skills; discuss collaboration tools and overheads, interface management, review procedures in a global context, and life-cycle management processes. Finally, the plan and business case must be verified. This is often done by a portfolio management group or the controlling function.

4. **Validate the business case**. This step is often neglected, however crucial it may be to close the loop between assumptions and a learning organization. The problem lies not in invalid assumptions, but in businesses failing to learn from previously made errors. Therefore, at critical life-cycle milestones, as well as at delivery and during service, cost and revenue must be reassessed with the goal of revisiting the entire initial planning stage (up to the level at which a product might be killed for not proving its assumptions). It is also important to lean toward risk management, uncertainty management, and accountability. Specifically, in a globally distributed project, this step assures that you and your business will learn from past obstacles in people management, turnover rates, or insufficient quality levels.

The business case is quantitative by nature. It builds upon assumptions and propositionswhich must be evaluated periodically rather than discussed solely at the beginning of the project. It must be looked at from different perspectives such as the validity, consistency, and completeness of the project. This is where software measurements come into the picture. They provide, for instance, the guidance for performing a feasibility study. They relate expected volume or size of the project to effort and schedule needs, thus indicating whether or not the proposed plan and delivery dates are viable. They indicate uncertainties, and, together with software engineering techniques, guide the risk mitigation. Considering that requirements typically change with 1%–3% per month is a starting point for planning releases and incremental deliveries.

 The global software engineering and IT business case is not a simple trade-off of the different costs of engineering. There are tangible benefits to going global in terms of flexibility, skills availability, market proximity, and labor cost. Additionally, there are extra costs in global software engineering and IT business due to overheads, frictions, rework, and misunderstandings.

Working in a globally distributed project means there will be overheads for planning and managing people; it means that you will face language and cultural barriers; it creates jealousies between the more expensive engineers who are afraid of losing their jobs while they are forced to train their much cheaper counterparts. On top of all of the above, there are risks related to intellectual property protection, security, and many other things as well. All of those elements must be considered when you are preparing your outsourcing/offshoring business case which comes on top of the regular product business case.

Part II

Development

Chapter 6

Requirements Engineering

Summary: Tell me how the project starts and I will tell you how it will end. We need to focus on the early phases, specifically, determining the requirements and making sure all stakeholders understand what has to be done. This chapter provides insight into the best practices and requirements in engineering for global projects.

Requirements engineering is the systematic approach to developing, specifying, analyzing, verifying, allocating, tracing, and managing the requirements (functional requirements, quality attributes, and constraints) of the system, and establishing and maintaining an agreement between the customer/user and the project team on the changing requirements of the system. Figure 6.1 shows the requirements engineering within the context of a globally developed product. We distinguish the product domain from the project domain because in most cases stakeholders and influence varies heavily between the two domains. Global software development looks primarily into the project domain whether it is colocated in an offshore location or distributed across locations.

The ultimate success factor for any global development project is to know what to do (i.e., eliciting, analyzing, specifying, verifying, and allocating the requirements). It is also necessary to assure that the impact of changes to previous commitments are analyzed and managed transparently for the sake of all stakeholders. This is indicated in Figure 6.1 by the different boxes which represent the requirements engineering activities throughout the life-cycle of a project.

Before the start of development, requirements are uncertain. That, almost by definition, is captured by an old requirements analyst slogan which claims, "I know it when I see it." These uncertainties, as can be observed in various industries, are increasing in today's quickly changing markets. Requirements uncertainties originate from various causes, such as cognitive limitations (i.e., users find it hard to imagine the product and to state their requirements; their opinions about their own requirements evolve by the very exercise of requirements elicitation) or changing circumstances so that requirements change (e.g., introducing the system changes the situation too, and therefore changes requirements!), but yield similar results [Lawrence01]. Because of these changes, work packages, and eventually the entire project, are delayed and do not fulfill the original expectations.

Global Software and IT: A Guide to Distributed Development, Projects, and Outsourcing,
First Edition. Christof Ebert.
© 2012 the Institute of Electrical and Electronics Engineers, Inc. Published 2012 by
John Wiley & Sons, Inc.

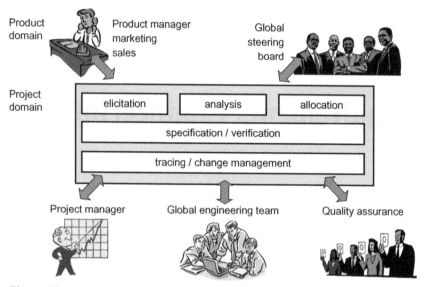

Figure 6.1 Managing the requirements in a global project or product.

Within global development projects the risks related to requirements are amplified due to delayed visibility of open issues, uncertainties, or misunderstandings. Open issues cannot be easily clarified by dropping in on another stakeholder's office; they must be formally handled [Damian03b]. The following requirements-related risks should be mitigated in global development projects while considering the adequacy of collaboration and communication. This means:

- Overlooking a crucial requirement.
- Not understanding the needs behind the requirements.
- Considering only functional requirements and overlooking nonfunctional requirements.
- Not inspecting requirements, thus detecting insufficiencies too late.
- Representing requirements in the form of designs, thus reducing the solution domain.
- Fragmenting requirements into dependent work packages designed by different teams.
- Continuous changes which undermine the initial planning and business case.
- Insufficient change management which leads to inconsistencies and defects.

From our experiences in global systems engineering projects, these risks are most effectively addressed by:

- Specifying requirements (i.e., grouping related requirements, permitting a higher-level understanding of relationships and dependencies, modeling impacts and dependencies, and consistently applying a specification template).

- Specifying the *understanding* of requirements (i.e., the receiver, such as an offshore team, will describe how it will approach the given requirements).
- Sorting requirements (i.e., determining the order of consideration based on criticality of need and level of associated risk, implementing in increments following the priorities, descoping those requirements with lowest priority).
- Assuring adequate collaboration and communication workflow management, such as distributed requirement databases, shared access control, and frequently updated and time-stamped baseline distribution of requirements, features and their individual status.
- Managing change (i.e., using automated tools to assist in the understanding and tracing of requirements from inception to allocation to delivery; evaluating requirements upfront on individual change risks; applying strict change management; determining the localization, scope, and impacts of changes).
- Designing for change (i.e., appropriate task organization in the distributed development teams, improved maintainability, modularity, and isolating features that are subject to changes).

The results and decisions from the bullet points above should be coined into a requirements engineering and management process as well as being embedded into the product life-cycle. This assures that you will understand and be trained in the various global teams (or different suppliers). It also serves as guidance with the ability to agree on a SLA and change process with customers and suppliers. Distinct standards for requirements engineering, such as IEEE 1233 and IEEE 830, focus on generic techniques to ensure that customer needs are recorded and traced throughout the development life-cycle. The key standard covering nonfunctional requirements and classifying generic quality attributes is ISO 9126.

Requirements that are properly expressed form a high-level abstraction of the functional and nonfunctional behavior of the product. Formalizing such a description helps in identifying reusable aspects of systems at a level independent of any particular solution or component structure. A template for a requirements specification is provided in Table 6.1. It is based on IEEE standards 830 and 1233 and what they demand with respect to requirements specifications. Data quality of project information and requirements lists is important to preserve integrity and consistency throughout the life-cycle.

To check for completeness and consistency of requirements and the traceability of work products, a minimum quality assurance is necessary. Inconsistencies and errors in requirements are most often found by testers because they think in terms of testability. If requirements are inconsistent or vague, they should be corrected on the spot. If a problem is detected during the project, it is called a requirements change and it has to be approved by the core team before any action is taken. Project information builds an online accessible history database upon which further impact analysis and project planning are based .

Table 6.1   A Requirements Specification Template for Global Development Projects

Requirement ID	Unique key to identify and retrieve the requirement
Requirement title	Short, concise, specific description
Status	Implementation status with history and owners
Details	Precise, understandable, traceable link to project / product
	Motivation from marketing requirements, link to roadmap
Constraints	Non-technical, non-functional requirements
	Economic, legal considerations; own / client business drivers
Dependencies	Related features, requirements, design decisions
Valuation	Balanced for cost and benefits
	Business reasoning, customer business case
Analysis	Impacts, effort, new constraints, make vs. reuse vs. buy
Priority	Clear priority based on cost and value
Traceability	Maintainable traceability to related work products
	Market requirements, component requirements, test cases, etc.
Impacts	Requirements and conditions on hardware, interfaces, etc.
Acceptance criteria	Quantitative targets, qualification test cases, SLA impacts
. . .	
Comments	Continuous collection during entire lifetime
	Must not create embedded conflicts to above sections

Impact analysis is based on requirements, priority setting, and portfolio management. What are the requirements? How do they relate between markets and correlate with one another? What is their impact? What markets have asked for them and for what reason? Are they necessary for a solution or just inherited from an incumbent approach, perhaps becoming obsolete in the meantime? To address these questions, requirements must be documented in a structured and disciplined way. They must be expressed to allow for both technical as well as business judgment aspects. Any incoming requirement should be reviewed with the product catalog and global product evolution in mind so as to also evaluate marginal value versus marginal costs. Underlying financial figures must be correct for both cost and value. Often, the value side of business cases is flawed and nobody follows through to see if a single requirement actually contributed to value creation as much as was expected by those who asked for it.

To effectively manage everlasting changes and creeping requirements (which normally translate into a quickly moving schedule, budget overruns, and decreasing SLA quality) is to stubbornly stick to the principle that engineering change requests must be based on allocated requirements. To support the management of variants, we recommend product line scenarios in which some of the tools we recommend later on can help with managing the baseline of reused and reusable requirements as well as those requirements that are market-specific. Linking those requirements to test cases reduces the overheads in managing the evolution of variants.

By definition, all requirements in global development projects must be accessible online along with other relevant product and project information. Beginning with simple spreadsheets, different tools can be used. We have seen entire projects which have been managed through the use of one spreadsheet. Such a spreadsheet has all requirements, their status, effort, responsible and mapping to increments, test cases, and work products. Reporting can be generated directly from such a spreadsheet. For bigger projects we recommend online accessible vaulting systems to trace requirements to work products. A requirements database helps with this effort. Contents include requirements, implementation status of each requirement, priorities, estimated cost, value assessment, mapping to releases (especially future releases to communicate the roadmap), relationships between requirements, and links to related implementation and test details.

Tools certainly help in managing requirements in a global context. They are, however, not a solution to requirements related risk management. For global development projects with more than a few engineers involved and for projects that are scattered between two and more locations, we recommend a professional requirements engineering tool that is capable of storing and organizing requirements and managing changes and traceability.

The impacts of a "simple" change proposal are highlighted in Figure 6.2. The complexity of the picture underlines why changes must be very carefully evaluated. Having a project plan that is directly linked with requirements is mandatory for all projects. If there is a change to the plan or to the content of the plan, both must be synchronized and approved by the entire core team.

In global software engineering and IT, change management is impossible to handle without automated tools, support and the discipline to maintain impact analysis, and traceability relationships. Traceability must always consider the hori-

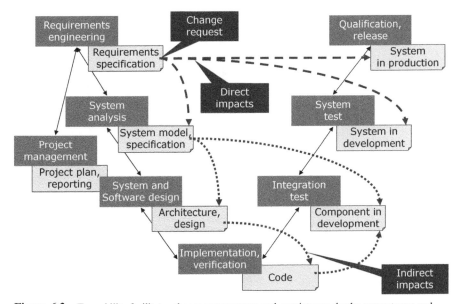

Figure 6.2   Traceability facilitates change management and consistency checks across teams and organizational boundaries.

zontal dependencies between requirements (or artifacts on same abstraction level) and vertical traceability from a work product on a higher abstraction level to one closer to the implementation (or downstream in the product life-cycle).

 Outsourcing/offshoring doesn't work without adequate tools, support, and discipline for change management.

For managing contracts and SLAs it is absolutely necessary to have time-stamped extracts of requirements, their applicability, their contract level, their mapping to various work products (e.g., design, test cases, project work packages, priorities, dependencies on other requirements or already implemented functionality, etc.). They should have an open interface to interface with collaboration tools used downstream of the project and to other related tools, such as project management. Open interfaces allow for the building of data exchange with suppliers using different tools.

Chapter 7

Estimation and Planning

Summary: Estimating size and resources is one of the most important topics in global software engineering and IT. You will not deliver according to expectations if you don't plan ahead, and, you cannot plan if you don't know the underlying dependencies and estimates. We will provide concrete guidance on estimation as well as some tools to check estimates and plans.

An estimate is a quantitative assessment of the likely amount or outcome of a future endeavor. The phrase is usually applied to forecast project costs, size, resources, effort, or durations. Given that estimates can, by definition, be imprecise, they should always include some indication of accuracy (e.g. ±x percent). Increasingly, the dynamics of the software market are shifting to include use of external components and adapting codes rather than writing codes from scratch. This has lead to new and extended kinds of technologies for the estimation. Gradually, estimation moves away from mere size-based estimation toward functional and component estimation. Standards are evolving because estimates play a crucial role in business and because enormous amounts of money are at stake.

Often estimates are confused with goals or plans. For instance, projects are scheduled according to needs but not necessarily in line with feasibility. Sometimes commitments are given to clients on something "very urgent and important" before anyone has checked how this "urgency" relates to previous commitments and capacity planning. Most failures in global software projects come from not understanding and considering this important difference between goals, estimates, and plans [Ebert07a, IDC07, Jones07, Hussey08, Rivard08]. Figure 7.1 shows these three different perspectives and how they relate to each other [SWEBOK11].

Estimation and planning for global software projects follows the typical processes of impact analysis, work breakdown, dependencies, and critical path analysis. This book will not repeat those in detail, especially as there are plenty of examples of good experiences and best practices available in literature [Ebert07a, Jones07].

A good starting point for best practices in estimation and planning is the CMMI [SEI11]. The process areas of project planning, integrated project management, risk management, requirements development, technical solution, and organizational

Global Software and IT: A Guide to Distributed Development, Projects, and Outsourcing,
First Edition. Christof Ebert.
© 2012 the Institute of Electrical and Electronics Engineers, Inc. Published 2012 by
John Wiley & Sons, Inc.

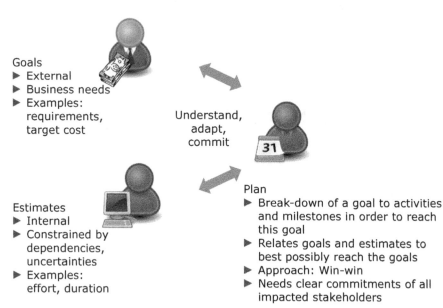

Goals
- External
- Business needs
- Examples:
  requirements,
  target cost

Understand,
adapt,
commit

Estimates
- Internal
- Constrained by
  dependencies,
  uncertainties
- Examples:
  effort, duration

Plan
- Break-down of a goal to activities
  and milestones in order to reach
  this goal
- Relates goals and estimates to
  best possibly reach the goals
- Approach: Win-win
- Needs clear commitments of all
  impacted stakeholders

Figure 7.1   Goals, estimates, and plans must match to achieve realistic commitments and deliveries.

environment for integration should especially be considered for planning in a global context. Additionally, for companies in the IT service domain, COBIT and ITIL are helpful toward learning about basic service processes and risk management [COBIT05, ITIL07].

Global development and sourcing projects should start with clearly defined business goals. Such goals are external to the specific software or IT project and set constraints which are necessary to take into account when making a plan. A business goal relates business needs, such as increasing profitability, to investing resources, such as starting a project or launching a product with a given budget, content, and timing. A goal may be, for instance, to reach a certain milestone at a given date or to extend testing by some time to achieve a desired quality level.

A global software company wanted to reduce engineering cost so it looked to outsource some of the test activities to a low-cost country. The supplier in that country was interested in building up a long-term relationship and growing toward more advanced assignments, such as software design. This was not what the client had in mind. In day-to-day business this different set of goals caused many conflicts because the client would send defective software for which the supplier often made proposals for redesign possibilities and tried to convince the client to act on those suggestions.

An estimate is the well-founded evaluation of how much time and resources would be necessary to achieve a stated goal. Estimates are typically generated internally and are not necessarily externally visible. They should not be driven by the goal because doing so could make the estimate overly optimistic. Of course, the underlying solutions which drive the estimates should be aligned with the goals. Estimates are generated by experts who are familiar with the product or project. In software and IT projects this could be the effort necessary to deliver at a given milestone.

A plan is the breakdown of a goal into activities and milestones that are constructed in order to reach this goal. The plan should be in line with the goal and the estimate, which is not necessarily easy and obvious, such as when a software project with given requirements will likely take longer than the target date that is foreseen by the client. In such cases, plans demand a review of initial goals as well as estimates and the underlying uncertainties and inaccuracies. Creative solutions with the underlying rationale of achieving a win-win position are applied to resolve conflicts. To be useful, the plan needs to achieve commitment with impacted stakeholders.

An ICT company wanted to outsource their network integration testing. Their clear business objective was to cut cost. They looked for a supplier with global coverage and found three companies capable of delivering this entire business process. In the evaluations and further negotiations the client looked to cut down on daily rates in order to achieve a cost reduction objective. SLAs were negotiated to sustain the quality level after the outsourcing would take place. The contract was closed and then the outsourcing started. The supplier soon realized that his efforts would be considerably higher than estimated because the test demanded more thorough preparation of each test line—again and again. Within a few months the margins shrank and they wanted to renegotiate. This, however, was not foreseen in the SLA and contract. Since this did not work, the supplier worked further toward building an exit from the SLA without losing his reputation. They found a strategy and within one year the contract was cancelled. Subsequent cost of the client was rather high because first they had to take the business back to their own premises to ensure business continuity before trying to find a new supplier with much higher rates.

 It is relevant in global software and IT projects that business goals are understood by all stakeholders and used to achieve a win-win situation. Goals must be translated to the respective task or process that is being globally executed. They help in arbitrating and short-term prioritizing and decision-making. Do not hide relevant goals. Avoid tying the supplier into a situation and SLA in which he can only lose. You, as a client, will also lose.

Global software and IT projects use four families of estimation techniques, namely, expert judgment, analogy, decomposition, and statistical (or parametric) methods.

- **Expert judgment** is based on the brainstorming of one or more experts who have experience with similar projects. An expert-consensus mechanism such as the Delphi Technique may be used to produce the estimate.

- **Analogy estimating** is based on the comparison of similar previous activities and on an analysis of the most relevant projects, products, and service attributes to try to figure out, from the experience of estimators, which could be the effort and cost values for the new project. Expert judgment requires skilled people who are able to properly understand relationships and implicitly evaluate qualitative and quantitative figures among projects to determine possible clusters of projects.

- **Decomposition** is a top-down estimation technique which tries to make the list of tasks initially planned more and more granular. The more granular the tasks associated to a certain requirement in a WBS, the closer the planned effort becomes with its final value, therefore reducing the mean relative error and the possible slippage in delivering the project's outcomes.

- **Statistical or parametric models** are a set of related mathematical equations in which alternative scenarios are defined by changing the assumed values of a set of fixed coefficients (parameters). Software project managers use software parametric models or parametric estimation tools to produce estimates of a project's duration, staffing, and cost.

Due to the risk in international sourcing projects and the many incidents between clients and suppliers, many estimation techniques are globally standardized by ISO. In 1998, ISO started to create the ISO-14143 family for function point–related estimations. This stated a series of common criteria for recognizing possible functional size measurement methods. Currently, five methods are also ISO standards: IFPUG (ISO 20926:2009), COSMIC (ISO 19761:2011), NESMA (ISO 24570:2005), Mark-II (ISO 20968:2002), and FISMA (ISO 29881:2010). All these methods size the functional user requirements for a software product as a sizing baseline which is then adjusted to estimate effort [Ebert07a].

Figure 7.2 gives an example of how different global development scenarios impact the project cost drivers. The first scenario (top) shows the cost for a fully colocated development. Evidently, there are no interface overheads because the team is sitting in one place. With an assumed total effort of 10,000 person-hours and a cost ratio of 30% if work is done in a low cost country, we find the distribution as depicted in the top part of the diagram. The total cost would be 10,000 cost entities. When globally distributed development takes place in two sites, the picture changes. While absolute effort (for simplicity) is kept unchanged, and design, project management, and interface management are primarily handled in the two sites, we face a total of 11,500 person-hours (due to the overheads of working at two sites), and a cost reduction of 19% toward 8,100 cost entities. With a fully offshored development (design and test) that preserves only the upstream activities in the high-cost country, the total effort further increases towards 11,000 person-hours, but with a total cost of only half the original cost, namely 5,000 cost entities.

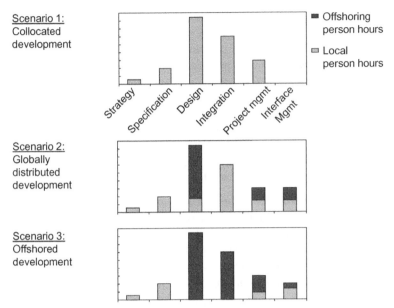

Scenario 1:
Collocated
development

Scenario 2:
Globally
distributed
development

Scenario 3:
Offshored
development

Figure 7.2   Cost structure for same development project handled in different global development modes.

Similar effects can be observed for quality, schedule accuracy, change management, and non-functional requirements [Damian03b, Ebert01b, Herbsleb00, Jones07]. The worst scenario in terms of performance is scenario 2, with split work across sites. We did a study of projects where we could distinguish between them according to the factors of collocation and allocation degree [Ebert01b]. Colocated teams achieve an efficiency improvement during initial validation activities of over 50%. With the same amount of initial defects after code complete, they would need half the effort for removing remaining defects for a defined quality level at the exit gate. Small projects with highly scattered resources show less than half the productivity when compared with projects with fully allocated staff. Cycle time is similarly impacted.

In global software projects, people and their cultures should be considered carefully. Oftentimes there is a general lack of historical data in organizations, therefore estimates are done mainly through analogy and experience. Only with experienced people can you start to build a proper historical database and regularly gather data there. To do so, you must focus on people in order to run estimates today and to plan how to design and implement historical databases for the purpose of catching and retrieving the experience within the organization during the years. Tools can help in reducing times and costs for data gathering; tools can partly produce reports after you decide which phenomenon and by which criteria they should be analyzed. I It would, however, be unrealistic to think they could properly do more than this.

What historical data should be collected and used? As a size measurement we recommend Function Points as they are well-defined and help to start with software product functional user requirements. Effort should be gathered in person-hours rather than in person-days. Do not store extra hours during the day or make those numbers incomparable for benchmarking purposes. Errors or incidents should be classified by severity and implementation priority for planning and scheduling purposes in a service desk process.

In judging estimates from external suppliers or teams in different sites, we recommend using benchmarking databases [Ebert07b, Jones07]. These databases include parameterized data sets from thousands of IT and software projects, many of which were done in a global setting. Often, Function Points are used as an underlying methodology to allow for the comparing of apples and apples. The most widely used databases for such estimation checks in global IT and software projects are:

- **QSM and SLIM Control**[1]. It is a proprietary empirical software estimation model in which effort is a function of size (e.g., Function Points, LOC), productivity, and time and a scaling factor. It is a nice tool to use to play with parameters, for instance, to see the impact on effort and delivery quality directly when advancing or relaxing a deadline.

- **SPR KnowledgePlan.**[2] Similar to QSM it is a proprietary software tool designed for sizing projects and to estimate work, resources, schedule, and defects. It allows you to evaluate project strengths and weaknesses and to determine their impact on quality and productivity.

- **COCOMO.**[3] The Cost Constructive Model (COCOMO II) is a parametric model used for software development projects. It allows the backfiring calculation from LOC to Function Points. Although the underlying empirical base is much lower than in the other databases and respective tools, it has a wide popularity due to its use in education.

- **ISBSG.**[4] The international software benchmarking database allows you to make online evaluations on schedule, duration, and so on of an estimate that is based on very few parameters. Compared with QSM and KnowledgePlan it demands much less by way of parameters, is in its free online accessible entry version, and can be easily used for a quick check.

 Use standardized functional size measurements, that is, function points of a certain type, and establish clear counting rules. Use international standards for sizing in case you work with different suppliers. This allows baselining the work to be done and gives you the ability to compare results later. Finally, derive effort and plans from these basis size measurements by analogy and by using work breakdown structure which relate to the project plan.

---

[1] http://www.qsm.com/tools/index.html
[2] http://www.spr.com/spr-knowledgeplan.html
[3] http://csse.usc.edu/tools/COCOMOSuite.php
[4] http://www.isbsg.org

Some additional hints derived from our outsourcing/offshoring experiences will help for estimation and planning:

- Assure a single requirements repository. Requirements are becoming increasingly unstable. They achieve shorter lead times and faster reaction in changing markets. The risk is that the project is built on a moving baseline, which is one of the most often quoted reasons for project failure. Global development projects need a central requirements repository and clear responsibility for making changes to it. The requirements must provide links to further information, a specified owner, the full impact analysis, responsibility for implementation, and the allocation to work packages and work products.

- Ask the global teams to estimate and plan the work they ought to perform. This achieves buy-in and also demands that they understand the assignment. Obviously, their results might deviate from what the project manager expects, which should rive a technical review of selected design alternatives and their impact. Do not cut such personal or team estimates without talking, but enforce that teams defend their estimates versus higher management.

- Plan your decisions based on work breakdown and actual skills. Plans are based on average performance indicators and history data. The smaller the project and the more the critical paths that are established due to requested expert knowledge, the higher the risk of having a reasonable plan from a macroscopic viewpoint that never achieves the targets on the microscopic level of individual experts' availability, effectiveness, and skills. It was shown in several studies that individual experience and performance contributes up to 70% of overall productivity ranges [Jones07, Ebert07a, McConnell03].

- Verify estimates and perform a feasibility analysis. Estimations are based on individual judgment and, as such, are highly subjective. Applying any estimation model expresses, first of all, the experience and judgment of the assigned expert. Even simple models such as Function Points are reported as yielding reproducibility inaccuracy of greater than 30% [Ebert07a, Jones07]. To reduce the risk related to decision making based on such estimates a Delphi-style approach can be applied that focuses multiple expert inputs on one estimate. Feasibility can be evaluated in simulating a project plan or relating it to previous experiences with tools such as QSM.

- Measure actual results and update your estimation rules. Most estimates are based on history data and formulae from operational databases. Faults, changes, effort, even the task breakdown are recorded by individuals who often do not necessarily care for data quality, especially when it comes to delivery and time pressure. Measurements must be verified and upon finished analysis, fed back to the estimation tool.

Traditional project planning and tracking looked at actual results versus plans. When the plans are adjusted after the facts it demonstrates that they are not reachable. This method creates too many delays and is not sufficiently precise to drive concrete corrective actions on the spot. For global development projects, such monitoring often means that difficulties accumulate for too long. Therefore, continuous predictions should be used to relate actual constraints and performance to historic performance results. Good forecasts allow for adjusting plans and mitigating risks long before the actual performance tracking measurements would visualize such results. For instance, knowing about average mean time to defect allows planning for maintenance staff, help desk and support centers, and service level agreements.

Chapter 8

Development Processes

Summary: Global software development and IT demand specific development and management processes. It is relevant to consider cultural and personal aspects in coining the right global development process. In this chapter we will emphasize the need for clear rules on collaboration regarding roles, interfaces, tools, and work products. Practical examples highlight how companies set up and maintain such rules.

Global software and IT projects typically have some sort of supplier-client relationship, even if there is only one company with a captive development center. It is important for clients and suppliers to have shared processes and to maintain clear rules on collaboration regarding roles, interfaces, tools, work products, and so on. Empirical studies highlight that success is higher when both the client and supplier firms exhibit at least CMMI maturity level three [Rottmann06]. Figure 8.1 shows the mutual dependencies between supplier and client process maturity [Ebert07a].

 Outsourcing insufficient engineering and management processes is a key reason for failed outsourcing projects. Insufficient processes are amplified as soon as distance and corporate boundaries add towards complexity.

From all our empirical research we can conclude that organizations on CMMI maturity level one or two should not expect that global software engineering would yield much benefit. Instead, it will reveal major deficiencies in processes and workflow, which create all types of difficulties, such as insufficient quality, delays, additional cost, canceled offshoring contracts, unmotivated workforces in both places (previous and new), and many more problems besides. The only viable alternative for such low-maturity organizations is to ramp-up the home companie's processes before proceeding with global software engineering and IT.

Different societies—and often persons on the microscopic level—have different values and underlying driving factors [House04, O'Hara94, Krishna04]. For instance,

Global Software and IT: A Guide to Distributed Development, Projects, and Outsourcing,
First Edition. Christof Ebert.
© 2012 the Institute of Electrical and Electronics Engineers, Inc. Published 2012 by
John Wiley & Sons, Inc.

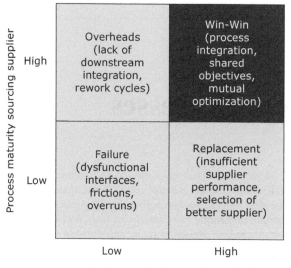

Figure 8.1 Process maturity of suppliers and clients must match.

time perception varies dramatically across societies around the globe. Some focus on the past or present, while others are very future-oriented. Though this can explained sociologically, such as the foreseeable or the always surprising effects of nature on the destiny of a certain region of the world, it impacts behaviors. Therefore, the concept of urgency is different in such societies. Creating hard deadlines or considering a milestone as a deadline might work well in some societies, but it may also fail without adequate training in another.

Administration and planning might traditionally be considered highly relevant in, for example, northern countries and in China (northern countries due to the need to plan for long winters, China due to thousands of years of highly sophisticated administrations) or, in other countries, they might be almost irrelevant. Another example of cultural differences would be trust. Some cultures do not care about written documents and primarily take a person and his word, while others demand written documents and evidence before they will accept results. Awareness of such differences allows you to consider them in terms of team building, setting a shared vision, and shared values and objectives. Shared values and training on such different societal attitudes is a key aspect in preparing the right development process and balancing the need for checkpoints with the level of acceptable and meaningful concrete deliverables. Needless to say, these societal differences are increasingly being reduced with growing globalization. This can be seen in the Indian software industry, which, over the decades, has adjusted extremely well to the northwestern way of planning and tracking.

Global development must balance managed processes with enough flexibility to ease the work for individual engineers, specifically, when engineers must act fast and don't have the time to synch around the globe's time zones. This is difficult and needs profound understanding (driven from business rationales) as to how to structure and tailor processes to avoid unnecessary overheads. Facilitate processes wherever possible, such as by creating standardized templates for work products, or tools for workflow management, Both of which reduce errors and improve productivity.

Global development benefits by chunking deliverables into self-contained work products that can be stepwise stabilized and integrated. It is based on the old Roman idea that self-contained pieces are easier to govern than a huge complex system, the so-called divide and conquer paradigm. This paradigm holds whether you do maintenance on a big legacy system, application and service development, or the engineering of a new system. Incremental development and related life-cycle models are known and applied for many years to address this "chunking" and stepwise stabilization [McConnell98, Royce98, Karlsson00].

Today, "chunking" and stepwise stabalization are enhanced by agile methods [Schwaber04]. Increments toward a stable build are one of the key success factors in global development. They ensure that deliveries from different teams or places in the world can be effectively integrated. Within periodic intervals, a validated baseline is made available for all team members upon which they build their enhancements or maintenance changes.

 Incremental development reduces delivery and quality risks because progress within the team is more continuous and can be more easily monitored. Utilize agile practices such as Scrum to build trust across sites and to ensure delivery in time, budget, and quality.

Traditionally, agile development methodologies have been demanded small colocated teams. This allows fast interaction between team members and, when necessary, immediate reaction and consideration of feature changes demanded by a customer. This seems to be in contradiction with the entire paradigm of global software engineering and IT—at least for any distributed development. It is certainly true from a microscopic perspective: Don't split team tasks and responsibilities across sites if it can be avoided. For instance, if code is developed in one place and unit tested in another, there is certainly the risk of inefficiency, misunderstandings, and inconsistencies. From the macroscopic view, distribution and global development are in line with the needs of agile development. It forces you to split the work in a way that will maximize team cohesion and minimize coupling. For instance, qualification testing or network integration in communication solutions can well be done at another place than the underlying application development. Requirements and business cases can be developed in different organizational and geographic layouts than the resulting designs and code.

In fact, hardware development has long proven that, with the right collaboration technologies, outsourced manufacturers can work with design teams in other physical places given that they have sound and integrated engineering change management, product data management, and the like.

Within global engineering projects, it is not frequently obvious how to implement an entirely incremental approach to architecture that is primarily driven by interacting classes or subsystems. Clearly, it would be advantageous to have isolated add-on functionality or independent components. In real-world systems, specifically in legacy systems that are maintained in low cost countries, development during top level (or architectural design) not only agree on interfaces and impacts on various subsystems, but also on a work split which is aligned with subsystems. The clash often comes when these subsystems should be integrated with all new functionality. Such processes are characterized by extremely long integration cycles that don't show any measurable progress in terms of feature content.

The following steps show how incremental development principles can be introduced and become beneficial for global engineering:

- Analyze requirements from the beginning in terms of how they could be clustered to related functionality, which could later be delivered as an increment.

- Analyze context impacts of all increments upfront before start of development (e.g., data structures that are common for all modules). The elaboration phase is critical to make real incremental development and a stable test line feasible. Obviously, not all context impacts can be addressed immediately without extending the elaboration phase toward what is unacceptable. Thus, it is necessary to measure context stability and to follow up with root cause analysis as to why certain context impacts were overseen. As a target, the elaboration should not take longer than one third of total elapsed time. The reminder of the project duration is related to the development activities.

- Provide a project plan that is based on these sets of clustered customer requirements and that allocates development teams to each set. Depending on the impact of the increments, they can be delivered to the test line more or less frequently. For instance, if a context impact is detected too late, a new production cycle is necessary which will take more effort and lead time than regular asynchronous increments of additional code within the originally defined context.

- Each increment is developed within one dedicated team, although a team might be assigned to several increments in a row. Increments must be completed until the end of unit tests and feature integration tests so that the various components can always be accepted to the test line. A key criterion for the quality of increments is that they don't break the build.

- The progress tracking of development and test is primarily based on the integration and testing of single customer requirements. This, for the first time, gives visibility to real progress because a requirement can only be checked off if it is successfully integrated in the test line. Traceability is improved because each customer requirement links to the related work products.

- Increments are extensively feature-tested by the independent test line before starting system tests. The test activity itself is done by means of daily (or frequent) build for all modules.

A lot could be added about development processes, but this is mostly sound software engineering knowledge that I will not repeat. For more information, I recommend checking the respective resources, such as [McConnell03].

Chapter 9

Practice: Global Software Architecture Development

Daniel J. Paulish, Siemens

Summary: This chapter provides a case study from Siemens and shows how best to apply architecture development in globally distributed software projects. The case study highlights relevant themes and guidance from previous chapters in a concrete project context. It offers valuable insights toward how to do things in your own company.It discusses some of the organizational and technical issues involved in doing global design and development. Finally, it describes a few techniques that have been successfully used on distributed projects to design software systems and manage the design and development after the high-level design phase is complete.

BACKGROUND

As software design and development teams are geographically distributed, coordination and control become more difficult due to distance, time zones, and cultural differences. Some project tasks can be distributed among collaborating staff located far away from one another, but some tasks, such as architecture design, are better done locally at a single site with staff sitting together in one room. Architecture design is a highly collaborative task that is usually done by a small team. It requires many discussions about design tradeoffs, real-time decisions, and specifications development.

Global Software and IT: A Guide to Distributed Development, Projects, and Outsourcing,
First Edition. Christof Ebert.
© 2012 the Institute of Electrical and Electronics Engineers, Inc. Published 2012 by
John Wiley & Sons, Inc.

Mike had just learned that his next assignment would be as a system design team member for a large transportation system project for a major North American city. He knew that there were already tens of thousands of contracted features in the requirements database, which was still growing. What was unique about this project, however, was that the architects with whom Mike would be working were located in four different countries around the world. He had never met any of these remote architects. Mike was understandably apprehensive about how he would efficiently collaborate with these distributed systems engineers. He was relieved to learn that the contracted features were all described in English, and that the customer was located just a short flight away. He suspected that he would be doing much traveling for this project, and he checked his personal calendar for the next few months.

Although it may be desirable to design a product at a single location, as projects become larger it may not be possible to house the development team in a single location. For large complex systems, it is not very likely that all the domain experts necessary to design a product line will be living in the same city. Thus, design processes for distributed projects must recreate the highly interactive and efficient communications of, say, the architecture design team gathered around the white board.

Architecture design for distributed development projects requires enhanced processes in two primary areas as compared to colocated projects.

Higher quality design artifacts: Engineers on distributed development projects will usually learn about the high-level design from reading design specifications. Thus, the artifacts generated from the high-level design process must be readable and understandable. Remote team members in distributed projects will not be able to ask questions of clarification of the designers who defined the system architecture as easily as in colocated projects. For distributed projects, models will more likely be used to describe the designbecause some team members with limited English language skills will not be able to easily read long specifications written in English. Defects introduced in design may not be so easily discovered by remote teams working on downstream processes. When remote teams with limited domain know-how develop the product, they may implement exactly what is described in the design specifications even though it may be incorrectly specified.

Improved collaborations: On distributed projects, central designers may not have the possibility for quick response communications and casual communications with distant designers. In fact, an architect working at one site may work while another architect at a different site in a different time zone is sleeping. For example, architect A has a question about a design that was described by architect B at another site. Architect A e-mails his question to architect B who is sleeping while architect A is working. Architect B comes to work the next day and answers the question by e-mail when architect A is sleeping. With such asynchronous communications, one can see how it can take substantial time before the requesting engineer receives a response to his question. Although architects in distributed sites will adjust their work hours to allow some overlap, we have noticed that most architects prefer to sleep when it's dark. Thus, collaboration tools are used to support question and answer communications, so that design decisions are not lost in a stack of e-mail messages.

Software architects perform design tradeoffs by drawing proposed design diagrams on a white board, and then discussing and modifying the design until it is stable enough to be documented within an architecture design document [Clements03]. Architects must design a system architecture that optimally meets both the functional and non-functional requirements [Berenbach09].

The following has been observed about how architects work on system design projects [Herbsleb05].

There are many design tradeoffs that must be performed. The design team will have many face-to-face meetings to determine which architecturally significant requirements are the most important to consider [Sangwan07]. Thus, high-level design is very iterative, requiring frequent communications among a design team whose members have differing skills and viewpoints as to how the system design will look. The frequent communication among the design team members requires that team members are colocated or that they come together for regularly scheduled design workshops. In a large survey among professionals on their experiences with distributed development, communication in the form of face-to-face meetings was frequently mentioned as a solution to diverse project problems [Illes-Seifert07].

A key role on a software systems design and development project is the chief architect. The chief architect is the primary technical decision maker for the project. The design team members will propose many alternative designs while considering how the architecturally significant requirements will be satisfied. As the leader of the system design team, the chief architect will decide on the design alternatives that will be used and documented for the project. "Just in time" decision making is required, since the chief architect needs to allow time for all the good alternatives to emerge from the team while still making timely decisions so that alternatives are not debated unnecessarily and the high-level design work can be completed within a time-boxed schedule [Paulish02].

Thus, architects will work on creating a system design within a small team lead by the chief architect. The team will have many face-to-face meetings to discuss the various design alternatives before documenting the system design for other remote designers who will do lower level design in accordance with the high-level design. Thus, system design is an activity that requires face-to-face contact in order to make progress. In distributed projects, the system designers must be brought together at a single location to be able to work together to do the tradeoffs and to consider alternative designs during the design workshops.

There are a number of organizations that are used for system design teams working on distributed projects. For example, we have had some success using an "extended workbench model" for distributed development (Fig. 9.1) on the Global Studio Project [Sangwan07].

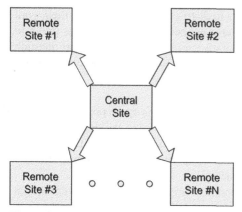

Figure 9.1   Example "extended workbench model" distributed development organization.

In that project, a small architecture team is part of a central organization in which members are assigned full-time from both the central and remote sites. The central organization operates with a chief architect as its technical leader and a project manager responsible for the entire product life-cycle. With the extended workbench model, the central team's architecture design tasks are staffed with some members of the future remote development teams who have temporarily relocated to work at the central site. Ideally, the time spent at the central site (e.g., 6 months) is used to "train" the future remote team members on the application domain, architecture, tools, and processes that will be used during the development. These team members will hopefully become team leaders of the remote development teams upon returning to their home sites. The design artifacts created by the central architecture team will be given to the remote teams for them to understand the high-level architecture of the system that they will be developing.

Design information is transferred from the central team to each remote component development team in the form of models and specifications. The documentation package is used to help communicate the work that will be done to the remote teams in accordance with the development plan. The work to be done is scoped to be implemented by a relatively small component development team (maximum of 10 engineers). These organizational approaches may change over time. For example, a component may be allocated to a distributed team in the beginning with the intent that, over time, the remote site will develop the skills to become a competence center in the functionality of that component [Avritzer08a].

Figure 9.2 gives an example organization showing the relationship between the central and remote teams for an extended workbench model. The project manager has the overall responsibility for the life-cycle of product development. The chief architect is the head of the architecture team and has overall responsibility for technical decisions affecting the product's functionality and performance. The members of the remote component development teams report to a local R&D resource manager

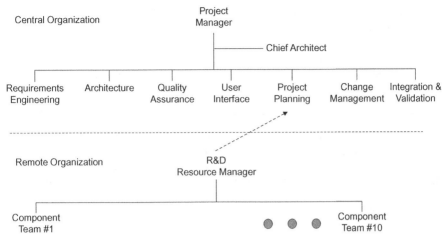

Figure 9.2   Example reporting relationships between central and remote teams.

at their site. The remote teams report to the project manager at the central location, usually through an assigned supplier manager.

When working with remote organizations that have unique domain and technical expertise, a "system of systems" approach may be used for distributed development [Avritzer08b]. With this approach, the software development process is still developed and managed centrally, but the system design team is extended with key domain experts who are resident at the remote sites. Their specialized domain knowledge drives the software architecture specification efforts during the early phase activities. Frequent communication between the central and remote teams and among the remote teams is encouraged. Unlike the extended workbench model approach, the central team is not required to coordinate the communications among the distributed teams.

Although in systems approach the system designers are spread across multiple sites, it is still necessary to bring them together periodically for the system design workshops. Typically, there will be more colocated meetings of the system designers at the beginning or early phases of the project. As the system architecture is documented and reviewed, the system design team members will spend more time at their home sites and will become more involved with lower level design and development activities.

There are many practices that are used to make the system design workshops more efficient. For example, jet lag can be a major concern when architects come together from different parts of the world for a design workshop. One practice used to combat jet lag is to colocate the system design team for three weeks at a time before giving them two weeks at their home site to work individually on documentation and to catch up with local obligations to their development team. We have been told by traveling architects that the 3/2 week schedule is preferable to the more common practice where a week-long design workshop is held every month. In this case, architects can lose efficiency as their bodies must adjust to different time zones more frequently.

When a high-level system design is completed, documented, and distributed to remote designers, there's always the possibility that the architecture will drift due to misunderstandings or lower level design changes. Thus, the central design team must provide an oversight function and conduct design reviews with the remote teams. In some cases, the high-level architecture may be modified to accommodate the lower level designs, but this should be a decision considered by the chief architect.

The two most critical roles on any development project are the project manager and the chief architect. The project manager is concerned about schedules, budget, organization, staffing, and meeting these objectives. The chief architect is concerned about the various technical decisions of the project. In a global software and IT project, these roles are pivotal and should be both well trained and well supported.

For global development projects, the project manager and chief architect must make decisions for a team that is geographically distributed and not under their direct control. Thus, in addition to the usual required management and technical skills, they must be able to work effectively with staffs from differing country and company cultures. Their communication skills will be stretched as they attempt to lead and interact with staff whom they may never have met and who may have performance incentives that are different from their own. We recommend that staff members assigned to these roles for global projects have intercultural experience or are given intercultural sensitivity training early in the project. Furthermore, they will need to be flexible and adaptable as project progress and status changes due to events that are beyond their control; for example, changes in political conditions in the countries in which their development teams are located [Sangwan07].

Design artifacts must be high quality since the author of a specification may not be easily accessible to answer questions from the readers (users) of the specification. High quality artifacts will likely be associated with a review process so that stakeholders and technical experts can review the documents before they are distributed to a large group of distributed developers. Agile techniques, such as Scrum, help in organizing global development teams towards high quality [Schwaber04].

For the Global Studio Project, we used Scrum teams to conduct daily stand up meetings to help coordinate the activities within the team. These short meetings typically address three questions: What have you done? what do you plan to do? And, is there anything standing in the way of making progress? For global development, we recommend a weekly coordination teleconference that is facilitated by the project manager with a representative from each component development team, called a "Scrum of Scrums." The audio portion of the weekly teleconference can be augmented with a desktop sharing tool so that presentation charts, diagrams, or documents can be viewed by all the participants.

We recommend using video conferences for "special" meetings. These meetings should include iteration kick-off meetings, review meetings, or meetings where technical documentation is exchanged or discussed between the central team and one remote team. Since the video conference equipment is usually a shared resource, these meetings would likely be scheduled in advance. In contrast, weekly teleconference would be scheduled in the same time slot each work week. If staff members are not at their work place during the fixed time slot, they can call in to the teleconference. When participants are not available due to vacation or illness, they should assign a proxy to participate in the weekly Scrum of Scrums meeting.

Many of the communications between the central and remote teams will necessarily be in the form of e-mail. This is particularly likely between sites, for example, in the United States and India because one team is likely to be working when the other team is sleeping. It is suggested that a secure intranet as well as virtual private networks are set up for such e-mails and development tools. This will provide some degree of protection of proprietary project communications and artifacts.

 Communication in distributed development projects should be supported by a mixture of different communication mechanisms, such as e-mail, telephone, collaboration web site (wiki), teleconferences, and video conferences.

We recommend that a collaboration web site (e.g., wiki) be set up for all team members to view decisions made on the project, store key documents, and support asynchronous discussions (e.g., forums). This collaboration site should also contain the tool set that will be used on the project as well as relevant training information. The collaboration web site can also link in to the development site. Here, team members will be able to submit code to a build, run regression tests, and generate release notes describing which features are implemented in each version of the software. For such projects, we recommend continuous integration techniques. Ideally, anyone on the project should be able to view the current status of the development by running the current build.

RESULTS

Distance and time zones can make communication between architects on distributed projects difficult. The informal "water cooler" communications are lost when team members are located at different sites. Thus, you must compensate for these lost communications with better specifications, collaboration tools, and periodic face-to-face meetings.

Intercultural and language differences can also hinder effective communication among the architects. Designs will be described in written and verbal forms, as well as in models (e.g., described in UML), that everybody on the team can understand. Work habits, educational backgrounds, and value systems will vary among the architects working at the distributed sites. Central site architects will need to have some understanding of cultural differences to be able to work effectively with the remote architects residing in other countries. We suggest having a kick-off meeting at the beginning of a project so that key team members can meet each other face-to-face before working together. One possible activity during the kick-off meeting is intercultural training.

Team size is a concern not only for a distributed project but for any project that has more than a few team members. As the team size gets larger, there are more communication paths among the team members. Thus, adding people to a software development project may be a way to get more work done, but individual productivity will decrease as team members have more people that they will need to communicate with to accomplish their work. For very large projects, some team members (e.g., the chief architect) are likely to spend most of their time communicating and very little of their time on developing project artifacts. Ideally, project managers recognize this negative productivity impact and strive to keep their development teams as small as possible. However, there is great pressure to bring new products to market quickly. Most project teams will likely be larger than is desirable. One solution to this problem is to break the project work into pieces that can each be done by a small team and then to have the pieces integrated by another team. The resulting organization is a collection of small teams that communicate between one another for predefined reasons or that have specialists who do the communicating. Based on our experience with large projects, we recommend, as rules of thumb, that no individual team is larger than 10 members and that the team members have their work places within 50 meters of each other [Allen84]. Furthermore, the team should have a work or conference room in which they can all fit for joint work tasks or stand up meetings.

For system design teams, we suggest that the size of the central high-level design team be limited to six architects, lead by a chief architect [Paulish02]. We've observed that large design teams can suffer from a "too many cooks in the kitchen" phenomenon. Smaller design teams can typically reach consensus, make design decisions more quickly, and document their decisions in the design artifacts. The team members must be selected carefully to represent different views, skills, domain expertise, and experience. In addition, for distributed projects, some team members will join the central design team for a limited time period with the intent that they will be leading their development teams when they return to their home country.

TAKE-AWAY TIPS

Some tips for architecture design for global software development projects are summarized below:

- Allow the chief architect to be the technical leader and decision maker for the entire project team.
- Select a chief architect who will be able to work well with the project manager and the remote team leaders and architects (i.e., good communication skills).

- Provide central oversight of the architecture so that it will not drift as lower level designs are done at the remote sites.
- Address the top five to ten concerns when defining the system architecture.
- Set up a kick-off meeting of the key members of all the distributed teams at the beginning of the project so that distributed team members have the chance to meet face-to-face.

Distributed development projects must compensate for the large communication paths from the central team architects to distant development teams. Software architecture is most efficiently done by a small team located at a single site, but today's need to rapidly develop new products demands that teams collaborate with each either across organizational and regional boundaries. Effective collaborations and good quality design artifacts are necessary for successful globally distributed projects.

Chapter 10

Practice: Software Chunks and Distributed Development

Audris Mockus AvayaLabs and David M. Weiss, Iowa State University

Summary: This chapter provides a case study from Lucent and shows how best to introduce distributed development in globally distributed software projects. The case study highlights relevant themes and guidance from previous chapters in a concrete project context. It offers valuable insights toward how to do things in your own company. This chapter shows how to define a quantitative analysis process to identify candidate chunks for distributed development across several locations. We discuss the nature of work items and their representations in change management systems before proposing a technique to distribute the work among multiple locations so that the number of work items spanning sites is minimized.

BACKGROUND

Software development organizations face considerable pressure and incentive to distribute their work [Carmel99]. In this chapter we look for technical solutions that will accommodate the business needs for distributed software development. The problem of distributing development work occurs when the work that is needed to evolve an existing software system cannot be performed by one team in one location because of resource limitations or business imperatives. Often, a highly skilled workforce is available in other countries where the same company has development locations. We investigate quantitative approaches to distributing work across the geographic locations in order to minimize their communication and synchronization needs. The same technique has applications in other areas, including distributing work to contractors in the same country, and assessing the state of an existing distribution.

Our main premise is inspired by Conway's work [Conway68], which suggests that the structure of a software product reflects the organizational structure of the company that produced it, and by Parnas's work [Parnas72], which suggests that the division of labor should be reflected in software modularity. In this chapter we

Global Software and IT: A Guide to Distributed Development, Projects, and Outsourcing,
First Edition. Christof Ebert.
© 2012 the Institute of Electrical and Electronics Engineers, Inc. Published 2012 by
John Wiley & Sons, Inc.

introduce ways to quantify the three-way interactions among the reporting structure of an organization, the geographic distribution of an organization, and the modular structure of source code. Our analysis is based on records of work items, where a work item is an assignment of developers to a task, usually to make changes to the software.

We conjecture that for software development to be most efficient the geographic distribution and reporting structure of the software, organization should match the division of work in software development: work items that are likely to change together, sometimes known as tightly coupled work items, which require frequent coordination and synchronization should be performed within one site and one organizational subdivision. This conjecture is supported by empirical evidence [Grinter99, Herbsleb00].

If one accepts this conjecture, then the question is how to identify such tightly coupled items. Our work is in large part an attempt to identify them by an empirical analysis of the changes made to software. Because of the empirical nature of our analysis, we refer to work items as "chunks" when they represent pieces of code that are being changed. Following the usage of the development projects whose software we have analyzed, we use the term "module" to mean a set of code contained in a directory of files. Note that this is distinct from the definition of information hiding module used by Parnas and others [Parnas72, Parnas85]. In fact, we believe that our chunks correspond to de facto information hiding modules.

The purpose of the typical work item in a software organization is to make a change to a software entity. Work items range in size from very large work items, such as releases, to very small changes, such as a single delta (modification) to a file. Figure 10.1 shows a hierarchy of work items with associated attributes. Boxes with dashed lines define data sources (VCS and CMS), boxes with thick lines define changes, and boxes with thin lines define properties of work items. The arrows define "contains," a relationship among changes; for example, each Maintenance Request (MR) is a part of a feature.

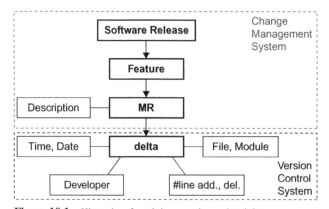

Figure 10.1   Hierarchy of work items and associated data sources.

The source code of large software products is typically organized into subsystems according to major functionality (database, user interface, etc.). Each subsystem contains a number of source code files and documentation. The versions of the source code and documentation are maintained using a version control system (see Chapters 13 and 15). We usually compute the lines changed by a delta by a file differencing algorithm (such as Unix diff), invoked by the VCS, which compares an older version of a file with the current version.

In addition to a VCS, most projects employ a change request management system (CMS) that keeps track of individual requests for changes, which we call Maintenance Requests (MRs). Whereas a delta is used to keep track of lines of code that are changed, an MR is intended to be a change made for a single purpose. Each MR may have many deltas associated with it, although each MR is made for a single purpose. Some commonly used problem tracking systems include ClearQuest from IBM and the Extended Change Management System (ECMS) [Midha97]. Most commercial VCSs also include support for problem tracking. Usually such systems associate a list of deltas with each MR.

There are several possible reasons for requesting a modification, including the need to fix previous changes that caused a failure during testing or in the field, and to introduce new features to the existing system. Some MRs are made to restructure the code to make it easier to understand and maintain. The latter activity is more common in heavily modified code, such as in legacy systems.

Based on informal interviews in a number of software development organizations within Lucent, we obtained the following guidelines for dividing work into MRs. Recall that an MR corresponds to a single purpose. Work items that affect several subsystems (the largest building blocks of functionality) are split into distinct MRs so that each MR affects only one subsystem; a work item in a subsystem that is too big for one person is organized into several MRs so that each one could be completed by a single person.

For practical reasons, these guidelines are not strictly enforced, so that some MRs cross subsystem boundaries and some have several people working on them. A group of MRs associated with new software functionality is called a feature. A set of features and problem fixes constitute a customer delivery, also known as a release. Put another way, each release can be characterized as a base system that is modified and extended by a set of MRs.

If every change to a work item could be made independent of every other change to the same or other work items, the software developer's life would be easy (and software would lose much of its power). Coordination is the set of activities used to understand the effect of a change on the different parts of a single work item, or the effects of a change on different work items. For a software release, all coordination is contained within the release, while for an individual delta on a file, coordination is often only with the other deltas for the file.

Changes made as part of an MR require tight coordination within the change and are preferably done by a single developer. For example, a change to a function's parameters would require a change in function declaration, in function definition, and in all the places in which the function is called. In contrast, the coordination between MR's, although needed, typically does not represent as much coordination as changes within one MR.

The tight coordination needed within an MR suggests that MRs are the smallest work items that may be done independently of each other. In particular, they could be assigned to distinct development sites or to distinct organizations. This hypothesis is supported by the evidence that MRs involving developers distributed across geographic locations take a lot longer to complete (see, e.g., [Herbsleb03]).

According to the general rules of dividing work into MRs described previously, the work items encompassing several MRs may reflect only a weak coupling among the parts of the code that they modify. Such work items may be accomplished by several people. They may also reflect the software's architectural division into separate, independently changeable units.

The tight coupling of work within an MR suggests the following measure of work-item-based coupling between entities in a software project. For two entities A and B the measure of absolute coupling is defined by the number of MRs that result in changes to or activity by both A and B. For example, if A and B represent two subsystems of the source code, the absolute measure of work item coupling would be the number of MRs such that each MR changes the code in both subsystems. The coupling for two groups of developers would be represented by the number of MRs such that each MR has at least one developer from each group assigned to it. In a similar fashion, a coupling is defined as being between a set of code and a group of developers, that is, the number of MRs that are performed by developers in the group and that modify the code.

To adjust for the size of entities A and B, measures of relative coupling may be obtained by dividing the absolute measure by the total number of MRs that relate to A or to B. We should note that coordination needed to accomplish MRs is also embodied in other activities and in ways that are not reflected in the preceding coupling measures. Examples of this would be coordination among MR's in a feature, or coordination during system integration and testing. However, the coordination needs are less likely to be as high between distinct MRs as within an individual MR.

RESULTS

Globalization is the process of distributing software development among several sites. Our main goal is to develop criteria and methods to allow project management so as to make better informed globalization decisions using quantitative evaluation of possible consequences.

We start by asking the question: What work could be transferred from a primary site that has resource shortages to a secondary site that has underutilized resources? We evaluate the costs and benefits of a particular transfer approach and use an algorithm to find the best possible transfer. In studying such transfers in Lucent Technologies we have observed that the following approaches are considered or used (the merits of each are discussed in [Mockus01]):

- Transfer by functionality, where the ownership of a subsystem or set of sub-systems is transferred. This was the most commonly applied approach in the software organizations we studied.

- Transfer by localization- where the software product is modified locally for a local market. An example of such a modification is to translate the documentation and user interface into a local language.

- Transfer by development stage, where different activities are performed at different locations. For example, design and coding may be performed at a different site than system testing.

- Transfer by maintenance stage, where older releases are transferred primarily for their maintenance phase when new features are no longer expected to be added to the release.

We want to describe a process that could help solve the globalization problem. We start by describing a number of factors that were mentioned by people who were involved in globalization decisions during our conversations with them. We present these factors to illustrate some of the complicating issues in globalization. After that we introduce several quantifiable variables and illustrate their use in a globalization decision.

We conjecture that globalization may lead to transfer of work that is in some way undesirable to the primary site. The last three globalization approaches noted in the preceding section reflect different types of "undesirable" work, such as localization, maintenance (often referred to as current engineering), testing, and tools support. We have observed several instances of functionality transfer (the first approach), where the areas that are not desirable to the primary site are transferred. Of course, they may have been transferred for other reasons as well.

We conjecture that the decision to transfer work may involve informal risk management strategies, especially if the transfer is taking place to a secondary site that has not worked with the primary site before or that has had problems working with the primary site in the past. The risk management strategies consist of identifying work that is "not critical" to the overall project in general and to the primary site in particular, so that the completion of the project, and especially the work in the primary location, will not be catastrophically affected by potential delays or quality problems at the secondary site. Examples of such "non critical" work include simulation environments, development tool enhancements, current engineering work, and parts of regression testing. To some extent, the risk management can be done by transferring a functional area, for example, a part of operations, administration, and management (OA&M).

For the work transfer to be successful, the receiving location needs to get appropriate training. If the work involves knowing the fine points of legacy systems, then significant support in training from the primary location has to be expected. Such a situation is likely to arise if the maintenance or testing stages are transferred. The amount of training may be especially high if the secondary location has a high turnover of programmers, thus requiring continuous retraining of the personnel. The training needs vary depending on how specialized the knowledge is that is needed to perform the work. How might one quantify the time and effort needed for developers to become fully productive? We show one way to do so for productivity and for other variables in the next section.

We looked at two aspects of globalization:

- When the competing globalization decisions are evaluated;
- When alternative globalization solutions are generated.

This section talks about the first aspect discussed above, while the second point, generation of alternative solutions, is discussed in the next section. The final globalization decision has to be made based on quantitative and qualitative considerations. For the most common globalization approach, division of functionality among locations, we focus on criteria and measures for several factors, including work coupling, effort, and learning curves. In a later section, we will discuss how to generate candidates that optimize our criteria.

We refer to any collection of files as a globalization candidate. The complementary part of the system contains all other files. Work items spanning locations tend to introduce coordination overheads and associated delays. Consequently, it is desirable to have as few of such work items as possible. This criterion can be approximated by the number of MRs that modify both the candidate and the complementary part of the software, which is the measure of absolute coupling between the candidate and the rest of the system (see preceding discussion). The candidates that minimize this measure are chunks because they have the minimal amount of coupling to the rest of the code base.

In addition to predicting future coordination needs, it is important to assess the current coordination overhead of the candidate part of software. This can be achieved by counting the number of MR's that involve participants from more than one location. Figure 10.2 compares two globalization candidates. The first curve shows the yearly trend of relative measure of work-item based coupling between the candidate and the complement, the second line shows the trend of the fraction of multi-site MRs within a candidate, and the third line shows the difference between them.

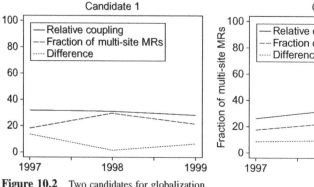
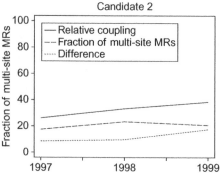

Figure 10.2   Two candidates for globalization.

Both candidates start with about the same degree of relative coupling, but candidate 1's relative coupling tends to decrease in time while candidate 2's tends to increase. In addition, candidate 1 requires considerably more multi-site MRs than candidate 2. This indicates that relatively more time and effort is wasted in candidate 1 because of multi-site work. We may want to assign such work areas to a single site with the expectation that it will reduce the amount of multi-site work and inefficiencies associated with it. Consequently, candidate 1 appears to be a significantly better candidate for distribution than candidate 2.

When assigning a part of the code to a remote location, it is important to ensure that the amount of effort needed on that part of the code matches the capacity of the development resources in the candidate location. It is also important that the candidate embodies some minimal amount of work; transferring a candidate that requires only a trivial amount of effort may not be worthwhile.

The amount of work needed for a candidate can be estimated by assessing historic trends of effort for the candidate. Assuming that a developer spends roughly equal amounts of effort for each delta, the total effort spent during a year can be approximated by adding the proportions of deltas each developer completed on the candidate during that year. For example, a developer who completed 100 deltas in a year, 50 of which apply to a particular candidate, would contribute 0.5 technical head count years to the candidate. The scale of effort is thus in terms of Person Years (PY). In our experience resources of between 10 and 20 PY were available in the remote locations, roughly corresponding to a group reporting to a technical manager.

The assumption that each delta (done by the same programmer) carries an equal amount of effort is only a rough approximation. In fact, it has been shown (see, e.g., [Graves98]) that in a number of software projects a delta that fixes a bug requires more effort than a delta that adds new functionality. However, in our problem, the approximation of equal effort per delta is reasonable because there is fairly large prediction noise because the effort spent on a candidate may vary over time. Furthermore, each programmer is likely to have a mixture of different deltas in the candidate, averaging out the distinctions in effort among the different types of deltas. In cases when more precise estimates are needed, models [Graves98] can be used to find a more precise effort for each delta.

When a chunk of code is transferred to developers who are unfamiliar with the product, a substantial adjustment in effort may be needed. In one of the projects that we studied, a typical rule of thumb to estimate the time until the remote new team reaches full productivity was 12 months. Figure 10.3 shows the empirical estimate of such a curve. The productivity is measured by the number of deltas completed by a developer in a month. The time is shifted for each developer to show their first delta occurring in month one. This allows us to calculate productivity based on developer experience with the transferred code. The horizontal axis shows the length of a developer's experience on the project in months and the vertical axis shows the average number of deltas over 50 developers who started working on the project within a three year period from 1995 to 1998. The jagged curve represents monthly averages, while the smooth curve illustrates the trend by smoothing the monthly data. The figure shows that the time to reach full productivity (when the learning

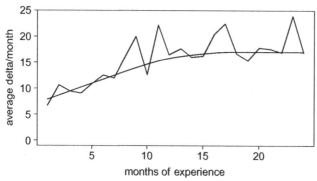

Figure 10.3 Learning curve.

When transferring a chunk of a complex system from one site to another, assume it will take about 18 months to achieve full productivity after the transfer. Even after this period, do not expect developers to handle more complicated tasks [Zhou10]. Many projects do not assign mentoring tasks to developers with less than 3 years in a project.

curve flattens) is approximately 15 months. Because developers in this project undergo a three month training period before starting work, the total time to reach full productivity is 18 months.

Now that we have some measures that we can use to evaluate candidates, we turn our attention to generating candidates that optimize a desired criterion. Such automatically generated alternatives can then be compared to existing candidates using qualitative and quantitative evaluations as described above.

Based on the previous analysis, we have the following criteria for evaluating candidates:

- The number of MRs that touch both the candidate and the rest of the system should be minimized.

- The number of MRs within the candidate that involve participants from several sites should be maximized.

- The effort needed to work on the candidate should approximately match the spare development resources at the proposed remote site.

Because the first two criteria both measure the number of undesirable MRs, we can minimize the difference between the first and the second criterion. In other words, let A be the number of multi-site MRs at present, and let B be the number of multi-site MRs after the candidate is transferred to a remote site. The increase in the number of multi-site MRs because of such a transfer can be expressed by the difference: B–A. The number B can be approximated by the number of MRs that cross candidate's boundary (the first criterion); the number A represents multi-site

MRs that are entirely within a candidate, and which, presumably, will become single-site MRs once the candidate is transferred to a new location (the second criterion); the third criterion simply defines the bounds on the effort of the candidate.

The algorithm generates possible candidates and selects the best according to the desired criterion. We use a variation of simulated annealing (e.g., [Kirkpatrick83, Metropolis53]) where new candidates are generated iteratively from a current candidate and the generated candidate is accepted as the current candidate with a probability that depends on whether or not the evaluation criterion for the generated candidate is better than for the current candidate.

As input to the algorithm we provide a set of files or modules where each file is associated with an effort in PY for the last year. The effort is calculated as described in the previous section. Another input consists of a set of MRs, where each MR is associated with the list of files it modifies and with an indicator of whether or not it is a multi-site MR. Finally, we provide a range of effort in PY for the candidate. Initially, the algorithm generates a candidate by randomly selecting modules until it gets within the bounds of the specified effort.

The new candidate is generated iteratively where the iteration consists of randomly choosing one of three steps:

- Add a module to the candidate set by randomly selecting modules from the complement of the system until one is found that does not violate the effort boundary conditions.
- Delete a module from the candidate set by randomly selecting modules to delete from the candidate until one is found that does not violate the effort boundary conditions.
- Exchange modules by randomly selecting one module from the candidate and one from the complement until the exchange does not violate the effort boundary conditions.

Once the new candidate is generated, the criterion of interest (coupling to the rest of the system) is evaluated and compared to the value for the current candidate. If the criterion is improved, the new candidate is accepted as the current candidate, if not, the new candidate is accepted as the current candidate with a probability $p < 1$. This probability p has to be greater than zero to make sure that in the long run all possible solutions are evaluated and that the algorithm does not get stuck in a local minimum. If the current criterion improves upon the criterion value obtained

When seeking component candidates for distribution, consider the Maintenance Requests (MR) performed on the respective candidate. Look for candidates with the following properties. (1) The number of MRs that touch the candidate and the rest of the system is minimal among candidates. (2) The number of MRs that involved participation from several sites is maximal among candidates. (3) The estimated required effort is about the same as the resources available at the new site.

in any previous iteration, the current candidate and the criterion are recorded as the best solution so far. This iteration is repeated a fixed number of times or for a certain period of time.

Two candidates are shown in Figure 10.2. The first candidate is optimal among candidates consuming approximately 10 PY per year and the second candidate is optimal among candidates consuming approximately 20 PY per year.

In previous sections, we have focused on the transfer of functional areas. It is interesting and instructive to evaluate alternative approaches in a quantitative fashion. In this section we describe an example evaluation of a localization approach.

The management team of a very large telecommunications project wanted to evaluate the possibility of having a development team located in a country in Asia to perform all customization work for that country. The feasibility analysis was based on the software features implemented for the entire region (all countries in Asia). The expectation was that the analysis would discover only a few functional domains where such features are implemented, thereby highlighting training requirements for the team. Good candidates for localization are products in which the localization work is concentrated in only a few functional domains, rather than being spread evenly over all functional domains.

By comparing a list of more than 300 features for Asian countries done in 1998-1999, with the remaining features done over the same period, we found that the former features modified almost all the functional areas (subsystems) of the product. Furthermore, the effort (as calculated from the number of delta) for Asian features mirrored the pattern of effort for the entire system, that is, the ratios of Asian feature effort to overall effort is relatively constant over the subsystems. Figure 10.4 shows a histogram of this fraction indicating that, while on average about 10% of the effort goes to Asian features; there is only one subsystem where more than 25% of the effort is devoted to such features. A similar pattern holds for modules and files. The only difference is that the precision is lower when predicting modules modified by Asian features.

Furthermore, different developers implement localization features over the years (possibly indicating shifting functionality). While 528 developers participated in implementing Asian features in 1998 and 1999, only 144 of them worked on such

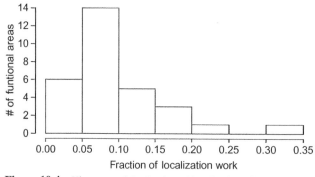

Figure 10.4   Histogram of the fraction of localization effort for an Asian market.

features both in 1998 and 1999. The large number of functional areas involved and the possibility of these areas changingover time indicate considerable obstacles when using the localization approach in the considered product.

Often bug fixing and testing are perceived as undesirable activities. Many organizations offshore the maintenance of deployed releases of software, but developing new releases is not offshored. Unfortunately, such decisions are rarely based on rigorous analysis of potential drawbacks and benefits. For example, an offshore team responsible for maintaining older releases may never develop sufficient skills to enhance the product and may struggle when the rest of the work is transferred to them. Consequently, it may be desirable to compare and, possibly, fine-tune candidates generated by the interested parties.

There are often a number of important social and organizational factors that need to be addressed in any decision to transfer work. For example, work that is considered undesirable or uninteresting by developers at a particular location may be proposed as a candidate for transfer.

TAKE-AWAY TIPS:

In large software systems, the alignment between work items and organizational and software structures allows us to state several important actions to take when considering candidates for transfer:

- Identify the current work structure and ensure that it matches the desired architecture.

 Practical questions to answer when considering the transfer of work to another location: (1) Does the current work structure match the initial architecture, and what is the current work structure? (2) Do the current work and software structures match the organizational structure? (3) Does the current work structure match the geographic distribution of the organization? (4) How to define a piece of software so that it is and remains an independent chunk that can be developed/changed independently: Is it a file, directory, or some other entity?

- Compare the current work and software structures and be sure that they match the organizational structure.
- Ensure that the current work structure matches the geographic distribution of the organization.

- Define and design the software into modules that can remain as independent chunks that can be developed or changed independently, and decide what the structural unit is for a module: Is it a file, directory, or some other entity?

Our approach applies to any project where some change data have been accumulated. Note that even in so-called greenfield projects the development proceeds by incremental change, so that once the project has produced a substantial amount of code, the algorithm could be applied to the change data.

Because of our strong emphasis on independent changeability, we think about what we have done as exposing the empirical information hiding structure of a software system. As a system evolves, decisions that are embodied in the structure of the code become intertwined in such a way that they are dependent on each other; a change to one usually means a change to the others. Evolution of the system impels the formation of chunks. The challenge for the software architect is to construct a modular design where the modules and the chunks closely correspond to each other throughout the system's lifetime.

Chapter 11

Configuration Management

Summary: This chapter underlines the relevance of good configuration management and change control especially in distributed projects. While configuration management is necessary for types of development and engineering, it must be quite strong in terms of methods and tools if teams are working in different time zones without the possibility of agreeing on whom is making which change. Concepts such as traceability help to see impacts of changes.

Configuration management is one of the key development process activities in a successful global project. In distributed development especially, chances are high that different versions of software are merged which creates inconsistencies and errors. Change review boards, versioning rules, branching and merging guidelines, and clean baselining and change control mechanisms must be installed. They ought to work the same way in all sites.

There are dedicated instruments to assure clean configuration management in global development projects. In this chapter we will list the most relevant instruments with the understanding that regular configuration management includes much more.

Rigorous change management assures that no change to any baseline happens without upfront agreement. Any changes and defects must be reported in a standardized change management system, such as Bugzilla or Synergy. They must have status flags with time stamps to allow consistency checks before approving them. They should be traceable to related work products (other change requests and configuration items), such as horizontally between related change requests or vertically (e.g., from a change request to the implementation and test cases). And, most important, no change is allowed without a documented approval. Often, changes happen through tunneling that takes place between engineers who know each other. This is not working in global development.

Access rights to tools and work products must be controlled. Global development increases the risk of intellectual property being exposed or compromised. We recommend installing role-based access policies because they are easy to install and to maintain. Archives must be protected with structured access rights to avoid inconsistencies from being introduced. Never give full visibility to an entire archive. If there is

Global Software and IT: A Guide to Distributed Development, Projects, and Outsourcing,
First Edition. Christof Ebert.
© 2012 the Institute of Electrical and Electronics Engineers, Inc. Published 2012 by
John Wiley & Sons, Inc.

high turnover to be expected, the role and access rights management should be feasible with batch jobs. In essence, this should be done periodically, without additional triggers to assure that responsibility changes or newcomers are immediately considered.

Most tools have operational databases that are hosted on servers. Make sure that these operational databases and warehouses are replicated across sites and that the replications are consistent with each other. Test specifically for those databases with frequent and high-load access to make sure that they work properly. This holds especially true for the code archive and change repository, both of which are continuously accessed by each engineer. Test how long it will take to replicate them in case of a network failure. Assure that engineers in all sites can continue working with localized copies of archives in case of network disruptions.

Backups must be distributed across sites. Never keep the archives and their backups at the same physical site. If separating them is not internally feasible, collaborate with an external provider to assure that your different archives and backups are distributed and accessible in case of emergency. Make routine checks on a periodic basis to verify their status, integrity, and accessibility. Test the entire restore and distribution mechanism on a periodic basis.

To assure configuration management is consistently implemented, configuration audits are placed in the project plan and performed periodically (at least at the bigger milestones). The following topics should be covered by such audits:

- **Infrastructure:** determine if the integrity of the baseline libraries is being maintained. Answer questions such as: Are the change and update records complete and accurate?

- **Project:** Is the project following its configuration management plan and protecting the integrity of its new and modified configuration items as intended? Is it producing its builds and releases according to the agreed-upon schedule?

- **Process:** Are configuration management activities being performed according to the organizational (and/or project) change and configuration process? Do the delivered work products conform to the established (and/or de facto) internal standards?

- **Baseline:** Are the baselined items accessible? Can previous versions be restored? Are changes always traceable to baseline items? Is one unique baseline status communicated to all stakeholders?

Configuration management is one of the disciplines that hugely benefits from using the right tools. In fact, it is hard to imagine having no support tools. When selecting these tools, make sure that they are not simple repositories, but that they are explicitly suitable and recommended for global (i.e., distributed) development. They must, at least, assure traceability to other tools (of a different supplier) and open interfaces so you can build your own connections.

Chapter 12

Open Source Development

Summary: Companies of various industries are investing in open source and effectively use it as viable ecosystem for access to skills and for creating new markets. Open source clearly is a global software and IT business with contributors from around the world and various packaging companies. We will provide concrete guidance on how to manage open source software, be it as a user or as a contributor.

The software industry has evolved toward complex supplier-user networks that cooperate and collaborate in many ways. These days, we hardly ever see the traditional way of software development where design, production, sales, delivery, and service are done by one company. Business models, engineering life-cycles, and distribution channels and services have dramatically changed. One key driver in these new value networks is free and open source software. The reasons for the fast growth of open source usage are manifold [Ebert07b, Forrester04]:

- Global competition and low entry thresholds drive companies to continuously try to reduce the costs of their software products and components. Open source software with comparatively low license and maintenance cost fosters life-cycle cost reduction.

- Time-to-profit means that you must cut out delays from the introduction of products and services. Using mature standard components allows focusing on the high-end which is where true value is created.

- Practically all industries are shifting—with the different speeds and cycle times—from hardware to software, and finally, to services. This implies that traditional hand-made proprietary low-level software is being replaced by standard solutions.

- The growing instability of global markets pushes users to select endurable solutions that will not be impacted by fads and hypes because both often drivecommercial software to annual revenue streams from selling unnecessary complexity. Open source software only delivers core features and thus achieves better performance and quality.

- Open source solutions with sufficiently big communities have better quality than their commercial counterparts. For instance, open source improves secu-

Global Software and IT: A Guide to Distributed Development, Projects, and Outsourcing,
First Edition. Christof Ebert.
© 2012 the Institute of Electrical and Electronics Engineers, Inc. Published 2012 by
John Wiley & Sons, Inc.

rity because more people review the source code than that of proprietary software. For that very reason, security breaches are typically fixed quickly and with broad notification to the user community.

- Students use open source in school, which substantially shortens their learning curve when they go to work for software companies. Engineers often have the same open source tools at home, which positively impacts the work climate and productivity.

Having shaped the global software industry for a decade, strong ecosystems have grown, covering technologies such as embedded software components, middleware, enterprise software and internet services.

Market leaders such as Google, IBM, Microsoft, SAP, and Siemens, as well as many small companies, engage in open source for multiple reasons. For instance, Mozilla's Firefox browser, with hundreds of millions of users, has become a rival of Microsoft's market-leading Internet Explorer, and has thus created a new push to an otherwise stagnating market. Major technology breakthroughs are based upon open source software. Many current engineering processes have evolved from the way open source is developed. This holds for iterative development and agile techniques as well as globally distributed software engineering.

Open source models have changed development processes. Agile development approaches, such as incremental development, gain acceptance because engineers learn them in their open source endeavors at home. Open source projects of different sizes and distribution degrees provide an almost controlled environment for experimenting in global software development as has been discussed in other chapters of this book. Many shared-development and knowledge-management platforms, including Eclipse and wikis, facilitate distributed development.

Innovative global business models are, perhaps, the most interesting open source contribution. A showcase example is Asterisk (www.asterisk.org), a key enabler for radical transformation in private branch exchange (PBX) telephony systems. Until recently, the hardware focus of business telephony allowed a few vendors to dominate this multibillion-dollar market. With IP telephony's arrival, most vendors want to closely bundle their traditional and IP hardware-based solutions to protect their long-term investments. On the other hand, millions of small and medium enterprises can't afford a PBX system, but still need its feature set. Asterisk has started to offer entirely PC-based systems that provide public switched telephone network (PSTN) connectivity through small processing cards instead of proprietary hardware boxes. Functionality is comparable to traditional PBX, flexibility to adapt and integrate with existing infrastructure is better, and scalability in terms of both traffic and features costs less because there's no expensive hardware investment.

Here are some concrete guidelines for practitioners using open source software in a global project context or contributing to open source projects:

- Apply clear decision criteria to open source decision making. For both technical and commercial criteria, examine your own product's overall life-cycle to make sure your open source decision is valid beyond the initial development phase.

- Decide on a distribution scheme. Before deciding to use GPL software, you must know how to handle packaging with it so that you can choose how to distribute your products. With most licensing schemes, you must distribute all copyrights from all contributors with the software. The more different components and contributions that exist, the more difficult this becomes. Using open source software involves many intrinsic challenges, so you might want to more narrowly focus your scarce engineering budget by turning to experts to handle issues such as configuration management, license reviews, liability transfer, or filtering new releases. Experts can help adjust your development processes to handle external components. Additionally, for small FOSS communities, professionals can work with both suppliers and users to improve interfaces and build decent change management and reliable road-mapping for industrializing your products.

- Check supplier availability over time. An open development tool might look attractive, but it may also prove disastrous over the years if it's not adequately supported.

- Disseminate technical, legal, and managerial information widely in your company. Not everybody has to read it, but you need to consider major impacts before introducing an open source component. License schemes, version status, configuration lists of all components in your products, bug information, and security warnings should be easily accessible and continuously updated.

- Manage and mitigate your legal exposure. You can't choose the license scheme you like because "copyleft" agreements, such as GPL, define most of the open source software you're using. First, understand the underlying licensing scheme and avoid those that aren't generally in mainstream use. GPL is used broadly and it benefits from known legal exposure and ways to cope with it.

- Create IPR awareness. Developers and their companies have been hurt by using open source without understanding basic copyright notions or other intellectual property rights. The right to use and modify software doesn't mean that copyrights are transferred. You must have a clear, indisputable legal status and governance regarding IPR and the use of open source software. Make sure that underlying open source components won't pollute your own source code. For instance, the status of proprietary code dynamically loaded with GPL (GNU General Public License) code is still fuzzy in the GPL license. If your business needs these proprietary drivers, maybe open source software isn't the answer for you. Contact the copyright owner and agree on a dedicated license scheme to clarify the legal impacts in such exceptional cases. Many popular open source components have dual licensing schemes that might be more appropriate.

- Even without open source usage, legal and commercial restrictions typically don't allow you to exclude liability of your products. However, most open source software comes without any liability, which means the distributor bears the entire risk without possible recourse to the licensor. Prepare for liability and fast bug fixing of your external components. Packaging companies offer services to handle all this, but you'll pay for it.

- Don't reinvent licensing schemes. If you use open source software in your products, you might want to create a community of contributors and, therefore, install a dedicated framework that will protect your copyrights and facilitate open development. There are more than enough license schemes available. Don't create new schemes that will only increase complexity and confusion among users. Instead, try to consolidate toward major schemes, such as GPL or LGPL.

- Avoid license schemes that are difficult to use or that might endanger your business model. For instance, the Artistic License includes ambiguities that can cause confusion on legal terms. Schemes such as BSD licensing or the Apple Public Source License might allow your open source software or extensions of it to move unexpectedly to the proprietary software domain.

- Control the introduction and use of open source software. Systematically qualify open source components before integrating them because versions and variants arrive more often in open source software than they do in proprietary software. For example, MySQL releases an update every four weeks and Eclipse releases one every six weeks. You must define upfront the refresh and update processes for introducing a new open source component version, and you must manage development and service life-cycle processes systematically in order to ensure that the chosen open source component, as well as your own components, can synchronize with each other and with your release and business cycles. Your configuration manager must explicitly authorize any external component on a per-version basis. Train your build or configuration manager and your quality teams on these additional open source related needs.

- Ensure that your processes support open source software usage. You must adapt your development and life-cycle management processes to cope with specific open source challenges. Configuration and change management must be able to handle bug fixes and open source update releases in various formats—source code, design descriptions, release notes, test cases, and so on. Quality control must verify and validate new upgrades before introducing them. When modifying open source software, your change processes must include making the changes public and your quality control must ensure that quality levels meet your standards. Test-driven development and code-analysis tools will help provide the quality infrastructure. When evolving open source software, don't overlook nonfunctional requirements such as performance or maintainability. If your products might be used in safety-critical systems or

 Open source software is of growing relevance in all software and IT projects. As a technical manager you should create awareness in your team to avoid legal exposure and to ensure the best possible usage schemes. As a software engineer, you might participate in an open source project to learn about global development styles and to experiment beyond the boundaries of your company.

within high-reliability standards, you must consider independent verification and certification.

Today, the open source approach has grown toward a global software engineering business model which can hardly be avoided for any software or IT project. Especially in the global software engineering context, community source software

Community source offers different levels of openness. For instance, BEA's Eclipse-based development environment lets engineers integrate FOSS and proprietary solutions. Nokia's Maemo[1] development platform is an interesting example. It is used to develop services and applications for Nokia's Internet Tablet. While Nokia controls the Maemo roadmap and overall technology evolution, it contributed less than 2% of the source code. Companies such as Sun, Hewlett Packard, and IBM created the rest of it, using FOSS libraries such as Linux.

is growing quickly. It uses the traditional open source approach with voluntary contributors and open licensing schemes, but it applies that approach to proprietary software that is shared in a closed user community.

Aside from cases in which proprietary software is mediocre or built on a weak business model, open source isn't cannibalizing of proprietary software. In fact, it creates new jobs and new demand for services. Close to one-fifth of all open source contributors earn money from their contributions [Ebert07b]. Last, but certainly not least, open source is an excellent vehicle, especially for young software engineers, for understanding architecture, coding styles, quality control mechanisms, and implementing your own ideas in a global setting.

[1] http://maemo.org

Chapter 13

Quality Control

Summary: Quality of a component or product must be designed from the beginning. Once designed, it must be rigorously and consistently controlled.. This is not easy in global settings with different stakeholders following their own objectives. In this chapter, we will discuss concrete practices to develop and control quality in global software and IT projects.

Competition, along with the customers' willingness to change suppliers whenever they are dissatisfied, has resulted in huge efforts to provide software on time and with the high quality the customer has specified and expects to pay for. A study by the Strategic Planning Institute shows that customer-perceived quality is amongst the three factors with the strongest influence on long-term profitability of a company. Customers typically view achievement of the right balance between reliability, delivery date, and cost as having the greatest effect on their long-term link to a company [Ebert07a].

Global software development challenges traditional quality control and asks for new solutions. Given the global competition, quality must be proven good enough for any component and for the entire system. Distributed ownership of these various software components does not allow close teamwork toward continuous builds or peer reviews. Often, the owners of interacting components know each other only from phone conversations, but still have to assure the right level of quality control.

Methodological approaches to guarantee quality products have lead to international guidelines (e.g., ISO 9001) and widely applied methods to assess the development processes of software providers (e.g., CMMI [SEI11]). Additionally, COBIT and ITIL are highly useful for defining basic processes in IT service companies [COBIT05, ITIL07]. Most companies apply certain techniques of criticality prediction that focus on identifying and reducing release risks. Unfortunately, many efforts usually concentrate on testing and reworking instead of proactive quality

Global Software and IT: A Guide to Distributed Development, Projects, and Outsourcing,
First Edition. Christof Ebert.
© 2012 the Institute of Electrical and Electronics Engineers, Inc. Published 2012 by John Wiley & Sons, Inc.

management [McConnell03, Ebert07]. It is useless to spend an extra amount on improving quality of a product to a level that consumers aren't willing to pay for. The optimum quality seems to be in between the two extremes. It means you must achieve the right level of quality and deliver it on time. It also means continuously investigating what this best level of quality really means, both for the customers and for the engineering teams who want to deliver it.

As a first step for any quality control activity, one must define the quality levels to be achieved. In global development projects, this is often done by means of SLA or by phase-end or hand-over criteria. These targets must be measurable regardless of the global collaboration model or contract model established with suppliers. It is key to set the right targets and to set them as performance indicators for R&D, the management in each location.

After knowing the target, it is relevant to know where the development with respect to defect reduction is at any moment. The general approach is called defect estimation. Defects should be estimated based on the stability of the underlying software components. All software in a product can be separated into four parts according to its origin. The base of the calculation of new/changed software is the list of modules to be used in the complete project (i.e., the description of the entire build with all its components). A defect correction in one of these components typically results in a new version, while a modification in functionality (in the context of the new project) results in a new variant. Configuration management tools such as CVS or ClearCase are used to distinguish the one from the other while still maintaining a single source.

Our starting point for defect estimation and forecasting the quality level comes from psychology. Any person makes roughly one (non-editorial) defect in 10 written lines of work. This applies to code as well as to a design document or an e-mail, as was observed by the personal software process (PSP) and many other sources [Jones07]. The estimation of remaining malfunctions is language independent because malfunctions are introduced per thinking and editing activity of the programmer, that is, visible by written statements. We could prove this independency of programming language and code defects per statement in our own environment when examining languages such as Assembler, C, and others. This translates into 100 defects per KStmt. Half of these defects are found by careful checking by the author, which leaves some 50 defects per KStmt delivered at code completion. Training, maturity, and coding tools can further reduce the number substantially. We found some 10–50 defects per KStmt depending on the maturity level of the respective organization. This is based on new or changed code and does not include any code that is reused or automatically generated. The author detects most of these original defects before the respective work product is released. Depending on the underlying personal software process (PSP), 40%-80% of these defects are removed by the author immediately. We have experienced in software that around 10–50 defects per KStmt remain. For the following calculation we will assume that 30 defects/KStmt are remaining (which is a common value [Jones07, Ebert07a].

To statistically estimate the amount of remaining defects in software at the time it is delivered by the author (i.e., after the author has done all verification activities, he can execute himself), we distinguish four different levels of stability of the software that are treated independently:

$$f = a \times x + b \times y + c \times z + d \times (w - x - y - z)$$

with

- x: the number of new or changed KStmt designed which will be tested within this project. This software was specifically designed for the aforementioned project. All other parts of the software are reused with varying stability.

- y: the number of KStmt that are reused but are unstable and not yet tested (based on functionality that was designed in a previous project or release, but never externally delivered; this includes ported functionality from other projects).

- z: the number of KStmt that are tested in parallel with another project. This software is new or changed for the other project and is entirely reused in the project under consideration.

- w: the number of KStmt in the total software build within this product.

The factors a–d relate the defects in software to size. They depend heavily on the development environment, project size, maintainability degree, and so on. Based on previous assumptions, the following factors can be used:

- a: 30 defects per KStmt (depending on engineering methods; should be based on own history data).

- b: 60% × 30 defects per KStmt (assuming defect detection before start of test is 60%).

- c: 60% × 30 defects per KStmt × (overlapping degree) × 25% (depending on overlapping degree of resources and test intensity).

- d: 1% × 30 defects per KStmt (assuming 1% of defects typically remain in a product at the time when it is reused).

With targets agreed upon and defects estimated, a variety of different defect detection techniques must be evaluated and combined to optimize cost, quality, and time. Preferably, defects should be detected close to the activity when they have been introduced (that is, before start of test). Since defects can never be entirely avoided, several techniques have been suggested for detecting defects early in the development life-cycle [McConnell98, Ebert01b]:

- Design reviews and inspections.

- Code inspections with checklists based on typical fault situations or critical areas in the software.

- Enforced reviews and testing of critical areas (in terms of complexity, former failures, expected fault density, individual change history, customer's risk and occurrence probability).

- Tracking the effort spent for analyses, reviews, and inspections, and separating according to requirements to find out which areas are not sufficiently covered.

The goal is to find the right balance between efficiency (time spent per item) and effectiveness (ratio of detected faults compared to remaining faults) by making the right decisions to spend the budget for the most appropriate quality assurance methods. In addition, overall efficiency and effectiveness have to be optimized. It must, therefore, be carefully decided which method should be applied on each work product to guarantee high efficiency and effectiveness of code reading (i.e., done by one checker) and code inspections (i.e., done by multiple checkers in a controlled setting). Wrong decisions can have two main impacts:

On one hand, the proposed method to be performed is too "weak." Faults, which could have been found with a stronger method, are not detected in the early phase. Not enough effort is spent in the early phase. Typically, in this case, efficiency is high and effectiveness is low. On the other hand, the proposed method to be performed is too "strong" or overly heavy. If the fault density is low from the very beginning, even an effective method will not discover many faults. This leads to a low efficiency, compared to the average effort that has to be spent to detect one fault. This especially holds for small changes in legacy code.

Globally distributed software development is highly impacted by work organization and effective work split. Often, not all necessary skills to design a complex functionality are available at one location. Instead of creating virtual development teams, we strongly advise (for reasons of productivity and quality) that you build coherent and colocated teams of fully allocated engineers. Coherence means that the work is split during development according to feature content, which allows you to assemble a team that can implement a set of related functionality—as opposed to artificial architecture splits. Colocation means that engineers working on such a set of coherent functionality should sit in the same building, in the same room, if it is feasible. Finally, full allocation implies that engineers working on a project should not be distracted by different tasks for other projects.

Projects at their start are already split into pieces of coherent functionality that will be delivered in increments to a continuous build. Functional entities are allocated to development teams, which are often based in different locations. Architecture decisions, decision reviews at major milestones, and tests are done at one place. Experts from countries with minority contribution will be relocated for the time the team needs to work together. This allows effective project management based on the teams that are fully responsible for quality and delivery accuracy of their functionality.

Colocating a development team to stimulate more interactions, however, is more expensive. We found, in our projects, that colocating peer reviews improves both efficiency and effectiveness of defect detection and thus reduces cost of non-quality. Looking into individual team performance, we can see that colocated teams achieve an efficiency improvement during inspections of over 50% [Ebert01b]. This means that with the same amount of defects in design and code, those teams, which sit at the same place, need less than half the time for defect detection. The amount of defects detected shows almost a factor of 2 difference in terms of defects per KStmt. Examining the low cost of defect detection during inspections compared to subsequent testing activities and the cost contribution of validation towards total cost, we found an impact of greater than 10% on project cost.

A final word on work allocation and ownership: Shifting verification activities to low-cost countries is highly inefficient. Often tasks are overly fragmented and the quality control activities are handled with poor results due to lack of knowledge. In the end, each delivery has to be checked twice, once at the time it is shipped to a low-cost country, and then again backward. All of these processes cost time and money and are demoralizing for the engineers on both sides because it always ends up ping-ponging back and forth. As mentioned before, we strongly recommend building teams, preferably in one place, and assigning them ownership for a work product including functionality and quality. Such teams should operate globally according to needs and skills availability, but not be internally split into first- and second-class engineering tasks.

Chapter 14

Tools and IT Infrastructure

Summary: Tools facilitate global software engineering dramatically. In fact, global development is impossible without adequate tool support. Tools are necessary due to several inherent characteristics of software engineering in different sites. In this chapter, we will provide a structured and systematic overview on different tools domains with many concrete examples. While the one or other example might become outdated over the years, it is still helpful to glean an understanding from this chapter as to the essence of tools selection and usage in global settings.

Software tools can be grouped along four dimensions, namely:

- Functionality: Comprising of and evolving into complex functionality, designs, and architectures. Examples include modeling tools, test environments, design tools, and so on.

- Communication: assuring understanding and exchange between stakeholders and amongst engineers. Examples include project management, requirements engineering, and change management tools.

- Work products: Managing a multitude of interdependent work products. Examples include tools for configuration management, versioning, debugging, and so on.

- Life-cycle: Software tends to evolve over time. A longer lifetime creates different versions or variants of the system, each of which must be managed until the end of its life. Examples of tools include some of the aforementioned tools, such as traceability tools, test configurators, or product data management.

These four dimensions becomeeven more complex in distributed teams, especially if they hardly ever (or never) meet. Even the smallest decision or reasoning for a

Global Software and IT: A Guide to Distributed Development, Projects, and Outsourcing,
First Edition. Christof Ebert.
© 2012 the Institute of Electrical and Electronics Engineers, Inc. Published 2012 by
John Wiley & Sons, Inc.

decision must be recorded and traced not only to originators but also to any other impacted artifacts, engineers, or product variants.

Performing outsourcing and offshoring without adequate tools and IT infrastructure will immediately cause problems and high overhead costs. Collaboration across enterprises and distributed teams often leads to fragmented processes and tool chains with heterogeneous interfaces and redundant and inconsistent data management which results in insufficient transparency. Activities such as project management, pre-development, and product engineering are rarely well-integrated due to the diversity of stakeholders with individual knowledge about projects, products, and processes. Consequently, engineering results such as specifications, documentation, and test cases are inconsistent, and items like signals and parameters are arbitrarily labeled. Changes create a lot of extra work because you have to make sure that nothing is overlooked. Reuse is hardly possible due to the many heterogeneous contents. This pattern is amplified when collaboration across supplier networks and complex healthcare workflows take place.

 The move to global software engineering is a useful catalyst to clean up an inventory of legacy tools once and for all.

To work efficiently, engineers need to handle a multitude of processes and different forms of knowledge that must be shared with colleagues across business processes and even beyond the borders of the enterprise. Tools are essential to collaboration among team members, enabling the facilitation, automation, and control of the entire development process. Adequate tool support is especially necessary for global software engineering because distance aggravates coordination and control problems, directly or indirectly, through its negative effects on communication. Tools and IT infrastructure help to integrate both processes and people along the entire life-cycle of a release or product. They can even reach beyond release and product to cover an entire portfolio. Global software and IT need both process and tools support. Figure 14.1 shows this impact based on a study at London Business School [Ebert10].

 Sustainable performance improvement in global software and IT projects demands simultaneous optimization of engineering and management processes and tools. Introducing tools simply for workflow management, PLM, and eventual collaboration might cause even higher cost due to insufficient usage. Merely improving processes will often only serve to create bureaucracy and overheads. For success in software and IT projects, processes must be supported by automated tools.

Now we will examine different tools and use cases and provide insight into concrete experiences with collaboration tools.

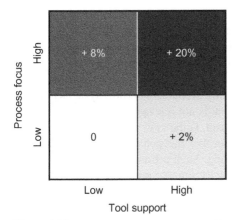

Figure 14.1   Tools without processes are nothing; processes without tools are not good enough.

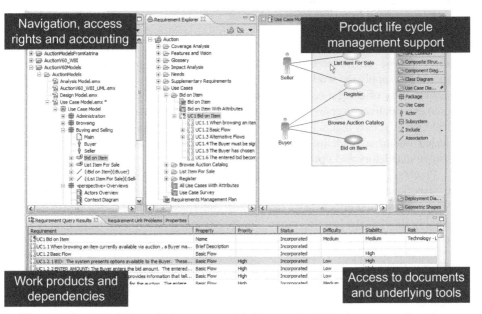

Figure 14.2   Example for tool suite to support global teams and collaboration across work products.

PROJECT MANAGEMENT

We strongly recommend installing a standardized project dashboard that allows navigating from a high level of abstraction (e.g., all ongoing projects, all active tasks, all offshore work packages, all distributed activities, etc.) down to impacted engineers, artifacts, tools, and processes. Navigation across different work products and supportive collaboration tools is realized with hyperlinks as portrayed in Figure 14.2

[Ebert10]. In fact, all professional engineering tools today allow linking into their contents by means of hyperlinks (i.e., URLs or even web services). A life-cycle picture shows the global overview of the processes, and many embedded hyperlinks allow navigation with a few clicks to the final element in which the reader is interested. Compared with static process models of the 1980s, which typically used standard data-modeling languages, the currently available workflow systems provide nicely visualized flows that hide anything that is not relevant for a specific view as much as possible. Usability, and not formalism, is the key.

A tailorable process framework can resolve the perceived conflict between organizational process and individual tailoring. Such a framework should be fully graphically accessible and should allow the selection of a process that will be applicable for components as well as an entire product that is based on selecting the appropriate parameters that characterize the project. The framework allows for automatic instantiation of the respective development process and product life-cycle, as well as a project quality plan and specific applicable measurements that are based on modular process elements such as role descriptions, templates, procedures, or check lists, which hyperlink with each other.

Usability of any workflow support system is determined by the degree to which it can be adapted or tailored toward the project's needs. There are organizational and project-specific environmental constraints. Those constraints make it virtually impossible to apply the workflow system in a way that is out of the box. Adaptation is achieved by offering a set of standard workflows, which are then selected (e.g., incremental delivery versus grand design; parallel versus sequential development; development versus maintenance). On a lower level, work products are defined or selected out of a predefined catalogue. The process models should distinguish between mandatory and optional components.

Processes and tools can be diverse across projects and, sometimes, across sites. Our experience drives us increasingly to standardizing tools across the enterprise because it has scale effects (e.g., license cost, interface simplicity), but it also considerably shortens the learning curve if engineers are moved to another project or if a new team of engineers is hired at some place in the world.

Collaborative project management tools such as ActiveCollab[1] and WorldView [8] offer a Web-based interface to manage project information for calendars and milestone tracking. Such tools give managers an overview of project status at different detail levels, such as team member locations and contact information. IBM LotusLive[2] provides an overview of ongoing project activities by using information extracted from developers' workspaces.

There are two open source platforms that are also used in project management, they are GForge,[3] AS and WebAPSEE.[4] The former is a platform that ties together different toolsets such as task managers, document managers, forums, or mailing lists;

---

[1] http://www.activecollab.com
[2] http://www.lotuslive.com/de/
[3] http://gforge.org/gf/
[4] http://sourceforge.net/projects/webapsee/

the latter aims to provide automated support for software process management, providing a high level of flexibility for changes on dynamic and enacting process models.

REQUIREMENTS ENGINEERING

Major RE tools such as DOORS[5] and IRqA[6] let multiple engineers use natural language text to describe project use cases and requirements and to record dependencies among and between them. These tools are expensive. As a result, companies often start by developing their own environments based on Spreadsheets and databases. However, such environments don't scale up and they create lots of hidden cost.

The professional tools show their power in global and distributed settings in IT and software projects. They help project teams to manage the requirements, to create use cases, and to mitigate project risk by displaying the requirements that may be affected by upstream or downstream changes of requirements. To be useful in global settings, requirements engineering tools should provide a document-oriented, Word-based interface with Web interfaces for users who need access to requirements information without the need of local installations. They encourage collaboration for geographically distributed teams through scalable Web interfaces, strong versioning support, and discussion threads.

DESIGN AND MODELING

Distributed design and modeling tools such as Objectif[7] and IBM Rational Tau[8] support virtual software-design meetings by capturing and storing all design-relevant information, role definitions, and version control coordination. It includes playback features to review a session once it has ended.

Prominent design and modeling tools, such as Gliffy[9] and Creately[10] support multiple diagram types such as UML or Business Process Modeling Notation. They also offer special features that simplify team communication and collaboration, such as tools for commentaries, creating blogs, and even managing knowledge. Furthermore, Gliffy can be integrated with the Jira distributed tracking system.

Model-based collaboration is what distinguishes collaborative software engineering from more general collaboration activities that share only files and not content [5]. Collaborative modeling tools such as Artisan Studio[11], Rational Software Modeler[12], and Visible Analyst[13] help developers create formal or semiformal soft-

---

[5] http://www.ibm.com/software/awdtools/doors
[7] http://www.microtool.de/objectif
[8] http://www-01.ibm.com/software/awdtools/tau/
[6] http://www.visuresolutions.com
[9] http://www.gliffy.com
[10] http://creately.com
[11] http://www.artisansoftwaretools.com
[12] http://www.ibm.com/software/awdtools/modeler/swmodeler
[13] http://www.visible.com/Products/Analyst

ware artifacts, including Unified Modeling Language (UML) models and customized software processes.

TEST AND VALIDATION

TestLink[14] is a popular tool for managing the entire testing process. It has a Web-based interface that, if you have a browser, is accessible everywhere. The tool organizes test cases into test plans. Users can import and execute groups of test cases by using one or more keywords that have been previously assigned by the users to the test cases.

On the other hand, Selenium[15] is a tool suite to automate Web application testing across many platforms. It includes an Integrated Development Environment (IDE) for writing and running tests, a remote-control tool for controlling Web-browsers on other computers, a Web-based quality-assurance tool, and an Eclipse plug-in to write Selenium and Watir[16] tests.

Finally, OpenSTA[17] is a distributed software-testing architecture that can perform scripted HTTP and HTTPS heavy-load tests with performance measurements from Win32 platforms.

CONFIGURATION MANAGEMENT

Global software engineering and IT imply that there is no longer a global owner of a specific work product across projects. Instead, many developers in different places simultaneously share the responsibility of enhancing functionality within one product. Often a distinct work product (or concretely, a file with source code) is replicated as variants that are concurrently updated and frequently synchronized to allow the centralized and global evolution of distinct functionality [Perry98, Herbsleb99].

Effective tools and work environments are thus the glue to successful global software development. Most commercial tools face problems when they are used in sites around the globe. Most big vendors have articulated similar problems to those that wo've faced. Almost no tool seamlessly foresees synchronizing and database for backing up contents without disturbing engineers who are logged on 24 hours a day, 7 days a week. Performance rapidly decreases when multi-site use is involved, due to heterogeneous server and network infrastructures.

The more distributed the project, the greater the need for secure, remote, repository and build management. Build tools such as Maven and CruiseControl let projects maintain remote repositories and create and schedule workflows. The workflows facilitate continuous integration for executing scripts, compiling binaries, invoking

---

[14] http://testlink.sourceforge.net
[15] http://seleniumhq.org
[16] http://watir.com
[17] http://opensta.org

test frameworks, deploying to production systems, and sending e-mail notifications to developers. A Web-based dashboard shows the status of current and past builds.

Distributed software engineering needs systematic configuration management. A version-control system lets team members share software artifacts in a controlled manner. Subversion (SVN[18]) is a popular open source version-control system that facilitates distributed file sharing. SVN adopts a centralized architecture in which a single central server hosts all project metadata. Developers use SVN clients to check out a limited view of the data on their local machines.

Currently, several systems use distributed version-control systems that operate in a peer-to-peer manner. Examples of distributed version-control systems include Git,[19] Mercurial,[20] and Darcs.[21] Unlike centralized tools that let developers check out a project from a distributed version-control system, the peer-to-peer systems provide a complete clone of the project's repository (called a fork) on local machines, not a just a portion of it.

Trackers are used to manage issues (or "tickets") such as defects, changes, or requests for support. The tracking function centers on a database that all team members can access through the Web.

Distributed trackers such as Jira[22] are a generalization of bug-tracking systems such as Bugzilla,[23] originally developed by the Mozilla project. A recorded issue includes an identifier, a description, and information about the author; it also defines a life-cycle to help team members track issue resolutions.

Managing corrections is a good example to help illustrate the observed challenges and solutions in global software engineering. Products are impacted by defects detected anywhere and at any time. There is a high risk that the same defects may be occurring again and again. The product line concept implies that feature roadmaps and deliveries of both new and changed (or corrected) functionality must be aligned and synchronized. Synchronization of deliveries, however, adds complexity to the development process. Corrections cannot be easily copied from one code branch to the other due to their impacts on ongoing development, such as new functionality with different local flavors that have already been added. Thus, effective synchronization of the individual corrections involves global visibility of all defects, impacts of defects, correction availability, and evaluation of impacts of the corrections. Nobody is forced to use corrections. A trade-off between stability and reliability is made before implementing a single change.

To facilitate easier communication of appropriate corrections, a worldwide defect database is mandatory and must facilitate synchronization of different types

---

[18] http://subversion.tigris.org
[19] http://www.git-scm.com
[20] http://mercurial.selenic.com
[21] http://www.darcs.net
[22] http://www.atlassian.com
[23] http://www.bugzilla.org

of dependency. Based on the detected failure and the originating fault, a list of files in different projects should be pre-populated and will tell you which other variants of a given file need to be corrected. Although this is rather simple with a parent and variant tree on the macroscopic level, due to localized small changes on the code procedure and database content level, careful manual analysis is requested. Those variants (e.g., within customization projects) are then automatically triggered. Depending on a trade-off analysis of failure risk and stability impacts, the developer responsible for the specific customization would correct these defects.

This approach immediately helps to focus on major field problems and ensure that, if applicable, they will be avoided in other markets. It, however, also shows the cost of the applied product line roadmap. Too many variants, even if they are maintained by groups of highly skilled engineers, create overheads. Obviously, variants need to be aligned to allow for better synchronization of contents (both new functionality and corrections) while still preserving the desired specific functional flavors necessary in a specific market.

COMMUNICATION AND SHARING

Communication tools are among the very basic needs for effective global teamwork. Collaboration techniques must be able to handle time zone challenges and standardizing project and team management practices so that all global stakeholders will benefit from increased efficiency. A lot of time is wasted in Global Software Engineering and IT projects due to cumbersome set-up of videoconferences or attempts to agree on an available time slot across a distributed group of engineers. Therefore, a mix of synchronous and asynchronous communication needs to be established.

Asynchronous communication tools include dedicated collaboration tools such as interactive requirements engineering repositories, workflow management tools, e-mail, blogs, mailing lists, newsgroups, Web forums, and knowledge bases such as wikis.

Synchronous communication tools include telephony, chat, instant messaging, video conferencing, and any type of online collaboration and meeting tools. Agree upon a fixed communication window for all members of a global team. This could be the same window across the company where everyone is available in case of urgent issues that need to be reviewed by the team. Such fixed windows work easily for two regions, such as Europe and Asia, or North America and Asia. It is more difficult to find a solution for three regions, specifically, if one of those is the American West Coast or Australia. A shared calendar is helpful for simple setup of remote meetings because it saves you from lots of e-mails in which many people are copied simply to read that somebody is unavailable due to a dentist appointment. Assure both for your teleconferencing and videoconferencing that events can be recorded and replayed. Experience has shown that team members who are not so fluent in English will often like to hear it again—even if it is only to improve their English proficiency.

Desktop sharing is absolutely mandatory for any global engineering team. There are numerous solutions that exist with the possibility of sharing computer screens and setting up teleconferences in parallel. We strongly recommend embarking on desktop videoconferencing via IP. It can be set up ad hoc when needed and has much lower cost (with same quality, if there is a good VPN) compared to the classic videoconferencing. Assure that simple directory services are available so that people can use videoconferences in ways that are similar to net-meeting and related tools.

WebEx[24] is the market leader for online meeting facilities. Both WebEx and WorkSpace3D[25] provide a rich interface for synchronous and asynchronous collaboration. They enable voice and video over IP communication while you view and edit documents, desktop and application sharing, co-browsing and whiteboard drawing, and meeting persistence for later replay.

The text-based eConference[26] is a lean tool that supports distributed teams needing synchronous communication and structured-discussion services. Such tools provide closed-group chat that is augmented by agendas, meeting minute-editing, typing-awareness capabilities, and hand-raising panels to enable turn-based discussions.

Office Communications Server (OCS) is an enterprise real-time conferencing tool from Microsoft[27] that provides the infrastructure for enterprise instant messaging, presence, file transfer, video calling, and structured conferences. It is available within an organization, between organizations, and with external users on public internet.

General communication tools (i.e., non-software engineering-specific) fall in the category of groupware, together with tools for document sharing and review, as well as concurrent editing and shared calendars. However, the term "groupware" is now used less frequently in favor of preferred wordings such as "collaborative software" or "social software." Popular multifunction collaboration platforms are IBM Lotus Notes/Domino[28] and Microsoft SharePoint.[29]

Recently, Web 2.0 applications have become quite common in open source and global software projects. They represent a valuable means to increase informal communication among team members. Web 2.0 extends traditional collaborative software by means of direct user contributions, rich interactions, and community building. Some key Web 2.0 applications are blogs, such as WordPress;[30] microblogs, such as Twitter (twitter.com); wikis, such as the Portland Pattern Repository,[31] social networking sites, such as LinkedIn,[32] and collaborative tagging systems, such

---

[24] http://www.webex.com

[25] http://www.tixeo.com

[26] http://code.google.com/p/econference

[27] http://www.microsoft.com/communicationsserver

[28] http://www.ibm.com/software/lotus/notesanddomino

[29] http://www.microsoft.com/SharePoint

[30] wordpress.org

[31] c2.com/cgi/wiki

[32] www.linkedin.com

as Delicious.[33] Increasingly, wiki platforms emerge as a practical, economical option for creating and maintaining group documentation.

COLLABORATIVE DEVELOPMENT ENVIRONMENTS

A Collaborative Development Environment (CDE) provides a project workspace with a standardized tool set for global software teams. CDEs combine different tools, and thus offer a frictionless development environment for outsourcing und offshoring. Several CDEs are available as commercial products or open source initiatives, and, increasingly, as online services hosted externally.

While traditional PDM and PLM/ALM tools interwork with many design and manufacturing tools, they only recently started to consider specific software engineering environments. Examples include Dassault Enovia MatrixOne,[34] Oracle Agile,[35] Siemens Teamcenter,[36] and Vector eASEE,[37] which interwork with dedicated software engineering tools, such as IBM's Synergy. More generic enterprise resource management (ERM) would not sufficiently support software engineering on the more specific workflows. CRM environments have recently integrated with defect tracking tools, but more is needed to also support requirements engineering end to end (e.g., a defect often results in a new requirement). Their scope is limited to various front-end processes. However, all of the tools that have been mentioned could be extended to facilitate interworking because they are event-driven.

CDEs are borrowing successful features that are typically available on social network sites. For instance, Assembla[38] notifies users of project-related events via Twitter; GitHub[39] offers a Twitter-like approach to monitoring a project's progress; Rational Team Concert[40] borrows Delicious's tagging feature, letting developers assign free keywords to managed items.

CDEs are often unsuitable in companies because of legacy tools or environments that must be enhanced by specific collaboration functionalities. In these situations, developers can choose from collaboration tools that map to typical life-cycle activities.

The need for workflow management support stems from the heterogeneity of underlying engineering tools and detailed processes that overlap considerably such as logon procedures, document management, and product data management. Software engineering processes must integrate with interfacing business processes from an end-to-end perspective. For instance, configuration management for software artifacts belonging to a single product line and reused in a variety of products must relate to the overall product data management (PDM). Software defect correc-

---

[33] delicious.com
[34] www..matrixone.com
[35] www.oracle.com/agile/index.html
[36] www.siemens.com/teamcenter
[37] www.vector.com/easee
[38] www.assembla.com
[39] github.com
[40] www.ibm.com/software/awdtools/rtc

tions must relate to overall service request management as part of the customer relationship management (CRM) solution.

Interworking with legacy and proprietary tools can be achieved by deploying an object request broker to give to such tools an open interface. However, the transactional interface between such tools often does not adequately support the fine-grained integration of data, thus avoiding replication of data as much as possible. For example, the product life-cycle view must include data from the PDM system, software documentation system, the defect tracking system, the personnel database (for the actors), the process assets library, and the authorized tools list, all in one view. For that reason, Eclipse is increasingly used as a reference platform to integrate existing (legacy or proprietary) tools with COTS tools.

KNOWLEDGE MANAGEMENT

One tool you won't want to miss is knowledge management. Information and knowledge must be effectively shared at a low retrieval cost. Demand for up-to-date and synchronized information available to your customers, your engineers and all your stakeholders is quickly increasing. Technical documentation in today's advanced global system providers is created from small modules that exist only once as a single source maintained by the appropriate expert. No single line of customer documentation would be written just for that one matter because it creates inconsistency. The best example of this is status reports in globally executed projects that need many inputs from various places and sources. Having an online reporting tool which integrates well with the project management, measurement, and various operational databases helps a lot.

Expertise is not always readily available. Appropriate knowledge management strategies and the respective tool-support help in finding the right answer to problems instead of forcing you to guess. We found, in several studies, that with distance, the tendency for ambiguity and guessing grows. Engineers are not the world's best communicators and, as such, often shy away from simply calling a peer in another place to clean up open issues. Instead, a day or more is wasted with figuring out the purpose of a design decision or requirement. Make a rule that decisions are documented right away and moved to an efficient knowledge management system that allows tagging and retrieval.

Knowledge centers are content management systems that let team members share explicit knowledge on the Web. A knowledge center, such as the Eclipse help system[41] or KnowledgeTree,[42] might contain internal documents, technical references, standards, FAQs, and examples of the best practices. Twiki[43] is another example of an enterprise collaboration web application platform used as a document management system and a knowledge base. Knowledge centers can also include

[41] http://help.eclipse.org
[42] www.ktdms.com
[43] http://twiki.org/

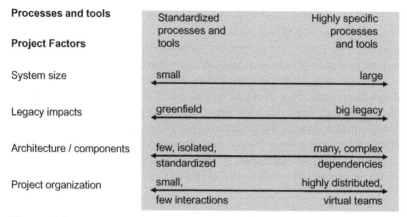

Processes and tools Project Factors	Standardized processes and tools	Highly specific processes and tools
System size	small	large
Legacy impacts	greenfield	big legacy
Architecture / components	few, isolated, standardized	many, complex dependencies
Project organization	small, few interactions	highly distributed, virtual teams

Figure 14.3   Selection of processes and tools depends on many parameters.

sophisticated knowledge management activities, such as expert identification and skills management, to acquire tacit knowledge in explicit forms.

There is no one answer to the question of which tools should be used for global software engineering. Various project factors determine different approaches to managing the involved software processes. Figure 14.3 details how different impacting factors not only characterize the project complexity, and thus the management challenges, but also how they determine the level of process integration and workflow management. Workflow management systems offer different perspectives to allow, for instance, navigation based on work products, roles, or processes [Ebert03].

Process diversity and tailoring of processes happens on various levels. A small example shows this approach. To successfully deliver a product with heterogeneous architecture and a mixture of legacy components built in various languages, certain processes must be aligned on the project level. This holds for project management, configuration management, and requirements engineering. Otherwise it would, for instance, be impossible to trace customer requirements that might impact several components through the project life-cycle. On the other hand, design processes and validation strategies are so close to the individual components' architecture and development paradigms that any standard would fail as well as all standards for one design or programming methodology have failed in the past. For efficiency reasons, the manager of that heterogeneous project or product line surely would not like it if, within each small team, the work product templates or tool-based workflows were redefined. Many workflow systems for unified processes fail on such low-level process change management. They do not allow integrating process needs on different levels into a hierarchy with guided selection.

Regardless of which tools are selected, they must interwork properly and thus reduce any manual effort, such as status reports or consistency checks. Put open interfaces, interworking capabilities, document exchange, transparent linking, and navigating into documents (or other artifacts) high on your wish list for the tools selection. Consider twice whether a legacy tool should be kept in times of growing globalization and exploding demands on productivity and cost reduction.

A warning around homemade tools: They sound terrific at their inception and are terrible at the installation phase. If you are not a toolmaker by products and business model, do not pretend to be one when it comes to your engineering. Go out to the Internet and evaluate the many available tools that easily span a prizing frame of zero (no license cost) to four- or even five-digit cost per seat of high-end design and test workbenches.

New collaboration tools and associated best practices are emerging almost daily. Two major trends can be observed. First, basically all engineering tools will provide collaboration features. These features help individual tools shared by a team, but they are implemented differently on each tool and do not allow data integration across tools. The second related trend is improved federation of engineering tools. Eclipse will help initially, but ensuring efficiency, consistency, and information security across multiple tools, teams, and companies will require a strong PLM/ALM strategy. Tools such as Teamcenter and eASEE allow secure federation and collaborative working with integrated data backbones.

No current tool supports all the activities necessary for global software engineering. Users must therefore prioritize their collaboration needs and the tools to support them. Introducing collaboration technology should be a stepwise process, starting with a collaboration platform to share applications. A consistent PLM/ALM strategy can evolve parallel to this process, providing mechanisms to guide and align technologies to the degree necessary. Such a strategy is valuable when working in external networks with participants from different organizations. Within one company, users should move to a CDE as part of their overall PLM/ALM.

Effective tool support for collaboration is a strategic initiative for any company with distributed resources whether the strategy involves offshore development, outsourcing, or supplier networks. Software needs to be shared, and appropriate tool support is the only way to do this efficiently, consistently, and securely.

Chapter 15

Practice: Collaborative Development Environments

Fabio Calefato and Filippo Lanubile, University of Bari

Summary: This chapter provides examples of practical experiences with tools from different companies and shows how to best use tools in globally distributed software projects. It highlights relevant themes and guidance from previous chapters in a concrete project context. Even if one tool or the other becomes outdated over time, this chapter still offers valuable insights toward how to do things in your own company.

BACKGROUND

Adequate tool support is paramount to enable collaboration between team members and to control the overall development process. This is especially true in global software engineering because of distance [Herbsleb01]. Distance has an impact on the three main forms of cooperation within a team [Carmel01]: communication, coordination, and control. Communication is the exchange of information, whether formal or informal, between the members. It can occur in either planned or impromptu interaction. Coordination is that act of orchestrating each task and organizational unit so that they contribute to the overall objective. Control is the process of adhering to goals, policies, standards, or quality levels that are set either formally (e.g., formal meetings, plans, guidelines) or informally (e.g., team culture, peer pressure).

 Distributed teams create overheads on communication, coordination, and control mechanisms, especially for informal purposes.

Due to distance, people cannot coordinate and control just by visiting the other team members. The absence of management-by-walking can result in coordination and control issues such as misalignment and reworking. When the control and coordination needs of distributed software teams rise, so does the load on all communication channels available. In fact, software projects have two complementary communication needs. First, the more formal, official communications are used for crucial tasks like updating project status, escalating project issues, and determining who has responsibility for particular work products. Second, informal 'corridor talk' allows team members to keep a "peripheral awareness" of what is going on around them, what other people are working on, what states the various parts of the project are in, and many other essential pieces of background information that enable developers to work together efficiently. In colocated settings, communication is taken for granted. As a result, its importance often goes unnoticed. When developers are not located together, they have fewer opportunities for communication. There is empirical evidence that the frequency of communication drops off with the physical separation among developers' sites [Herbsleb03]. Therefore, distance exacerbates coordination and control problems directly or indirectly through its negative effects on communication. In other words, communication disruption due to distance further increases and aggravates coordination and control breakdowns [Carmel01].

Distance can have an effect on three distinct dimensions: geographical, temporal, and socio-cultural. Geographical distance is a measure of the spatial dispersion that occurs when team members are scattered across different sites. It can be operationalized as the cost or effort required to exchange visits from one site to another. Temporal distance is a measure of the temporal dispersion that occurs when team members wish to interact. It can be caused by time-zone differences or time shifting work patterns (e.g., one site having a quick lunch break at noon and another site a two-hour lunch time at 1 o'clock). Socio-cultural distance is a measure of the effort required by team members to understand the organizational and national cultures (e.g., norms, practices, values, spoken languages) in remote sites.

Cooperation difficulties due to distance can only be partially tackled using appropriate techniques. For instance, coordination and control issues can be counteracted by respectively adopting architectural frameworks that enable a better division of labor between teams, and by choosing an agile development process. However, global development would not be feasible without adequate tool support [Ebert06]. In fact, developers need constant tool support during the whole software life-cycle in order to model, design, and test software functionalities; manage a myriad of interdependent artifacts; and communicate with each other. In the next section, we present a number of tools and collaborative development environments that are available today to enable effective global software development.

Tools provide a considerable help to software development activities. Software engineering tools that assist distributed projects fall into the following categories: software configuration management, bug and change tracking, build and release management, modelers, knowledge centers, communication tools, and collaborative development environments.

A software configuration management (SCM) tool includes the ability to manage change in a controlled manner by checking components in and out of a repository, the evolution of software products, storing multiple versions of components, and by producing specified versions on command. SCM tools also provide a good way to share software artifacts with other team members in a controlled manner. Rather than just using a directory to exchange files with other people, developers can use an SCM tool to be sure that interdependent files are changed together and to control who is allowed to make changes. Furthermore, SCM tools make it possible to save messages about what changed and why. Open-source SCM tools have become indispensable tools for coordinating the interaction of distributed developers. Until early 2000s, the world of SCM tools has been quite stale [O'Sullivan09]. Concurrent Version System (CVS),[1] which was released in 1990, is the ancestor of the many open source SCM tools available today, and, despite some severe drawbacks (e.g., limitations in renaming and deleting folders), it is still in wide use today, although it is now used as a legacy system. Subversion (SVN)[2] came out a decade after CVS with the goal of overcoming the negative aspects of CVS. Both SVN and CVS adopt a centralized, client-server approach. A single central server hosts all project's metadata. Developers see a limited view of the data from the central server on their local machines. In early 2000s, however, a number of projects (e.g., Git,[3] Mercurial,[4] and Darcs[5]) were started to develop distributed SCM tools that operate in a peer to peer manner.

Bug and change tracking is centered around a database that is accessible through a web-based interface by all team members. Other than an identifier and a description, a recorded bug includes information about who found it, the steps it will take to reproduce it, who has been assigned to it, and in which releases the bug exists and it has been fixed. Bug tracking systems, such as Bugzilla[6] and JIRA,[7] also define a life-cycle for bugs to help team members track the resolution of defects. Trackers are a generalization of bug tracking systems that include the management of other issues such as feature requests, support requests, or patches.

Tracking bugs and other issues in a project is as important as code development. When Mozilla organization first came online in 1998, one of the first products that was released was Bugzilla, an open source bug system implemented to replace the in-house system which was then in use at Netscape. Only upon creating the bug repository were the people involved in the project able to move on to the development of the new browser. Since the birth of Bugzilla, a bug is not actually a bug until it has been reported to the issue-tracking system. In fact, it is a common scenario to forbid developers to commit any piece of code that has no issue description attached. Today, issue tracking systems have become so dependable that companies often also use it to assign and track administrative tasks.

---

[1] http://www.nongnu.org/cvs/
[2] http://subversion.tigris.org/
[3] http://git-scm.com/
[4] http://mercurial.selenic.com/wiki/
[5] http://darcs.net/
[6] http://www.bugzilla.org/
[7] http://www.atlassian.com/software/jira/

Figure 15.1   Project-build information within a dashboard.

Build and release management allows projects to create and schedule workflows that execute build scripts, compile binaries, invoke test frameworks, deploy to production systems, and send e-mail notifications to developers. Build and release management tools can also provide a web-based dashboard to view the status of current and past builds (Fig. 15.1). Build tools, such as CruiseControl[8] and its ancestor like the UNIX make utility, are essential tools to perform Continuous Integration [Fowler06], and serve as an agile development practice which allows developers to integrate daily, thus reducing integration problems.

> The larger the project, the greater the need for automating the build and release function.

Model-based collaboration is what distinguishes collaborative software engineering from more general collaboration activities which only share files and not content [Whitehead07]. Collaborative modeling tools such as Artisan Studio,[9] Rational Software Modeler,[10] and Visible Analyst[11] help developers to create formal or semiformal software artifacts including visual UML modeling software artifacts and customized software processes.

Product and process modeling encompass the core features of what was called Computer Aided Software Engineering (CASE) from requirements engineering to visual modeling of both software artifacts and customized software processes. Collaboration in software development tends to be centered around the creation of formal or semiformal software artifacts. According to [Whitehead07], model-based collaboration is what distinguishes software engineering collaboration from more

---

[8] http://cruisecontrol.sourceforge.net/
[9] http://www.artisansoftwaretools.com/products/
[10] http://www-01.ibm.com/software/awdtools/modeler/swmodeler/
[11] http://www.visible.com/Products/Analyst/

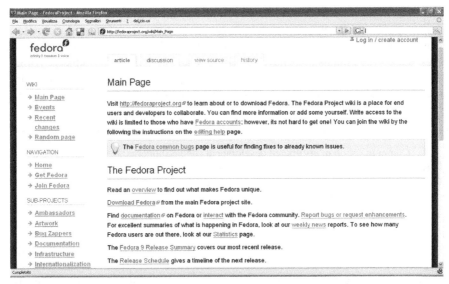

Figure 15.2   Fedora Project documentation based on wiki.

general collaboration activities which lack the focus on using the models to create shared meanings.

Knowledge centers are mostly document-driven and web-enabled which allows team members to share explicit knowledge across a work unit. A knowledge center includes technical references, standards, frequently asked questions (FAQs), and best practices. Ther use of wiki software for collaborative web publishing has emerged as a practical and economical option to consider for creating and maintaining group documentation. Wikis are particularly valuable in distributed projects as global teams may use them to organize, track, and publish their work [Louridas06]. Figure 15.2 shows the home page of the Fedora project wiki where both developers and users may contribute and find information. Knowledge centers may also include sophisticated knowledge management activities to acquire tacit knowledge in explicit forms, such as expert identification and skills management [Rus02].

Communication tools increase productivity in global teams. Software engineers have adopted a wide range of mainstream communication technologies for project use in addition to, or replacement of, communicating face-to-face. Asynchronous communication tools include e-mail, mailing lists, newsgroups, web forums, and blogs; synchronous tools include the classic telephone and conference calls, chat, instant messaging, voice over IP, and video conferencing. E-mail is the most widely used and successful collaborative application. Thanks to its flexibility and ease of use, e-mail can support conversations while also operating as a task/contact manager. However, one of the drawbacks of e-mail is that, due to its success, people tend to use it for a variety of purposes, often in a quasi-synchronous manner. In addition, e-mail is 'socially blind' [Erickson00] in that it does not enable users to signal their availability. Before becoming an indispensable tool ubiquitous in every workplace, e-mail was initially used by the research community niche and was actually opposed by management. Likewise, chat and instant messaging have followed a similar evolution path. At first mostly used by young people for exchanging 'social' messages, these synchronous tools have spread more and more in the workplace. While e-mail is socially blind, these tools, in contrast, provide a lightweight means to ascertain availability of remote team members and contact them in a timely manner.

 Communication in distributed development can be supported by providing stakeholders with a variety of different options. Do not expect one tool to fit all. The involvement of many sites means there are many different cultures, habits, and, most of all, language skills.

General communication tools (i.e., non-software engineering-specific) fall in the category of 'groupware' which refers to the class of applications that support groups of people engaged in performing a common task [Ellis91]. However, nowadays the term "groupware" is disused in favor of preferred wordings such as "collaborative software," "social software, " or "Web 2.0" [Murugesan07], all of which also include systems used outside the workplace (e.g., blogs, wikis, instant messaging).

Interoperability and a familiar user interface provide strong motivations to integrate task-specific solutions and generic groupware into collaborative development environments (CDE). A CDE provides a project workspace with a standardized toolset to be used by the global software team. The earliest CDE was developed within open source software (OSS) projects because OSS projects, from the beginning, have been composed of dispersed individuals. Today, a number of CDE are available as commercial products, open source initiatives, or prototypes to enable distributed software development.

With over 230,000 hosted projects and two million registered users, SourceForge[12] is the most popular CDE at the time of this book's publication. The original mission of SourceForge was to enrich the open source community by providing a centralized place for developers to control and manage OSS projects. SourceForge offers a variety of free services: web interface for project administration, space for web content and scripts, trackers (for reporting bugs, submitting support requests or patches to review, and posting feature requests), mailing lists and discussion forums, download notification of new releases, shell functions and compile farm, and supports CVS, Subversion, Git, Mercurial, and Bazaar[13] configuration management tools. Figure 15.3 shows the personal page of the author, which provides access to a standard toolset which can be used on every project. The commercial versions for corporate use, called SourceForge Enterprise Edition and CollabNet Enterprise

---

[12] http://sourceforge.net/
[13] http://bazaar.canonical.com/

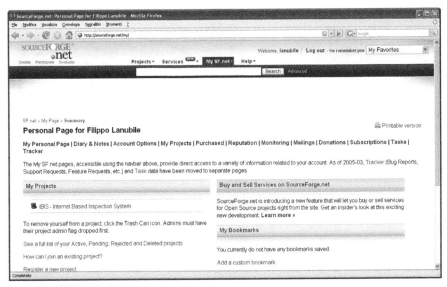

Figure 15.3   Personal SourceForge portal.

Edition, add features for tracking, measuring, and reporting on software project activities.

Distributed SCM gained popularity in 2002 when Linus Torvalds made the controversial decision to use BitKeeper, a proprietary, closed source tool by BitMover Inc., for supporting the Linux kernel development, the pinnacle of free open source software. In 2005, when BitMover announced that it would stop providing a version of the tool that was free of charge to the community, Torvalds decided to start the development of a new distributed SCM, which later became Git. The main reason for starting a new SCM development project was that none of the available free systems met Torvalds' needs, particularly the requirements on performance and safeguards against data corruption, either accidental or malicious.

GForge[14] is a fork of the SourceForge.net project. It has been downloaded and configured as in-house server by many industrial and academic organizations (see Fig. 15.4). Like SourceForge, it also offers a commercial version, called GForge Advanced Server. It supports CVS, Subversion, and Perforce[15] configuration management tools. A notable feature of GForge is its integration with the CruiseControl build tool.

Ohloh[16] is an online community platform built upon a web services suite. Its aim is to map the status of the OSS development world by retrieving data from

[14] http://gforge.org/projects/gforge/
[15] http://www.perforce.com/
[16] http://www.ohloh.net/

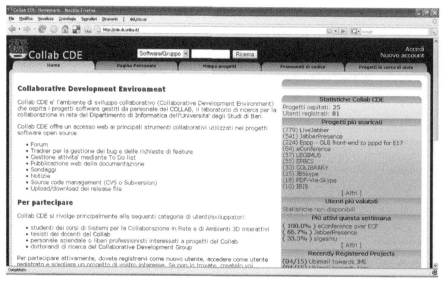

Figure 15.4   A GForge-based CDE.

public CDEs (Fig. 15.5). As such, Ohloh provides statistics about a project's longevity, licenses, and software measurements, such as source lines of code and commit statistics, so as to inform about the amount of activity for each project. It also allows for evaluation of trend popularity of specific programming languages through global statistics per language measures. Contributor statistics are also available with the aim of measuring developers' personal experiences on the basis of commit statistics and mutual ratings (in form of "kudos" received from other developers in the community). As of January 2010, Ohloh counts over 440,000 members and lists over 430,000 projects.

Trac[17] is a CDE that combines an integrated wiki, an issue tracking system, and a front-end interface to SCM tools, usually Subversion, although it supports a number of other configuration management tools through plug-ins. Also, CruiseControl can be integrated via plug-ins to support source code building. Project overview and progress tracking are allowed by setting a roadmap of milestones which include a set of so-called tickets (i.e., tasks, feature requests, bug reports, and support issues) as well as by viewing the timeline of changes. Trac also allows team members to be notified about project events and ticket changes through e-mail messages and RSS feeds. Figure 15.6 shows a screenshot of a project with active tickets grouped by milestone and colored to indicate different priorities.

Google Code[18] is a Google application that offers a project hosting service with revision control (only SVN and Mercurial are supported), issue tracking, a wiki for documentation, and a file download features (Fig. 15.7). Google code service is free

---

[17] http://trac.edgewall.org/
[18] http://code.google.com/

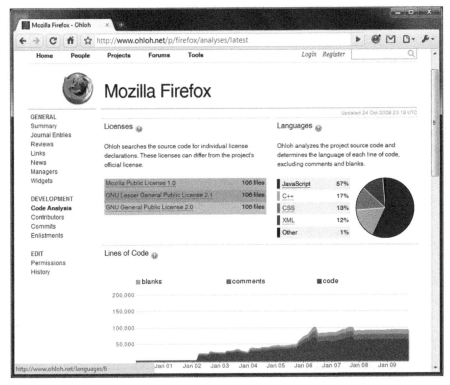

Figure 15.5 Ohloh's statistics non Mozilla Firefox code base.

(3) Active Tickets by Milestone - eConference over ECF - Trac - Mozilla Firefox

File Modifica Visualizza Cronologia Segnalibri Strumenti ? del.icio.us

Milestone M3 (12 matches)

Ticket	Summary	Component	Version	Type	Owner	Status	Created
#49	Implemented Multichat editor	core-ui		enhancement	alessio_angelini	assigned	04/12/08
#50	Implement agenda	core-ui	1.0	task	alessio_angelini	assigned	04/12/08
#4	A conference can be called	core-ui	1.0	user-story	alessio_angelini	assigned	12/24/07
#6	A participant can be given or removed the rights to speak	core	1.0	user-story	pasquale_fersini	assigned	12/25/07
#8	A participant may send messages at conference time	core	1.0	user-story	luca_bacco	accepted	12/25/07
#10	An invitation for a conference call has been received	core	1.0	user-story	luca_bacco	accepted	12/25/07
#14	A conference caller can grant or refuse RFS	core	1.0	user-story	pasquale_fersini	assigned	12/25/07
#20	Implement the pending invitations	instantmessenger-ui	1.0	user-story	pasquale_fersini	assigned	12/26/07
#84	New conference participant event	core		defect	alessio_angelini	new	05/26/08
#41	MVP Convert: Create an InvitationManager to handle the invitations	instantmessenger-ui	1.0	enhancement	pasquale_fersini	accepted	04/09/08
#51	Create a base testcase class for Integration tests of econference	dev-support	1.0	task	mario_scalas	accepted	04/12/08
#58	Fix order among toolbars	core-ui		defect	pasquale_fersini	new	04/17/08

Milestone M4 (23 matches)

Ticket	Summary	Component	Version	Type	Owner	Status	Created
#9	A caller may grant speech rights as he wishes	core	1.0	user-story	pasquale_fersini	assigned	12/25/07
#12	A caller may remove speech rights as he wishes	core	1.0	user-story	pasquale_fersini	assigned	12/25/07
#15	A caller choose the scribe	whiteboard	1.0	user-story	pasquale_fersini	assigned	12/25/07
#16	The scribe updates the whiteboard	whiteboard	1.0	user-story	pasquale_fersini	new	12/25/07
#62	Implement automatic updating	core	1.0	enhancement	mario_scalas	new	04/18/08
#70	Implement the UserManager	core	1.0	task	pasquale_fersini	new	04/23/08
#65	Creation of non-persistent chatroom in the ConferenceWizard	core-ui		defect	alessio_angellini	new	04/20/08

Completato

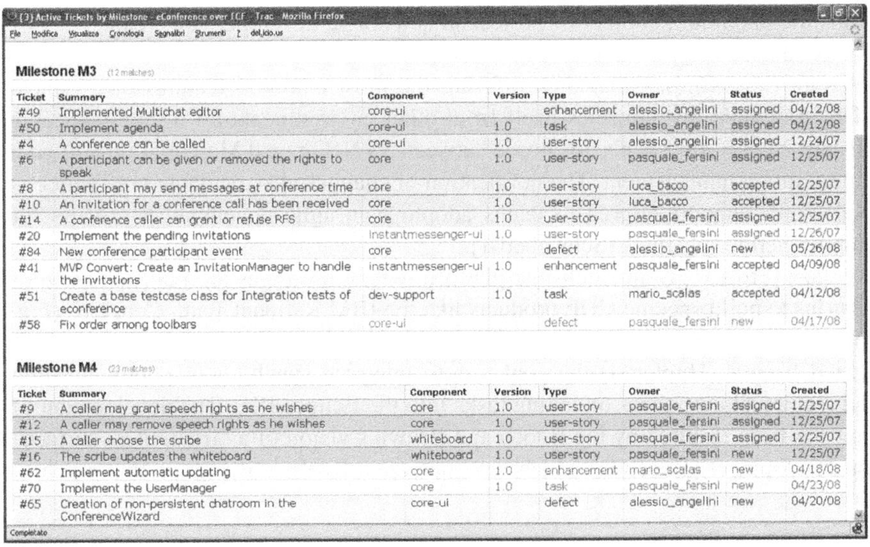

Figure 15.6 Active tickets in Trac grouped by milestone.

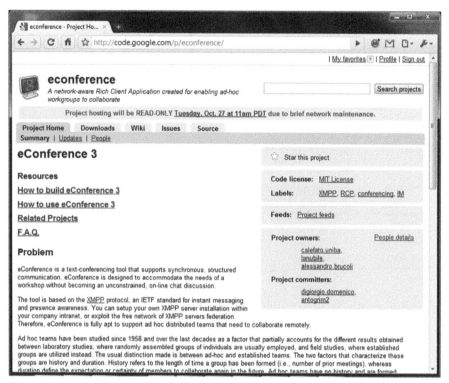

Figure 15.7   An example of project summary page in Google Code.

for all OSS projects that are licensed under one of the following nine licenses: Apache, Artistic, BSD, GPLv2, GPLv3, LGPL, MIT, MPL, and EPL. The site also limits the maximum number of projects that a single developer can create.

Assembla[19] is yet another CDE service for both open source and commercial software (Fig. 15.8). Other than offering the most common features of a typical CDE, Assembla distinguishes itself from other environments for a few noticeable aspects, namely, the chance to choose between SVN, Git, and Mercurial for software configuration management. The notification of changes also available via Twitter as well as the support offered to teams adopting an agile development process for running Scrum meetings [Schwaber01].

Jazz [Frost07] is an extensible platform which leverages the Eclipse notion of plug-ins to build specific CDE products like the IBM Rational Team Concert[20] (Fig. 15.9). The present version has a wide-ranging scope, but in the former version of Jazz [Cheng04, Hupfer04] the goal was to integrate synchronous communication and reciprocal awareness of coding tasks into the Eclipse IDE. The development of Jazz has been inspired by the Booch and Brown's vision of a "frictionless surface" for development [Booch03] which was motivated by the observation that much of

---

[19] http://www.assembla.com/
[20] http://www-01.ibm.com/software/awdtools/rtc/

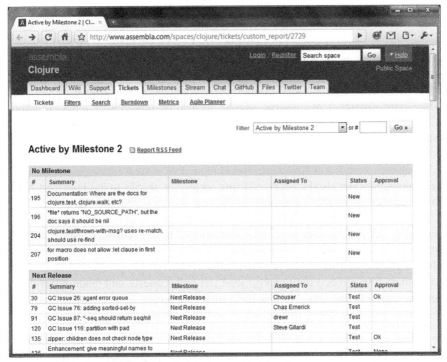

Figure 15.8 Active tickets in Assembla grouped by milestone.

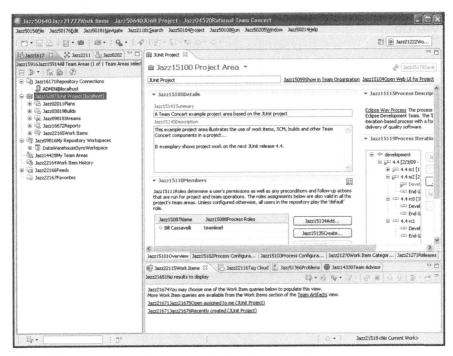

Figure 15.9 A screenshot of the Jazz client Rational Team Concert.

the developers' effort is wasted in switching back and forth between different applications to communicate and work together. According to this vision, collaborative features should be available as components that extend core applications (e.g., the IDE), thus increasing the users' comfort and productivity. Jazz uses a proprietary source code management solution, which can also be replaced by other common SCM tools (e.g., SVN and Git). The Jazz client is a rich client application, called Rational Team Concert (see Fig. 15.9), which is built upon the Eclipse RCP platform. Aside from the development-specific features, Jazz also offers a built-in RSS reader and integrates with Lotus Sametime and Google Talk instant messaging networks. Jazz repositories can also be accessed using a browser, thanks to the Jazz Rest API, which exposes and makes accessible all the core services from the Web.

GitHub[21] is a CDE service that describes itself as a "social network for programmers" (Fig. 15.10). Like the other CDEs mentioned before, GitHub hosting service only offers Git as source code management to both open source and commercial software projects. However, GitHub also aims to foster developers' collaboration by letting them fork projects through Git, send and pull requests, and monitor development through a twitter-like, "follow-this-project" approach.

Figure 15.10   Main page of Ruby on Rails project in GitHub.

[21] http://github.com/

Finally, to conclude this section, we mention some other noticeable CDEs, such as Launchpad,[22] which is known for hosting the Ubuntu project; GNU Savannah,[23] the central point for the development of most GNU software; Tigris,[24] which is a CDE specialized on hosting open source software engineering tools; and CodePlex,[25] Microsoft's recent take on collaborative open source development.

Web 2.0 extends traditional collaborative software by means of direct user contribution, rich interaction, and community building. Some key Web 2.0 applications are blogs, microblogs, wikis, social networking sites, and collaborative tagging systems. The use of Web 2.0 applications has become quite common in open source and global software projects as they represent a valuable means to increase the amount of informal communication exchanged between team members. For example, wiki platforms, such as Confluence,[26] have emerged as a practical and economical option to consider for creating and maintaining group documentation [Louridas06].

RESULTS

Although all the products reviewed in this chapter are successful and effectively adopted by many distributed development teams, companies today are relying more and more on collaborative development environments. Capgemini, a multinational consultant and outsourcing company, has managed to successfully introduce the use of CollabNet, the enterprise version of SourceForge, by starting with a few pilot projects which focused on a subset of the most needed CDE features. CollabNet was gradually spread to the various seats of Capgemini. Deutsche Bank has also reported to have successfully adopted the CollabNet CDE thanks to the ability to collect all the metrics necessary to quickly target specific wastes in the project management and apply rapid corrections. At InfoSupport, a Dutch-based consultant company, the adoption of the Jazz CDE has significantly reduced maintenance costs and time-to-market. First, rather than spending resources in trying to make several successful tools coexist, the adoption of Jazz ensured an integrated set of tools with a coordinated release lifecycle and no risks of present and future reciprocal incompatibilities. Second, the availability of a web-based thin client of Jazz allowed customers' InfoSupport to access relevant information within the CDE.

TAKE-AWAY TIPS

In this chapter we presented a number of tools and collaborative development environments that are available to support distributed teams. As a general guidance, we can draw a few major lessons that can prevent GSE/outsourcing efforts from falling to pieces.

---

[22] https://launchpad.net/
[23] http://savannah.gnu.org/
[24] http://www.tigris.org/
[25] http://www.codeplex.com/
[26] http://www.atlassian.com/software/confluence/

Two aspects that drive the successful adoption of an issue tracking system are *ease of use* and *extensibility*. On the one hand, a polished and intuitive user interface lowers the entry level of expertise, thus allowing the tool to be opened to the customers as well. On the other hand, choosing products that offer extension API allows companies to customize tools to meet their corporate standards, for instance, in terms of security (e.g., single sign-on integration) or culture (e.g., polling to prioritize new features).

Wikis have mostly found their way in distributed projects as document repositories and online help systems. Successful adoption of an enterprise wiki needs strong support for *file uploading* and *WYSIWYG editing* features. In fact, on the one hand, in wikis people found an easier way to share documents in a central place through the web browser rather than using e-mail or storing them in a network folder. On the other hand, wikis have dramatically reduced the webmaster bottleneck, and the related costs, by reducing the expertise needed to update web pages, thus getting more people involved in page editing.

The idea of adopting no SCM in a distributed project is out of question. We reviewed the mainstream SCM tools, which can be broadly classified as centralized and distributed, depending on whether they need a central repository or not. Unlike centralized SCM tools, when developers check out a project from a distributed revision control system their local machines contain a complete clone of all project's repository (called a fork), not a just a portion of it. The major difference between a centralized and a distributed SCM tool is that, with the former, committing a change also implicitly means publishing it onto the central repository. Conversely, with a distributed tool, commit and publish are decoupled because a developer, after committing a change to the local repository, still has to explicitly decide when to share it with others. In general, distributed SCM tools are preferred when developers need to travel often. Therefore, companies should select an SCM that reflects the degree of distribution of the project to manage. Highly distributed projects, involving three or four remote sites or more, definitely benefit from using distributed SCM. In addition, since distributed SCM tools have been designed with the purpose of making repositories merge a routine operation, they are generally much more performing than centralized counterparts at computing diffs and applying patches. Such differences in performance increase as the number of files in a repository reaches tens of thousands or more. Therefore, the adoption of distributed SCM tools is highly recommended for managing very large projects.

Because they are essential to enable distributed development, SCM tools were the first to be integrated within CDE products. CDEs successfully combine most of the technologies mentioned earlier in one place (e.g., issue trackers, communication, and knowledge management tools). They thus provide a frictionless surface in development environments with the goal of increasing the developers' comfort and productivity. CDEs provide developers with awareness notifications via feeds or e-mails about the changes occurred to artifacts (e.g., documents being shared or modified), workspace (e.g., event notifications in case of build failures, new commits), and team (e.g., coworkers' profiles, blogs, activities, bookmarks, wikis, and files). By aggregating this information in one place, CDEs provide an overall group awareness to developers who have few or no chances to meet. They are useful for speeding up the establishment of organizational values, attitudes, and trust-based inter-personal connections, thus facilitating communication as well as the overall distributed software development process [Calefato09]. Although at first glance enterprise CDEs might be discarded due to high license costs, companies should not overlook the hidden costs due to the effort of integrating several pieces of free software, extending them to meet their corporate standards, and contacting different tech-support teams.

Finally, the area in which most of the CDE platforms need improvement is in the integration of build tools (only available in GForge, Trac, RTC, and Codeplex) and modeling tools (only available in Trac).

Part III

Management

Chapter 16

Life-Cycle Management

Summary: Software development involves profound technological knowledge, teamwork, processes, methods, and tools. To reduce complexity, it looks just as rational to put all engineers in one location, share the objectives, agree on one process and technology to apply, and let the project run. Reality, especially in times of global development of solutions with lots of different players, components, interfaces, and anything else that could possibly increase complexity, is different. This is where product life-cycle management enters the picture. It assures that one product life-cycle is defined, agreed upon, and consistently implemented in order to have consistent interfaces, agreed roles and responsibilities, defined work products, and thus, a possibility to share and collaborate in a global dimension.

Product life-cycle management (PLM) and application life-cycle management (ALM) both ease collaboration of distributed teams because processes and rules can be relied upon and must not be reinvented for each task [Ebert03]. Training materials can be developed and shared. This is something which seasoned practitioners and managers, as well as young engineers—perhaps in different parts of the world or in different companies—can rely upon.

As an example, let's look at the development of Internet information systems. Requirements elicitation of such web-based systems shows differences to more conventional approaches as described earlier in this chapter. Often, requirements for web-based information systems are "created from scratch" by developers themselves rather than being discovered through the normal process of identifying system stakeholders and gathering their requirements. Ad hoc elicitation during development has life-cycle impacts. Evolutionary life-cycles dominate and are often used in an explorative approach. The development cycle for a web-enabled application is short, that is, only a few months and highly iterative, which leaves very little time for any formal requirements gathering and their consolidation. In such a compressed timeframe, adaptations of web applications to different geographical locations, cultures, or varying knowledge and background (i.e., skill level) of prospective users,

Global Software and IT: A Guide to Distributed Development, Projects, and Outsourcing,
First Edition. Christof Ebert.
© 2012 the Institute of Electrical and Electronics Engineers, Inc. Published 2012 by
John Wiley & Sons, Inc.

are done by explorative development. Internet information systems create prototypes of a running solution which is a simplified executable for exploring more requirements or constraints. They do this based on explorative product life-cycles.. Often, such an iterative approach without a full view on architectural impacts and business rules to govern future usage initially yields inadequate quality and performance. Other development cycles to improve quality should therefore be considered

Effective collaboration in a global context means that the different functions of the enterprise plus potential external partners (e.g., outsource manufacturing) need to agree on processes, tools, and practices. They need to apply common access to knowledge, performance measurements, and decision-making protocols. They need to share information, communication, and underlying resources. The overarching process guidance comes from gate reviews in the product life-cycle, which explains the slogan of product life-cycle management.

Many standards have been set up over the last two decades to facilitate product life-cycle management. Life-cycle processes are currently driving the underlying specific standards. ISO 15288 summarizes the system life-cycle processes, while ISO 12207 is the standard for software life-cycle processes. Both ISO and IEEE currently work diligently to align underlying process standards with these life-cycle standards. From an overall process viewpoint, formal approaches to guarantee quality products have lead to international guidelines (e.g., ISO 9001) and currently established methods to assess the product/solution engineering processes of suppliers (e.g., ISO 15504, SEI CMMI, ITIL, COBIT). The related systems engineering process is described in IEEE 1220.

Practitioners do not look for heavy process documentation, but rather for process support that describes exactly what they have to do, at the moment they have to do it. Modular process elements must be combined according to a specific role or work product to be delivered. Still, the need for an organizational process, as described by CMMI maturity level 3 [SEI11], is strongly emphasized and reinforced. We generally recommend not embarking on global software development if the impacted organizations are not at least on maturity level 3 and have defined life-cycle processes (which are requested when operating at maturity level 3).

Global development, in many cases, exhibits supplier-client relationships, even if the supplier is part of the home organization. An example of this is software centers in different parts of the world that contribute to product development with shared or split responsibilities. Companies such as SAP, IBM, or Alcatel-Lucent have these models in place and manage internal suppliers following defined processes and a standardized product life-cycle [Ebert07a, Zencke04, Forrester04]. The product life-cycle with its defined phases is key for (internal or external) supplier agreement and planning. Figure 16.1 shows a simplified product life-cycle and the different needs per phase from a supplier/contributor and contractor/owner perspective.

The product life-cycle must be mandatory for all projects. This implies that it is sufficiently agile to handle different types of projects. Standardized tailoring of the life-cycle to different project types with predefined templates or intranet web pages simplifies usage and reduces overheads. Its mandatory elements must be explicit and auditable. Some online workflow support facilitates ease of implementa-

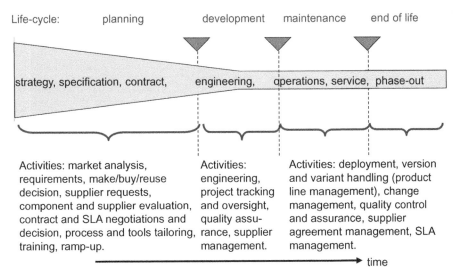

Figure 16.1 Life-cycle management for global software and IT products and services.

tion and correctness of information. Gate reviews (decision reviews) must be well prepared. They must not result in lengthy meetings, but should rather be prepared with online checklists so all attendees are prepared and can quickly decide the go/ no go for next phase. Project information should generally be available online.

Chapter 17

Supplier Selection and Evaluation

Summary: A key success factor in global software development and IT management is how to master the relationships with suppliers. Supplier selection includes contracting and procurement strategies because management has to decide between make versus buy and also the life-cycle of these products or services. Based on the offer and contractual risks, managers on both the procurement and technical side have to decide whether a client relationship and subsequent sourcing is profitable and whether related risks can be managed over a long period of time. In this chapter we will provide concrete guidance on supplier selection and evaluation.

Supplier relationships can evolve over time because the business situations of the partners change and new technology and new vendors enter the marketplace. Often, outsourcing situations lock the client to some degree, making it expensive for the client to change its vendor. Very early on in an outsourcing project, a client becomes tied to its chosen vendor even though the client may try to manage costs and dependencies by competitive arrangements by introducing additional suppliers. Although organizations try hard, it is hardly possible to assess every risk andto plan for contingencies in a contract over a long period of time.

Supplier relationships often oscillate between trust and control. Figure 17.1 shows an oscillating evolution. Naturally, there is not one single path, but the layout is archetypical for most supplier relationships. Depending on outsourcing content, some stability can be reached over time, but the customer organization must be clear that behaviors occasionally need to change otherwise performance and cost won't be competitive. This being understood, mature customer organizations consider such evolution in the contract set-up to avoid lock-in at a point where the relationship needs a change.

Global Software and IT: A Guide to Distributed Development, Projects, and Outsourcing,
First Edition. Christof Ebert.
© 2012 the Institute of Electrical and Electronics Engineers, Inc. Published 2012 by
John Wiley & Sons, Inc.

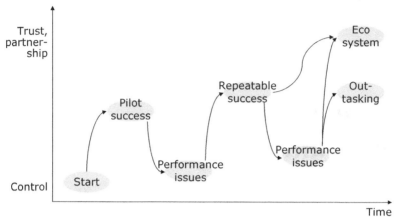

Figure 17.1 Supplier relationships evolve over time between control and trust.

 It is important for clients and suppliers to use shared processes and to collaborate with sufficiently high process maturity for the outsourcing of software develop-ment. Different empirical studies highlight that success is higher when both the client and supplier firms exhibit at least CMMI maturity level 3. Additionally, for companies in the IT service domain, COBIT and ITIL are helpful toward basic service processes and risk management.

Over the past 10 years the impacts of process maturity on supplier relationship and global software and IT performance have been analyzed in different industry settings [Ebert07a, Rottmann06]. There is a clear correlation of maturity leveland performance results on both sides. The supplier might exhibit a CMMI maturity level of five; if the customer has insufficient processes, the relationship will be risky at best. They will often be canceled very fast.

Such changes are not easy though. Often, the customer forms a hybrid organiza-tion or eco-system that is somewhere between a market and a hierarchy with its suppliers. Renegotiations can be used to mitigate incomplete contracting issues. It is also possible that the contract between the parties evolves toward individual agree-ments within a frame contract. The supplier selection phase determines not only an initial contract, but also the influence mechanisms and relationship management over long contractual periods. Managers should therefore be very careful in selecting a supplier and setting up the respective contract.

Global software development is not necessarily outsourcing. This means that not in all cases is there a need to select external suppliers. Unless you collaborate with an internal offshoring site, this chapter can be skipped. However, even in the case of full internally managed global development, it might be insightful to apply some of the following checklists to your internal software departments and check the professionalism of their local management. Many of the checklists simply help to detect deficiencies and to improve. We will come back to supplier agreement management and the entire life-cycle impacts of managing a supplier in a later chapter.

When selecting external suppliers, a key prerequisite is in identifying which supplier best fits your needs. There are a few simple rules to follow:

- Select a supplier that fits with the size and business model of your own company. For instance, a very big business process outsourcing supplier might be less interested in providing specialized services to a small company. The supplier might be willing to do so, but after a while behaviors will be less supportive to the needs of the small or medium enterprise. They would have done better with an intermediate used to working with small enterprises or by using a supplier who specializes in this type of management.

- Select a supplier with sufficient process and methodology know-how. As a rule, the supplier of engineering services must have high process maturity. Demand a recent CMMI appraisal valid for the entire company and evaluate results. Additionally, for clients looking for suppliers in the IT service domain, COBIT and ITIL are helpful toward basic service processes and risk management.

- Assure process flexibility. It is not of much help if you select a supplier that demands to use exactly the same processes and tools across all projects. A good supplier is capable of adjusting its processes and interfaces to your tools. Of course, they should be able to help you in improving processes and optimizing tools, but this is decided on a needs basis.

- Select a supplier with sufficient domain knowledge in your own field. Having domain expertise allows you to put skilled engineers who need less knowledge to understand technical aspects related to the product or service on your project rather than those who only understand the design and programming language.

- Demand a list of engineers working on your project with skills, current subject experience, previous projects, and so on. Insist that these engineers are allocated to the project in case you want to build skills over a time. Note that defined engineers and names typically increase cost per head because it reduces flexibility at the supplier side.

- Use a supplier that is physically present at your own site. It often takes substantial effort to continuously travel to the supplier site or to have only video conferences. Having a local supplier's sales team, as well as some engineering skills, eases requirements and change management.

Some simple checks for supplier selection should be applied throughout the different processes of supplier selection and agreement management:

- Did you ever work with this supplier and would you do it again? What were the lessons learned from that previous contract? Alternatively, demand this check from a reference client who you know and trust.

- What expertise and references are available from the supplier in your own domain?

- What is the turnover rate at the supplier site? Is it acceptable or rather high? How are skills managed in light of this turnover rate? What turnover rates will be assured by the contract?

- How stable is the supplier and its management or shareholders? Did it recently change, reorganize, or merge with another company? Avoid any supplier that is currently hampered by big acquisitions.

- What business processes are in place at the supplier to elicit requirements and to cope with change? Does this fit your needs?

- Is the supplier able and experienced in handling global development teams? Can it manage teams with members from different companies?

- Do the supplier and its employees have the necessary formal qualifications your customers and markets demand (e.g., ISO 9001, CMMI maturity levels, COBIT and ITIL implementation, etc.)? Is the supplier periodically audited? Check some recent audit results.

- Are the legal constraints acceptable for you and your company? Suppliers often demand that the site for legal disputes be in a part of the world where you are not so experienced. Check which site makes sense for you and your lawyers. Check if there are some sample legal cases that show typical behaviors. Specifically, focus on anything related to protecting your intellectual property. Manage the risk of any impact on your intellectual properties, such as whether a key engineer may defect, upfront.

- Is the infrastructure sufficient for your own purposes? Does it scale up to the high interaction needs during shared development or testing? Is it protected and auditable? Are the tools interfaces to your own tools sufficient? Have they been tested in real-world scenarios before?

- What prices are demanded for the services? Are they competitive? How will you avoid a lock-in position once the supplier has understood your technology, products and business?

Generally speaking, there are many checks which should be performed prior to the contract signature and determine a first "go/no-go" for the selection. Most can be done offline as part of a request for quotation. You might still want to visit the suppliers' sites to directly see offices and talk with engineers or management. In that case, make sure you speak with those engineers and team leads who will later be working on your project. Trust your feeling when looking into offices or cafeterias; they provide messages about culture and behaviors.

Contracts are finally agreed with both technical and non-technical / commercial elements. The technical aspects are coined into a service level agreement that you should manage carefully.

Chapter 18

Supplier Management

Summary: Supplier management is often neglected and only considered relevant where there are formal handovers of software components or IT services. In fact, hardly any software and IT project can survive without supplier management. A small company may use COTS or open source components, a bigger company may distribute work allocation across departments, and yet another company may collaborate with its customers on requirements specifications. In this chapter, we will show sourcing and supplier management in a distributed context. Checklists are introduced to facilitate your own selection criteria.

In managing a sourcing relationship, both client and supplier should use their respective power and processes in order to obtain optimal results. For the commercial supplier, the optimal outcome may be best measured in financial terms, either in the short term or the long term. The optimal results for the customer are more difficult to assess and evaluate due to looking into different dimensions, such as business case, motivation, and sustainability. Perhaps the best way to characterize the optimal outcome from the client's point of view comes from the project group or the individual level: a successful project, delivered within a reasonable schedule and budget, gives personal and professional satisfaction. The customer organization must define what it considers the positive outcome to be the long-term success of the sourcing projects with its stakeholders. At times it means you must bite the bullet and pay a bit more in order to achieve trust and get much better results overall, as opposed to too much control (see Chapter 7).

 Supplier and sourcing management is a core competence for any software and IT manager today. It is certainly not something to "delegate" to a procurement organization. The technical manager is the key stakeholder and is held accountable for culture, climate, results, and performance. Procurement and purchasing manages contracts, but not people, processes, results, or relationships.

We will look specifically at the case in which an external supplier must be managed. This does not preclude captive sourcing relationships, such as an engineering organization in India working within, and for, a big global enterprise. The major difference with such captive sourcing and supplier management is that too often the internal clients do not realize that they ought to manage their captive suppliers as if they were external suppliers, while the captive suppliers, on the other hand, behave as if they were separate units.

The starting point for any supplier management is a framework of life-cycle processes, responsibilities, and clear decision criteria. Product life-cycle management (PLM) protects and guides the different stakeholders in global development. Figure 18.1 shows the relevant phases along the product life-cycle and the respective activities related to supplier management. Four major phases are distinguished, namely, supplier strategy, supplier selection and contracting, contract management, and evaluation and relationship management.

A client or customer organization must provide a realistic and precise expectation of functional requirements and quality attributes (e.g., reliability). They should clearly state that payment will be provided only for systems that meet the agreed upon functionality (e.g., requirements, acceptance tests, SLA conditions). They should demand milestone presentations of progress for continued funding.

Supplier organizations, on the other hand, must insist on a signed contract with requirements. They must agree before contract signature on clear and reasonable acceptance criteria. The contract must be explicit that the supplier owns the software until final payment. They must clearly agree on liabilities and support after handover. They have to express disagreement and unrealistic conditions openly and not con-

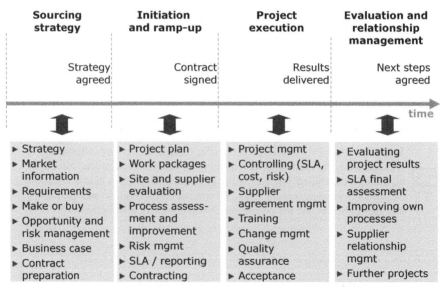

Figure 18.1   Supplier agreement management along the product life-cycle.

tinue with diverging assumptions. They should always strive for win-win results and therefore offer compromise approaches once needs are understood. In cases of component delivery, they should include a software key that will operate after the date of contracted software acceptance.

As a client, you should be cautious not to manage primarily by means of the SLA. We were called in to a worldwide leading ICT company in a difficult situation. An outsourcing supplier for their testing and documentation was underperforming. It was way below the SLA, and the obvious mechanism would have been to put clear targets and then take consequences if they are not met within a few weeks. The ICT company however, was smart enough to consider that there could be reasons why such a company suddenly underperforms. When we looked to the supplier, we found that he was best in class and had been carefully selected. In fact, it would have been difficult for our client to get rid of that outsourcing supplier because there were already some lock-ins that were visible which would have made it expensive to switch. When we brought the different needs together, we found that quite early in the sourcing agreement our client had focused very much on cost reduction. The supplier, eager to win the contract, agreed, and later found that the margins would be too low in the long run. They decided internally to prepare a graceful cut by failing on certain SLA conditions where both parties would be "guilty" due to unclear specifications and interfaces. Upon identifying this root cause, we worked toward a renewed contract with win-win schemes built in. A major change was to keep the low rates (win for the client) but include an incentive for quality and performance (win for the supplier). They agreed, and after some mixed workshops, which we facilitated, to really obtain a re-launch with fresh minds and perceptions. It worked out well.

As a client you should always consider the golden rule of supplier management: You pay for what you get. Don't get trapped in contracts that look "cheap," but later bring tons of extra cost due to lousy processes and insufficient delivery quality. Preconditions of any successful supplier management are good processes on both sides, that is, for the client and the supplier. Insufficient client processes cannot be externalized. They will not scale up from a single site to several sites. Often, those low-maturity processes can be handled in localized development without many overheads due to colocated teams, but they will fail with globalization.

If your own processes (being the client) are on a CMMI maturity level one or two you better ask for a consultant who can help you in installing effective engineering and management processes. Most suppliers offer such support, but this is not necessarily a sustainable solution, as they have different interest and business models. Independent of what your processes look like, it is relevant to review them carefully with your suppliers and agree to interfaces on work product, engineering, and tool level. The exchange of information must be carefully planned. A change management tool is not enough. It needs rules for documentation, design reviews, change management boards, and so on. Install workflow management and online accessible project, work product, and process information to assure proper knowledge management. Interactive process models, such as RUP and others have proven very helpful to communicate and install processes [Ebert03, Royce98].

For your own processes and their improvement, consult with the CMMI [SEI11] that has different process areas suitable for supplier management. Specifically, version 1.3 of 2011 strengthens supplier management topics. They range from selection and contract management to building a shared vision and effective collaborative teams. The CMMI has rich evidence from big global systems development projects with different contractors working on one assignment. For companies in the IT service industries, COBIT and ITIL will also help towards orchestrated processes [COBIT05, ITIL07].

Figures 18.2–18.4 provide some sample checklists for supplier and contract monitoring. The first checklist (Fig. 18.2) is used to highlight specific supplier-

☑ Sudden behavioral changes
☑ Contractual agreements are not kept
☑ Difficulties and issues are not communicated
☑ Frequent rejection of inputs, specifications, etc.
☑ Above average turn-over rate of engineers on your projects
☑ Reduced contact with supplier senior management
☑ Demand to re-prioritize requirements
☑ Overly exact and restrictive interpretation of SLA
☑ Increasing amount of escalation
☑ Financial situation of supplier worsens
☑ Other clients leave your supplier
☑ Supplier gains new and more relevant clients

Figure 18.2 Checklist: Indicators for supplier risks.

☑ Is progress according to agreed milestones and deliverables?
☑ Are right skills and engineers available as agreed?
☑ Is technical expertise on right level?
☑ Are agreed quality levels of deliverables proven?
☑ Are the budgeted cost and schedule kept?
☑ Is quality, cost and content of work products adequate?
☑ Which risks materialize? Which risks are mitigated?
☑ Are agreed standards and processes implemented?
☑ Is security and intellectual property sufficiently protected?
☑ Are governance mechanisms installed and followed?
☑ Which improvements are proposed by supplier?
☑ Is there any way to improve relationship management?

Figure 18.3 Checklist: Supplier evaluation during the project.

☑   Did the supplier give the perception of not being qualified?
☑   Have schedule and budget constraints been kept?
☑   Have all deliverables been according to SLA and quality levels?
☑   Has effort been in line with estimates? Why not?
☑   Which risks materialized? Which risks could be mitigated?
☑   Which improvements are proposed by the supplier?
☑   Which improvement are suggested by own team?
☑   Has the work split and allocation been adequate?
☑   Are there possibilities to improve relationship management?
☑   Are there possibilities to improve communication?
☑   Is this the right supplier to grow with or to continue with?

Figure 18.4   Checklist: Supplier evaluation at project or contract end.

created risks during contract execution. They are a kind of formalized gut feeling to detect changes which (specifically if several appear) point to growing risks. The second checklist (Fig. 18.3) provides some checks for supplier evaluation during an ongoing project. The third checklist (Fig. 18.4) is used at contract termination or project end to summarize lessons learned for future supplier management.

Consider sufficient time and budget resources for training the supplier on your processes. A very strong training tool is the scrum process with short team meetings everyday in which recent results and future steps are briefly reviewed. Any uncertainty should be brought up in such reviews, which should take not more than 15–30 minutes and can even be conducted by telephone conference across sites [Schwaber04].

Build a supplier program management to handle the necessary review and decision processes. Agree with your supplier review and acceptance processes to assure the right quality level. Installing such processes after the contract signature will create the perception of policing the supplier. You can ask third parties in case of questions or needs for escalation.

Chapter 19

Practice: IT Outsourcing—A Supplier Perspective

S. M. Balasubramaniyan, Wipro

Summary: This chapter describes practical experiences from an outsourcing supplier's perspective. The scope of the engagement described in this case study was such that it could comprehensively cover relevant themes and guidance from previous chapters in a concrete project context. It offers valuable insights of outsourcing partnerships that can help toward doing things successfully in your own company.

BACKGROUND

One of the key components of Distributed Software Management is the outsourcing of part or full life-cycle of the Application/Product and/or the associated infrastructure to partner organizations. In this case study, the transformation of IT infrastructure and applications by a large global organization in close association with Wipro as their primary outsourcing partner, has been taken as the case in point. Commencing historically, with a predominant advantage of cost arbitrage, the compulsions of outsourcing took multiple dimensions later. Like most successful organizations world over, irrespective of their domain and operations, this organization has given a strategic position for IT outsourcing due to its overweighing merits over the drawbacks.

The drivers for outsourcing were many for this company. The complexities of the system and the software that drives it have increased manifold and it was practically impossible for the organization to do everything by them. From a "Vertical Integration" approach, the company moved over to an "Assemble the best pieces" approach. Through the collaboration of the best players in the industry, who have core competencies in their own areas of focus, the company derived the best results.

The second aspect in this relationship was the non linear increase in the need for educated and trained workforce to support the high growth business strategies.

Global Software and IT: A Guide to Distributed Development, Projects, and Outsourcing,
First Edition. Christof Ebert.
© 2012 the Institute of Electrical and Electronics Engineers, Inc. Published 2012 by
John Wiley & Sons, Inc.

The thrust given for technical education and the ability to train large numbers of skilled people in the developing nations had benefited large corporations such as this organization to leverage the combined benefits of appropriate competencies at much reduced cost.

In the initial days of IT enabled business operations, the trend in this organization was also to have most of the IT implementation through proprietary architecture, infrastructure, and tools. However, with the need for working in a global environment, it has become imperative that one adopts Global Standards and Open architecture for implementation. This approach has substantially improved the development and implementation timelines as well as the cost. Additionally, a good support from the industry is available for any issues or specific needs for platform and standards based developments. The investment in developing Solution frameworks with a focus on customized solutions for the specific needs of their clients by Wipro helped to meet the above objective.

As in the case of progress in any domain, the collaboration tools and infrastructure have been developed in parallel to the advancement in the Information Technology itself. These tools and methods have transformed the "Cube Farm" of IT management from a colocated system to a globally distributed system. This has substantially helped the realization of globally distributed software development. The availability of audio and video conferencing, configuration management systems, and multi site project management tools can be cited as the examples for the same.

With the increasing need for improving the outcome of application or product development per unit cost or unit effort, distributed development, through outsourcing, has given a quantum advantage in recent times. Given that the options and the mode of outsourcing have grown with experience, organizations need to study and adopt what is best for them. In this engagement, the outsourcing client leveraged the ready-to-cook solution frameworks, large infrastructure for customization in low-cost locations, nearshore presence of Wipro's personnel for requirement gathering and final implementation.

 IT outsourcing must be treated as a strategic step in the operations of an organization and not as a tactical cost saving effort. Any simple cost savings approach, rather than an overall sustainable cooperation, fails after some time.

There are multiple ways in which an organization can evolve the strategy considering the various operational factors like IT budget, the work force requirements, technology transitions, spread of operations, vendor management and availability of partners, business growth, and the proportionate scale of IT operations. The client, in this case study, needed a large experienced workforce for a short duration to design the transformation of their IT landscape that would need very low maintenance cost.

The strategic position for IT Outsourcing also enables an organization to consider the risks in it. The risk profile for IT Outsourcing would vary from one organization to another. A structured approach to Risk assessment and judicious decision making together with carefully planned Risk mitigation are required to be included in the planning process. In this case, timely development and implementation of the new systems in line with the retirement plan of the legacy systems was the major risk evaluated and mitigated through phased implementation plan.

The success of IT outsourcing starts with making the right choice of work to be outsourced. Since this is an important starting point in any collaborative work, many studies have been conducted and one of the good models to follow has considered two factors, namely, Interaction Requirements and Management Requirements (Fig. 19.1).

The evaluation of the IT work in the above model helps the organization that is outsourcing, as well as the IT service provider, to make an objective assessment of the suitability or the potential risks to the successful outsourcing. Where the need for interaction between partners and the management of relationships are low, the work considered for outsourcing is most amenable for success. When these factors are high, the risk to the success of outsourcing is the highest. This model helps the partners to take care of the failure modes to ensure that the probability of successful outcome is high.

It is not a prescriptive situation to outsource or not based on the above model, but it helps the partners to consider the risks involved and the efforts to be taken to plan, mitigate, and prevent the occurrence of any of the identified risks.

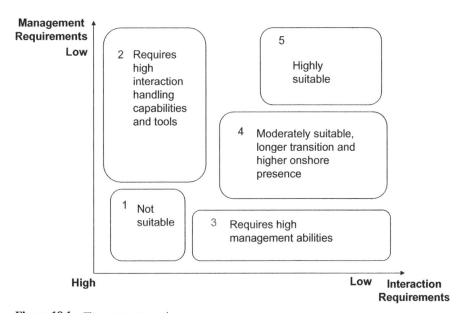

Figure 19.1   Fitment to outsourcing.

Preparedness for outsourcing applies to both organizations. While the supplier partner who takes up the outsourced work needs to be adequately equipped for successfully meeting the obligations in the engagement, an equal part is played by the outsourcing organization in ensuring that the collaboration succeeds. The lack of preparedness on both sides is, most often, the cause of failure in outsourcing relationship.

In the engagement described in this case study as a part of the planning process, key and decision making representatives of the client organization and Wipro, the IT partner chosen, sat together to evaluate the risks to the engagement. Through various deliberations, it was determined that the IT transformation project scope is of relatively low management requirement and relatively high interaction requirement. Accordingly, a Program Management Office was created to enable relevant stakeholders in either organization to be brought together at the right instances to make suitable decisions to move the engagement forward. Collaborative tools such as Weekly voice conferencing, MS Project plan, and remote secure login and the like were used to manage the risks.

 In IT outsourcing partnerships, the proposition is either "Win-Win" or "Lose-Lose". There is practically no sustainable situation where one partner wins and the other loses from the business perspective. Therefore, it is essential that both the outsourcing organization as well as the service provider organization consider the business imperatives of one another and plan the collaboration accordingly.

In IT outsourcing, the organization which takes up outsourced work needs to make investments in work force training, infrastructure, project managerial capabilities, processes aligned to the partner's working, cultural fit, and executive oversight. Service Provider organizations such as Wipro invest in Talent Transformation in a big way for making their workforce ready for their clients' technical and business needs. Customer specific Offshore Development Centers (ODCs) provide the opportunity for creating the right environment for a client's engagement through tools, processes, and infrastructure. The cultural fit is taken care of through cross-cultural training, both for the client's personnel as well as Wipro's personnel.

For the outsourcing organization, since it is a strategic decision, adequate support needs to be given to the partners in terms of a road map of partnership, investment for induction of partners to the organization's culture, adaptability to the distributed management of applications and products, clear articulation of success factors, and very importantly, consideration for partner's business imperatives. Identification and appointment of sponsors at senior management level in the client's organization took care of this aspect in this case.

To arrive at the right combination of organizational characteristics for successful, long-term and value adding collaborations, the product or the IT engagement can be viewed from the perspective of its own life-cycle. The imperatives of collaboration and the characteristics that the relationship would need to take at different phases of the above life-cycle are different. At the inception stage of a product or IT application life-cycle, the outsourced engagement yields the best benefits but it is also the phase in which outsourcing is most challenging. In the growth phase, the outsourcing can be leveraged for growth acceleration such as widening global reach and customization for different markets. In the maturity phase, the outsourced-to partner can ensure that the installed base is maintained, sunset product and services are extended in life, and additional savings/revenue is obtained. Customer engagement and loyalty and product/service continuity is the key engagement objective in this phase.

When the right combination is achieved, the best value added collaborative capabilities emerge. Table 19.1 summarizes the best possible combination in each of the above life-cycle phases.

The IT transformation engagement described in this case study fitted into the Growth Phase of the IT life-cycle of the client's organization. Accordingly, the team in Wipro had experienced architects and program managers as the key team members adapted a solution framework which was developed in the practice groups for faster implementation. The relationship spanned the development, implementation, and support to ensure a long-term commitment. A Program Management Office was created which worked with the sponsor organization of the client in a collaborative way. Enough empowerment was given to Wipro through business engagement models such as Fixed Price modules to distribute the responsibilities between the two parties. Speed of implementation in line with the IT evolution strategy was the key business proposition.

RESULTS

Studies in the area of successful IT outsourcing are pointing towards three factors that can determine the success of a partnership.

The first factor is the cost leadership. Cost continues to be the primary reason for outsourcing decisions and will continue to be so for a long time to come. In the IT outsourcing scenario, the cost leadership could be achieved through optimized total cost of ownership (TCO). TCO considers multiple cost factors in the engagement like workforce cost, transition cost, infrastructure cost, operational cost, and sustaining cost. Therefore, the ability of partners in obtaining appropriate advantages in each of the above considerations can determine the cost leadership. A client-specific Offshore Development Center, a proven framework for transition, and a long-term engagement commitment which, in this case, led to distribution of cost structures, helped the client to derive the cost advantage,

The second consideration is the capability enhancement for the partnership. As mentioned in the beginning of this section, today's applications and products require

Table 19.1 Outsourcing Activities Across the Life-Cycle

Life-Cycle Considerations	Inception Phase	Growth Phase	Maturity Phase
Principle Purpose	Leverage Core Strengths / IP Portfolio	Domain Competencies / Experience	Cost Benefits
Stake in Outsourced Work	Distributed Ownership of Implementation	Flexibility and Agility in response to Market	Extending the life cycle of application / product
Mode of Engagement	Centrally Coordinated	Decentralized Responsibilities	Ownership Transition
Organisational Fit	Aligned Shared Vision / Long Term Planning	Investments alignment / Medium Term Planning	Skills revectoring/ Tactical planning
Choice of Partners	Trusted, Preferred and Strategic Partners	Mature Partners / Long term commitments	New Partner possibilities / Engagement commitments
Enabling Considerations	Investment in Core competencies, Tools, Methods, Systems and Processes	Investments in Diverse tools and processes; Choice from a bag of options	Partner invested; Adhocset up for the engagement purpose
Management Style	Executive level commitments; Empowered relationship	Communication and Collaboration driven	Customer–Vendor level relationship

complementary capabilities to build and maintain. During the growth path of an organization, it is possible that the organization decides to focus on its core competencies and look at partners for supplemental competencies. Therefore, the collaborative working through outsourcing would enhance the capability of the organization. In this IT transformation deal, a few key personnel of the client organization were dedicated to the engagement to ensure a speedy and fault-free beginning of the project. This commitment helped, in a long way, for downstream quality of the transformation solution and implementation.

The third factor is the supplier partner's knowledge of the playing field of the outsourcing organization. The ability to expand the market reach, as well as the value provided through industry and market knowledge that can be vectored into the work being outsourced and the time it takes to market the advantage provided, are clear enablers for successful outsourcing. Depending on the IT outsourcing strategies of an organization, the selection of partners needs to be made without choosing too many or too few. Wipro was engaged in the domain of this client for more than a decade and, therefore, the solution framework that was developed by the practice group and used to build the transformation solution had the correct requirement of the client carefully built in. It made the solution appropriate and needed minimal customization and rework.

As the partnership mode of working matures and the horizon of the collaboration expands, it becomes apparent that the considerations of partnership are not the same in all instances of outsourced partnership. To get the best value out of the outsourced partnership, deeper insights need to be made as the relationship realizes the cursory benefits of outsourcing. In this case, the approach taken during defining and implementing the IT transformation was different from the approach taken during the sustenance phase of the implementation. Low cost of maintenance was the primary business driver and low cost resources, remote support, and deployment of diagnostic and analytical tools enabled the achievement of this.

Probing deeper, the considerations in the outsourced partnership, the following aspects emerge:

- Principle purpose of outsourcing: The purpose of outsourcing could be for tactical cost considerations or for the domain/platform experience of the supplier organization or for the IP/core competency of the supplier. The value proposed by each collaborating organization or each partnership could be vastly different.

- The stake in outsourced work: The choices could be among expanding the life-term of the application/product, agility and flexibility required to respond to market requirements, and sharing the ownership in a large complex implementation. Here, the context of the work being outsourced would be the key.

- Mode of engagement: The role and responsibilities of partnering organizations need to be considered. The situation may warrant the program to be centrally coordinated or with decentralized responsibilities or completely left to be managed by the supplier organization. The maturity of the IT application or the product is the key for this decision.

- Organizational fit: How well the vision and objectives of the supplier organization align with those of the outsourcing organization would be a strategic fit for large and long tenured collaborations. In certain domains, like technology outsourcing and product development, this aspect would be a key consideration.

- Choice of partners: Organizations categorize different partners on a scale of preference for different kinds of outsourced works. Strategic partners share the road map of the outsourcing organization, while a tactical customer–vendor relationship exists for non-core engagements. In some instances, one may have to carefully select and establish a long-term relationship, whereas in some situations, new vendor opportunities can be explored.

- Enabling Considerations: Depending on the tools, methods, systems, processes, and even political considerations, the decision on outsourcing may have to be taken. Oftentimes, the geographical considerations and political environment of the partner organizations could become limiting factors.

- Management Style: This is one of the key considerations in relationships where the supplier is mature and large. The display of management commitments, Executive level connects and shared visions and goals would determine the success and, sometimes, the continuity of outsourced partnership itself.

The governance of outsourced engagement is another key success factor. While many of the aspects of governance are mastered over a period of time with experience, it is essential to be cognizant of the relationship enablers that make the outsourced relationship successful.

- Learning Curve: Collaborative capabilities are something an organization learns over a period of time. It is not an inherent characteristic of most organizations. Therefore, the experienced among the partners need to hold the hand of the other to take the relationship through the initial hard path to comfort. Often, the first projects of outsourced engagements are not successful, but it is essential how much the partners have learned out of their mistakes and are able to apply in subsequent engagements. This determines the success of long-term outsourced relationships. The experience of Wipro in the business domain of the client in this case study ensured that the engagement derived the benefit from the learning curve for well over a decade.

- Organization Structure: At the commencement of an outsourced relationship, both the organizations need to position appropriate people who would interface on a peer term basis. Clear escalation paths need to be defined. Management review structure and hierarchy need to be put in place. This pre-requisite, if done well, will largely ensure that the relationship is successful. The sponsor organization in the client's and the Program Management Office (PMO) in Wipro can be cited as an example.

- Engagement Score Card: An objective measurement system with clearly defined parameters closely related to the objective of the engagement would ensure that the perceptions on either side do not dislodge the collaborative engagement. It is necessary that the measurement system is periodically revisited to make it relevant to the current state of engagement and revised if necessary. All management reviews are held keeping this score card in view so that the course corrections and mutually agreeable evaluation of the current status and actions can be evolved and agreed upon. One typical engagement score card is the balanced score card. One can use a variation of it by taking into consideration the objectives of the engagement at any point of time.

- Soft Skills and Cultural Fit: In a global and distributed environment, temporal and cultural misfits take a heavy toll on relationships. It is essential that the personnel on the outsourcing and Supplier organizations learn one another's cultures and adapt themselves to the situation. Best results are obtained when both parties move to a common neutral platform and it is not a situation of one party totally adapting to the other. IT outsourcing being technically oriented, often the soft skills like communication, presentation, attire, etiquette, leadership styles, attention to details, and the like are often neglected and they become the source of outsourcing engagement failures. The cross-cultural training of India for the client's personnel interfacing with Wipro project team was a key success factor in this direction.

- Program Management: The establishment of a PMO and steering committee to consider and resolve issues in the conduct of the outsourcing engagement is another important enabler for success. The coordination, tracking of progress against the objectives of the engagement, the dependencies management, change management process, logistics, security details, and the like, if addressed in time, would substantially improve the success probability of outsourced engagement.

 History has it that many of the engagements have fallen off, not due to technical or financial considerations, but due to inability of both partners to govern the relationship.

Notwithstanding the fact that any program management would need to include the following aspects, it is all the more important to give adequate focus in an outsourced environment since two different organizations, and therefore, two different cultures are involved.

- Risk management: Risk management should commence from the stage of prospecting of cooperation and should continue as a live agenda in any review or discussion. The risk identification, the mitigation, and the preventive steps should be neatly documented and be visible to all stakeholders.

- Transition management: Any outsourced working would need a structured transition of knowledge from the outsourcing to the supplier entities. Planning a successful transition is the key responsibility of either organization.

- Knowledge management: A vital concern of outsourcing organizations is the loss of knowledge in partner's organization due to staff turnover and project modes of working. A well established knowledgment management system will largely alleviate the fear of loss of information and knowledge of the product or application transitioned.

- Business models: A variety of options for business and commercial models would greatly enhance the business value in an outsourcing relationship. Often, the ability not to take risk by the supplier and a lack of convincing approach by the outsourcing organization, lead to precipitation of issues in the collaboration. This aspect takes a firmer position as the relationship matures. Outsourcing organizations would demand that the partners place their stakes in the relationship through variable project costing, risk and reward model and the like.

- Business continuity: Equally applicable in monolithic development environment, it gains importance due the nature of business to partners. Cost effective and innovative solutions in case of contingencies would greatly help the purpose of outsourcing.
- Alliances: Complex solutions, development, and support need integration of off-the-shelf products customized for the purpose. A good alliance with key COTS product vendors would accelerate the solutions development and value created.

In critical engagements, the partner with a nearshore center or who works out of the client's location is a viable solution. However, they are likely to erode the benefits of offshored outsourcing over a period of time and need to be strategically used for induction of new relationships.

TAKE-AWAY TIPS

Successful organizations across world adopt multi-pronged strategies for market leadership, time-to-market advantage, cost competitiveness, delivery excellence, global presence and reach, portfolio management, and a highly profitable existence. Globally distributed software and product management through outsourcing and offshoring play a vital part in it.

Successful IT outsourcing decisions are not likely to be tactical ones. Carefully determining what to outsource, whom to outsource, and what benefits are expected to be derived from it need to be thought through and planned. Preparation toward partnered relationships where imperative cultural and business differences are likely to be present is essential. An outsourced relationship often needs to be planned long–term, which automatically brings in the need to find the solution to the question on its long-term sustainability. Value addition to cursory benefits will need deeper considerations and the phase in the life-cycle of the product or application under consideration. Also, the surround consideration needs to be equally taken care to temper the engagement to improve the probability of success of IT outsourcing.

The "Next Level Partnership" considerations surface at the crossroads of a relationship when the question "What next?" is raised. The objectives of a nascent or a new outsourced collaboration would have been achieved and both partners look for the next higher value added engagement. Typically, the answers to this question result in expanded scope of engagement, involvement of partners in the upstream cycles of the IT or product decision making process, higher responsibilities for the suppliers, and building stakes in each others' organizations.

Chapter 20

Monitoring Cost, Progress, and Performance

Summary: Monitoring cost, progress, and performance of global software projects is a control activity concerned with identifying, measuring, accumulating, analyzing, and interpreting project information for planning and tracking activities, decision-making, and cost accounting. We will provide guidance for monitoring cost, progress, and performance in global and distributed IT and software projects.

Global development projects do not fail because of incompetent suppliers, project managers or engineers working on these projects; neither do they fail because of insufficient methods or tools. Primarily, they fail because of the use of wrong management techniques. Management techniques derived and built on experience from small colocated projects are inadequate for monitoring global software development. As a result, service level agreements are not met and the delivered software is late, of low quality, and of much higher cost than originally estimated.

Dedicated management techniques are needed because software projects yield intangible products. Project (or supplier) monitoring and control is the basic tool for gaining insight into project performance and is more than only ensuring the overall technical correctness of a project.

Monitoring and control answers few simple questions derived from the following management activities:

- Decision-making. What should I do?
- Attention directing. What should I look at?
- Performance evaluation. Am I doing that is either good or bad?
- Improvement tracking. Am I doing better or worse than last period?
- Planning. What can we reasonably achieve in a given period?
- Target setting. How much can we improve in a given period?

Global Software and IT: A Guide to Distributed Development, Projects, and Outsourcing, First Edition. Christof Ebert.

Is there sufficient insight into your software and IT projects? If you are like the majority of those in IT and software companies, you only know the financial figures. Too many projects run in parallel, without concrete and quantitative objectives and without tracking of where they are with respect to expectations. Project proposals are evaluated in isolation from ongoing activities. Projects are started or stopped based on local criteria, and not by considering the global trade-offs across all projects and opportunities. Only one-third of all software engineering companies systematically utilize techniques to measure and control their product releases and development projects [Ebert07a].

There is a saying that "you cannot control what you cannot measure." This might sound a bit awkward because certainly management is more than semi-automatic number crunching. However, if there is little or no visibility in the status and forecast of projects, it is apparent that some common baseline measurements need to be implemented for all projects in an organization. Such core measurements would provide visibility into the current versus planned status of engineering projects, allowing for early detection of variances and time for taking corrective action.

Measurements reduce surprises by giving us insight into when a project is heading toward trouble, instead of discovering it when it is already there. Standardized measurements provide management with indicators to control projects and evaluate performance in the bigger picture.

Many organizations that consider software development as their core business often have too much separation between business performance monitoring and evaluation and what is labeled as low-level software measurements. Similar to a financial profit and loss (P&L) statement, it is necessary to implement a few core measurements to generate reports from different projects that can easily be understood by non-experts. Maintaining consistency across projects allows you to easily aggregate data for assessing contract and business performance and assisting with estimating which culminates in a kind of engineering balance sheet. This allows for better predictability of future projects and quantification of the impact of changes to existing ones.

What is the purpose of a progress review? It is all about understanding the project's status and upcoming activities so that adjustments can be planned and implemented as necessary. The kinds of things that are discussed in these reviews include:

- Is the project on track (size, effort, budget, schedule, etc.)?
- Have there been any changes to the project or its requirements that people need to know about?
- Is there anything going on in the organizational/customer/project environments that people need to know about?

- What are the near-term activities, and are we adequately prepared to perform them?
- What is the status of project issues/risks that were previously identified?
- Are there any new issues or risks?

To effectively and efficiently monitor global development projects, the following steps need to be done:

- Set objectives, both short-and long-term for products and process.
- Understand and agree to commitments and their changes (e.g., requirements).
- Forecast and develop plans both for projects and for departments.
- Identify and analyze potential risks.
- Set up and commit to a service level agreement (independent of contract format).
- Set up and agree on a contract which relates milestones, deliverables, SLA, and payment.
- Motivate people to accomplish plans.
- Coordinate and implement plans.
- Compare actual measurements with original objectives.
- Determine if the project is under control and whether the plan is still valid.
- Predict the development direction of process and product relative to goals and control limits.
- Evaluate project and process performance.
- Investigate and mitigate significant deviations.
- Identify and implement corrective actions and reward/penalize performance.

An initial set of internal project indicators for this goal can be derived from the Software Engineering Institute's (SEI) core measurements and measurement literature [Ebert07]. They simplify the selection by reducing the focus on project tracking and oversight from a contractor and program management perspective. Obviously, additional indicators must be agreed upon to evaluate external constraints and integrate with market data. Here is our short list of absolutely necessary project measurements:

1. **Requirements status and volatility.** Requirements status is a basic ingredient to tracking progress based on externally perceived value. Always remember that you are paid for implementing requirements, not for generating code.
2. **Product size and complexity.** Size can be measured as functional size in Function Points, or code size in lines of code or statements. Be prepared to distinguish according to your measurement goals with code size between what is new and what is reused or automatically generated code.

3. **Effort.** This is a basic monitoring parameter to assure you stay in budget. Effort is estimated upfront for the project and its activities. Afterward, these effort elements are tracked.

4. **Schedule and time.** This is the next basic monitoring measurement to ensure that you can keep the scheduled delivery time. Similar to effort, time is broken down to increments or phases which are tracked based on what is delivered so far. Note that milestone completion must be lined up with defined quality criteria to avoid detecting poor quality too late.

5. **Project progress.** This is the key measurement during entire project execution. Progress has many facets and should look to deliverables and how they contribute to achieving the project's goals. Typically, there are milestones for the big steps and earned value and increments for the day-to-day operational tracking. Earned value techniques look to the degree of how results such as implemented and tested requirements or closed work packages relate to effort spent and elapsed time. This then allows estimating cost to complete and remaining time to complete the project.

6. **Quality.** This is the most difficult measurement, as it is hardly possible to forecast accurately whether the product has already achieved the right quality level which is expected for operational usage. Quality measurements need to predict quality levels and track how many defects are found compared to estimated defects. Reviews, unit test and test progress, and coverage are the key measurements to indicate quality. Reliability models are established to forecast how much defects need still to be found. Note that quality attributes are not only functional, but also relate to performance, security, safety, and maintainability.

Projects typically aggregate information similar to a dashboard. Such project dashboard allows having all relevant information related to project progress against commitments including risks and other information summarized on one page, typically online accessible with periodically updated data. Examples for project dashboard information are performance of milestones against the planned dates, or showing the earned value at a given moment.

Project dashboards provide information in a uniform way across all projects, thus not overloading the user with different representations and semantics that he has to wade through. They provide information at the fingertips so you are ready to make decisions. They help to examine those projects that underperform or that are exposed to increased risk. Project managers would look more closely and examine how they could resolve such deviation in real time within the constraints of the project. All projects must share the same set of consistent measurements presented in a unique dashboard. Lots of time is actually wasted by reinventing spreadsheets and reporting formats when the project team should, instead, focus on creating value.

A project dashboard must not be time consuming or complex. Measurements such as schedule and budget adherence, earned value, or quality level are typical

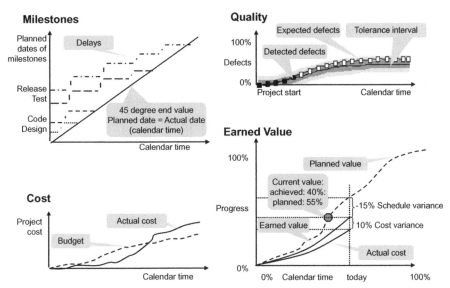

Figure 20.1   Measurement dashboard (part 1): Overview measurements for schedule, cost, quality, and earned value.

performance indicators that serve as "traffic lights" on the status of the individual project. Only those (amber and red) projects that run out of agreed variance (which, of course, depends on the maturity of the organization) would be investigated and further drilled down in the same dashboard to identify root causes. When all projects follow a defined process and utilize the same type of reporting and performance tracking, it is easy to determine status, identify risks, and resolve issues without getting buried in the details of micromanaging the project.

A selection of the most relevant project tracking measurements is provided in Figures 20.1 and 20.2 and Table 20.1 [Ebert07a]. Projects typically aggregate and provide information similar to a dashboard. Such a project dashboard allows you to have all relevant information related to project progress against commitments, including risks and other information summarized on one page, typically one that is online accessible with periodically updated data. Examples for dashboard measurements include milestone tracking, cost evolution, a selection of process measurements, work product deliveries, and faults with status information. There can be both direct measurements (e.g., cost) as well as indirect measurements and predictions (e.g., cost to complete).

We distinguish three views on project measurements with different underlying goals, namely:

- Aggregated view. This is the typical dashboard with all relevant information on one page (see Fig. 20.1). It is standard for an organization or enterprise to ensure that information is presented uniformly with same measurement definitions and visualization semantics, thus ensuring that no time is lost in answering questions around scope, content, or data quality.

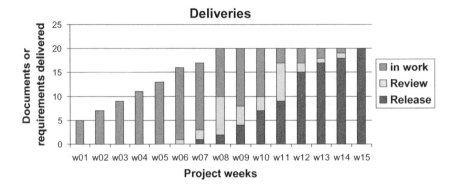

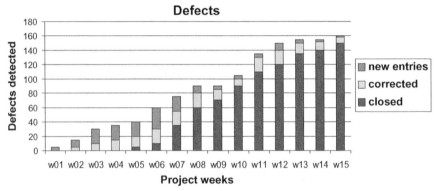

Figure 20.2   Measurement dashboard (part 2): Work product measurements on delivery and quality for a project over project time; status information is indicated with different shades.

- Work product progress. This are the typical bar charts indicating how much progress is visible from looking to work products, requirements, increments or detected defects (see Fig. 20.2).

- In-process measurements. This is the most sophisticated view that is typically only used in organizations with sufficiently mature processes in order to control and optimize processes within the project. Such measurements vary depending on the current focus and process improvement activities (see Table 20.1).

Figure 20.1 shows a simplified dashboard as it is used to track projects. It covers the major dimensions of any SLA, namely, milestones, cost (expenses), quality, and earned value. Such tracking measurements are periodically updated and provide an easy overview on the project status, even for very small projects. Based on this set of measurements several measurements can be selected for weekly tracking work products' status and progress (e.g., increment availability, requirements progress, code delivery, defect detection), while others are reported periodically to build up a history database (e.g., size, effort). Most of these measurements are actually byprod-

Table 20.1   Measurement dashboard (part 3): In-Process Measurements Comparing Actual Values with Targets

Metrics	Targets	Actuals	Comment
Size [KLOC]			
Effort [PY]			
Time-to-market [months]			
Tested requirements [%]			
Design progress [% of est. effort]			
Code progress [% of est. size]			
Test progress [% test cases]			
Inspection efficiency [LOC/h]			
Effort per defect in peer reviews [Ph/defect]			
Effort per defect in module test [Ph/defect]			
Effort per defect in test [Ph/defect]			
Defects detected before integration [%]			
Number of defects in design			
Number of defects in peer reviews			
Number of defects in module test			
Number of defects in test			
Number of defects in the field			

ucts from automatic collection tools related to planning and software configuration management (SCM) databases. Project-trend indicators based on such simple tracking curves are much more effective in alerting managers than the delayed and superficial task completion tracking with PERT charts.

Figure 20.2 expands this project view toward a more WBS and work-product driven perspective. Do not get lost in such work products tracking as long as the overall project perspective is not established. Table 20.1 and its measurements are more advanced and links process performance with project performance. Different core measurements and process indicators are combined to get a view into how the project is doing and how it performs against the estimated process behaviors. It not only reveals under-performing projects easily, but it also helps to see risks much earlier than with after the fact tracking alone. In-process checks are always better than waiting until it is too late for corrections.

These project control measurements are periodically updated and provide an easy overview on the project status, even for very small projects. Based on this set of measurements, few measurements can be selected for weekly tracking work products' status and progress (e.g., increment availability, requirements progress, code delivery, defect detection), while others are reported periodically to build up a history database (e.g., size, effort). Most of these measurements are actually byproducts from automatic collection tools related to planning and software configuration management (SCM) databases.

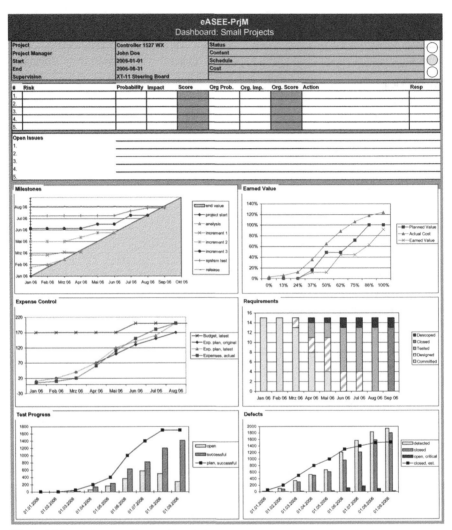

Figure 20.3 Tailorable project dashboard view with eASEE combining the most relevant information.

Figure 20.3 shows a tailorable project dashboard that has all necessary information on one sheet, namely risks and open issues, budget and expense control, milestone control, earned value tracking, requirements and their respective implementation status, test planning and tracking, and defects status. Built into the commercial eASEE PLM tools suite, it receives parts of its data from operational databases and others from the internal data backbone.[1] This ensures sufficient data quality to compare project status across all projects of a portfolio.

[1] www.vector.com/easee

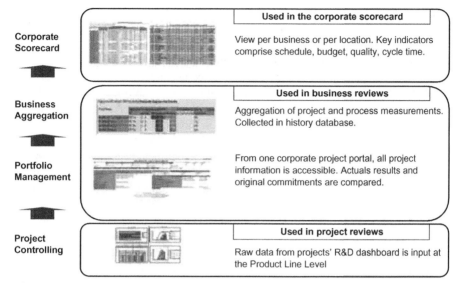

Figure 20.4   Measurements provide a consistent view on all engineering projects, product lines, and business units.

Figure 20.4 provides a practical example that we have established for a major Fortune 100 company. The corporate scorecard was the starting point and the necessary links to distributed operational data were established stepwise with a decent effort on ensuring data quality by means of periodic reviews, governance, and tool support. This small example also indicates that different processes such as corporate control, strategy management, portfolio management and project management are ultimately related. What goes wrong on one level must be visible on the next higher level—if it is beyond the acceptable noise level.

Aggregation is not intended for micromanagement or command and control from the top, but rather to ensure that the same data is utilized across the company. This has advantages not only on the cost side due to less rework and redundant data collection mechanisms, but also to ensure that risk management is based on exactly the same insight into operational and strategic baselines and that decisions can be tracked one day in case of external investigations. Ensure that numbers are consistent across these different hierarchies. Often aggregation hides insufficient data quality which is then only revealed when it is too late to improve those underlying processes.

The single best technology for getting control over deliveries, shared work packages, deadlines, and other resource constraints is to set formal objectives for quality and resources in a measurable way [Royce98, Ebert07a]. Planning and control activities cannot be separated. Managers control by tracking actual results against plans and acting on observed deviations. Controls should focus on significant deviations from standards and at the same time suggest appropriate ways for fixing the problems. Typically, these standards are schedules, budgets, and quality targets established by the project plan. All critical attributes established should be both measurable and testable to ensure effective tracking. The worst acceptable level should be clear although the internal target is in most cases higher.

Effective project tracking and implementation of immediate corrective actions requires a strong project organization. As long as department heads and line managers interfere with project managers, decisions can be misleading or even contradictory. Frequent task and priority changes on the practitioner level with all related drawbacks are the consequence. Lack of motivation as well as inefficiency are the concrete results. A project or matrix organization with dedicated project teams clearly shows better performance than the classic line organization with far too much influence of department leaders.

Quality must be monitored closely because it is typically the first failure point in any shared or collaborative global project. Phase entry criteria must be defined and agreed upon in a way that allows for rejection of any subsequent activity if the component quality is inadequate. Related test process measurements include test coverage, number of open fault reports by severity, closure delay of fault reports, and other product-related quality, reliably, and stability measurements. Such measurements allow judgments in situations when, because of difficulties in testing, decisions on the nature and sequence of alternative paths through the testing task should be made, while considering both the entire testing plan and the present project priorities. For example, there are circumstances in which full testing of a limited set of features will be preferred to an incomplete level of testing across full (contracted) functionality.

Next to the targeted and achieved quality level, cost must be controlled. The use of cost control is manifold and must go beyond simple headcount follow-up. In decision making, cost information is used to determine relevant costs (e.g., sunk costs, avoidable versus unavoidable costs, variable versus fixed costs) in a given project or process, while in management control the focus is on controllable costs versus non-controllable costs.

Avoid complex aggregation of different cost parameters. Instead, use simple straight-forward key figures to measure and report status of business objectives and SLA. Ensure that key figures are balanced to avoid local optimization. Combine key figures that look backward, such as progress tracking, with those that look forward, such as cost to complete.

Often heterogeneous cost elements with different meaning and unclear accounting relationships are combined into one figure that is then optimized. For instance, reducing "cost of quality" that includes appraisal cost and prevention cost is misleading when compared with cost of non-quality because certain appraisal cost (e.g., module test) is a component of regular development. Cost of non-quality, on the other hand, is incomplete if we are only considering internal cost for fault detection, correction and redelivery because we must include opportunity cost due to rework at the customer site, late deliveries or simply binding resources that otherwise might have been used for a new project.

Activity-based accounting allows for more accurate estimates and tracking than using holistic models, which only focus on size and effort for the project as one unit. Make sure that your accounting in outsourcing/offshoring tracks the cost or effort of the major activities, otherwise you will be unable to contain cost and improve processes. Effects of processes and their changes, resources and their skill distribution, or factors related to each of the development activities can be considered, depending on the breakdown granularity. Functional cost analysis and even target-costing approaches are increasingly relevant because customers tend to pay for features instead of entire packages as before. Not surprisingly, cost reduction can only be achieved if it is clear how activities relate to costs. The difference is to assign costs to activities or processes instead of departments.

All activities that impact the development process must be considered to avoid uncontrollable overhead costs. Cost estimation is derived from the size of new or reused software related to the overall productivity and the cost per activity. Although activity-based accounting means more detailed effort reporting throughout each project, it allows for a clear separation between value adding and non-value adding activities, process value analysis, and improved performance measures and incentive schemes. Once process related costs are obvious, it is easy to assign all overhead costs, such as integration test support or tools, related to the processes where they are necessary and again to the respective projects. Instead of allocating such overhead to projects based on overall development effort per project, it is allocated related to activities relevant in the projects. For instance, up-front design activities should not contribute to allocation of expensive test equipment.

While dealing with controlling cost, often the question comes up of which tracking system is to be used. Most companies have rather independent financial tracking systems in place that provide monthly reports on cost per project and sometimes even on an activity basis. The reports are often integrated with timesheet systems and relate effort to other kinds of cost. Unfortunately, such financial systems are in many cases so unrelated to actual engineering activities that neither the activities clusters nor the reporting frequency are helpful for making any short-term decisions. We therefore introduce in such companies simple project dashboards which provide a look to risks status combined with key figures with a balanced view on progress versus plans and outlook versus objectives.

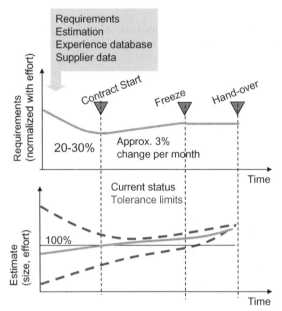

Figure 20.5   Managing changes in scope and content.

Variance analysis is applied to control cost evolution and lead-time over time (Fig. 20.5). It is based on the initially agreed set of requirements (or features to be implemented) and the standard costs to perform a single activity within a process under efficient operating conditions. We can allocate effort to each requirement based on up-front effort estimation. With each requirement that is delivered within an increment, the value of the project deliveries would increase by the amount of effort originally allocated to the requirement. The reasoning here is that the effort should correlate with our pricing. This certainly is not reality, however, it is a good predictor for value generated. Why, after all, should one spend a large part of project effort on a small marginal value to the customer? If the value of delivered requirements is bigger than what was supposed to be invested in terms of engineering effort, the project is ahead. If it is less it is behind. The same approach is taken for schedule. Both parameters combined give an excellent predictor for time and cost to complete a project.

Typically, such standard costs are based on well-defined outputs of the activity, for instance, test cases performed and errors found in testing. Knowing the effort per test case during integration test and the effort to detect an error (which includes regression testing but not correction), a standard effort can be estimated for the whole project. Functionality, size, reuse degree, stability, and complexity of the project determine the two input parameters, namely, test cases and estimated number of faults to be detected in the specific test process. Variances are then calculated as a relative figure: variance = (standard cost − actual cost) / standard cost.

Variance analysis serves to find practical reasons for causes of off-standard performance so that project management or department heads can improve operations and increase efficiency. It is, however, not an end in itself because variances might be caused by other variances or be related to a different target. Predictors should thus be self-contained, such as in the given example. Test cases alone are insufficient because an unstable product due to insufficient design requires more effort in testing.

A major use of cost control measurements combined with actual performance feedback is the tracking of earned value (see also Figure 20.1). Earned value compares achieved results with the invested effort and time. For simplification, let us assume that we have an incremental approach in the project with customer requirements allocated to increments. Let us further assume that we deliver increments on a frequent basis, which are integrated into a continuous build. Only when such increment is fully integrated into the build and tested is it accepted. Upon acceptance of an increment, the status of the respective requirements within this increment is set to "tested." The build, though only internally available, could at any time, with low overhead, be finalized and delivered to a customer. The value measurements then increase by the relative share of these tested requirements compared to the sum of all project requirements. If, for instance, 70% of all customer requirements are available and tested, the earned value is 70%. Weighting is possible by allocating effort to these requirements. Compared with the traditional progress tracking, earned value doesn't show the "90% complete syndrome" (where lots of code and documents are available, but no value is created from an external perspective), because nothing could be delivered to the customer as is.

Chapter 21

Risk Management

Summary: Globally distributed software development poses substantial risks to project and product management. As companies turn to globalized software and IT, they find the process of developing and launching new products becoming increasingly complex as they attempt to integrate skills, people, and processes that are scattered in different places. We will highlight here some typical risks and provide guidance for risk mitigation and risk management in global settings.

Globally distributed software development amplifies typical software project and product related risks, such as project delivery failures and insufficient quality. Worse yet, it creates new risks, such as inadequate IPR management or lock-in situations with suppliers. These risks must be identified in due time and have to be considered together with the sourcing strategy and its operational implementation.

While the classic centralized software development approach once allowed solving problems in the coffee corner or around the white board, global teams today are composed of individuals who are culturally, ethnically, and functionally diverse. They work in different locations and time-zones and are not easily reachable for a chat on how to design an interface or how to resolve a bug that prevents test from progressing. This explains that, for instance, only 30% of all embedded software is developed in a global or distributed context, while the vast majority is colocated. The reason is very simple. Embedded software poses much higher risk on safety and reliability; thus companies prefer risk management in their own—known— environment, rather than adding risk through global teams. How can these risks are mitigated and thus flexibility be improved?

Risk management is the systematic application of management policies, proce- dures, and practices to the tasks of identifying, analyzing, evaluating, treating, and monitoring risk. Global development projects pose specific risks on top of regular risk repositories and check lists. They relate to two major underlying risk drivers, namely, insufficient processes and inadequate management.

Not all eventualities can be buffered because in the global economy, developing and implementing products must be fast, cost effective, and adaptive to changing needs. Therefore, there is a need to utilize different techniques to effectively and

Global Software and IT: A Guide to Distributed Development, Projects, and Outsourcing,
First Edition. Christof Ebert.
© 2012 the Institute of Electrical and Electronics Engineers, Inc. Published 2012 by
John Wiley & Sons, Inc.

efficiently mitigate risks. This chapter systematically introduces risk management in global software and IT context. Governance and legal regulations play a crucial role in mitigating risks in global projects. Methods include using basic project, supplier, and quality management techniques, process frameworks (e.g., CMMI), ITIL, COBIT, product life-cycle management, effective communication processes, SLA based escalation, competence management, and innovation management.

Most countries today enforce to companies with headquarters in that country or which are quoted at a local trading places to comply with rules on risk management. A good example is the Sarbanes-Oxley Act in the United States, which holds the CEO and CFO of such companies personally liable for providing correct information about the status of the company and for ensuring that the internal control and risk management system is working properly. Failing to prove compliance can result in lawsuits and severe punishment. Offshoring or outsourcing therefore must support these mechanisms for internal control and risk management. This can be translated to the following rules:

- Establish and maintain an efficient and effective control and risk management system which includes supplier management.
- Enforce the internally applicable compliance rules also to suppliers so that full transparency can be maintained.
- Provide transparency of the business processes and resulting documentation and work products.
- Document decisions with impact on governance, compliance, and finance risks.
- Ensure that industry best practices are followed to effectively and efficiently mitigate risks, including the supply chain, as it has immediate impact on finance performance and legal exposure of a company.

The latter specifically applies also for mitigating software product liability risks, which in some countries can end in very costly lawsuits if, for instance, products create risks to public safety or health, or even have already caused damages. From a legal perspective, best practices translate into applying international standards such as CMMI, COBIT, or ITIL, consistently and in a way that can be easily audited.

Governance and compliance are the personal responsibility of a CEO or managing director and his finance deputy. It is enforced by a set of processes and checks, including periodic external audits.

Based on many projects, we have established a global software and IT risk top-ten list. Depending on the specific layout of global software and IT (e.g., with or without external supplier), the ranking list of these top-ten risks is as follows: Project delivery failures; insufficient quality; distance and culture clashes; staff turnover (mostly for captive centers); poor supplier services (only for outsourced development); instability with overly high change rate; insufficient competences; wage and cost inflation; lock-in (only for outsourced development); inadequate IPR management.

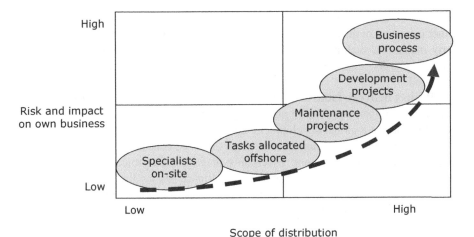

High

Risk and impact
on own business

Low

Business
process

Development
projects

Maintenance
projects

Tasks allocated
offshore

Specialists
on-site

Low   High

Scope of distribution

Figure 21.1   Business risks depend on the degree of distribution.

4. Flexibility: JIT
   organizational networks.

   Risks:
   ► Poor supplier
     services
   ► Lock-in
   ► Distance and culture
     clashes

3. Talent: Race for skilled
   people. Value creation
   happens where the skills
   are.

   Risks:
   ► Staff turnover
   ► Insufficient
     competencies
   ► Wage and cost inflation

1. Efficiency: Speed to
   profit ahead of
   competitors.

   Risks:
   ► Project delivery
     failures
   ► Insufficient quality

2. Presence: Global growth
   strategy.
   Learn from new
   markets.

   Risks:
   ► Instability with overly
     high change rate
   ► Inadequate IPR
     management

Figure 21.2   The top-ten global software and IT risks and their underlying drivers.

Figure 21.1 shows the relationship of business risks on the scope of the distribution. The broader the scope, the bigger the business risks for the client.

These risks can be clustered according to major drivers which then allow selecting the most adequate mitigation strategy. Figure 21.2 shows the top-ten risks sorted on the four major drivers for global software and IT.

We will now have a closer look at these risks and identify specific mitigation patterns [Ebert08]. Our empirical research provides data from a longitudinal study across close to one hundred projects and products of different size and managed either in captive or distributed mode. We can highlight with this data that specifically early indicators, such as requirements change rate, early defect removal and skill level, key risks related to project performance, and attrition can be effectively mitigated.

Project delivery failures. A standard risk for many projects, the risk of being late or over budget, amplifies in probability and impact due to the intrinsic difficulties of managing a global development team.

As mitigation, project and team managers must be educated in estimation, planning, dependency management, uncertainty management, project monitoring, and communication. The latter is crucial as experience shows that projects fail not because of unknowns, but because of not willing to know or to communicate known facts [Ebert07a, Hussey08, Rivard08].

We have seen from ramping-up internal software teams in Eastern Europe, India, and China that solid processes not only accelerate introduction of outsourcing/ offshoring but also serve as a safety net to assure right training, good management practices, and so on. We conducted a controlled experiment when ramping up offshore development teams in China. Our experience was that the building of such a globally distributed development team was fastest and most reliable in the case where the demanding organization was on CMMI maturity level 3. The same was done with lower-maturity demanding organizations with the effect that the CMMI maturity level 2 organizations could manage with some external support, while the maturity 1 organization failed due to highly inefficient interface frictions and lots of rework. For companies in the IT service domain COBIT and ITIL enhance CMMI-SVC toward basic service processes and risk management.

We recommend maintaining an organization-wide risk repository with all project risks together with identified mitigation actions. At the start of a new project, the project manager has to take this organization wide risk repository and check what specific risks are applicable to his project together with any new items. The second, a more medium-term approach, is to train all project managers. Using the CMMI or COBIT and certifying in professional project management is an effective mitigation.

Another important and easy mitigation action is building on past project experiences. The key parameter for project success is schedule adherence. We suggest doing a periodic root cause analysis (RCA) on completed projects to identify the key issues that contributed to delays. On these issues we can do a Pareto analysis to define focused actions for the most critical and repeating issues. Figure 21.3 shows the impact of project delivery risk mitigation indicating a clear reduction in spread of schedule deviation over years, as we increasingly apply our learning from previous projects toward future projects.

Insufficient quality. Working in different places or with teams in different organizations means, that many work products are moved across such places and teams with the risk of insufficient quality. Often the underlying rationale is that teams suppose that there will still be sufficient validation "downstream" so that quality deficiencies accumulate.

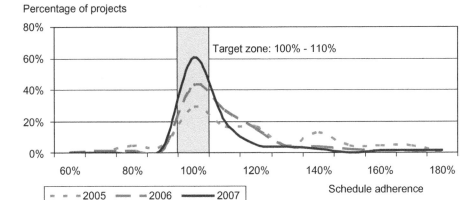

Figure 21.3   Improved project performance in terms of schedule adherence.

Many global development projects suffer from a "ping pong" approach of work products being thrown back and forth due to poor quality. These stories repeat each other—independent of countries and culture. The designer in the Mexican team claims that the U.S. specification was not good enough, while the integration tester in India kicks back the product because Mexico again delivered insufficient code quality.

The major risk mitigation to such repeated rework and increasing mistrust is to force quality gates on work product level. A work product is only accepted if it has the right quality level. Incoming work products are inspected at least in samples to check consistency and quality. Service level agreements and responsibility assignments reduce the "ping pong" effect because at the least it is clear who should do better.

We look to early defect removal (EDR) as the measurement of defects found before the start of the test compared with total estimated defects and compare it with upfront-defined threshold [3]. It will provide warning signals so that corrective actions can be initiated well before the product becomes due for delivery to customer. Having worked with this concept over many years in different companies, we observe a strong negative correlation of −0.9 between mean EDR and mean schedule adherence for a set of around fifty projects in the timeframe of 2004–2007. Figure 21.4 shows this trend over four year period which indicates that EDR is indeed an advance indicator to reflect on quality, and thus schedule variance of the product.

Distance and culture clashes. Globally distributed software development is highly impacted by work organization and effective work split. Working in a globally distributed project means overheads for planning and managing people. It means language and cultural barriers [O'Hara94, Hussey08, Sangwan07]. It creates jealousy between the more expensive engineers being afraid of losing their jobs, while

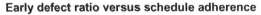

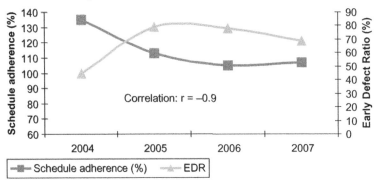

Figure 21.4   Optimizing early defect removal in global development contributes to improved schedule adherence.

they are forced to train their much cheaper counterparts. The barriers to such harmonization and cooperation are not to be underestimated. They range from language barriers to time zone barriers to incompatible technology infrastructures to heterogeneous product line cultures and not-invented-here syndromes. An obvious barrier is the individual profit and loss responsibility that in tough times means primarily focusing on current quarter results and not investing in future infrastructures. Incumbents perceive providing visibility a risk, because they become accountable and more subject to internal competition.

As risk mitigation we recommend collaboration and communication. Collaborate across disciplines, cultures, time, distance, organizations. Communication starts before the outsourcing/offshoring project is kicked off. Fears, hopes, barriers must be articulated. Assess your organization carefully on such distance and culture risks. This demands a fully new skill set, currently not taught at universities (e.g., managerial, teaming, sharing without losing) [Sangwan07]. Cultural sensitization, periodic workshop between clients and suppliers, and networking between various teams has been the effective risk mitigation strategy. Provide space for engineers to share their emotions with team leaders openly. Establish early warning systems to detect upcoming barriers and fears.

Collaboration also means effective and efficient tools support. The exchange of information between sites must be carefully planned. The closer tasks and software components are linked, the more need for good data communication. Tasks with high overlap should not been done with too much time distance. Especially with a high work time overlap, online collaboration has high demands on fast, reliable quality of service for video, engineering tools and online collaboration. A change management tool is not enough because engineering demands collaboration on content and knowledge. Plain supplier management platforms as they are offered today for handling online market places and tenders are also insufficient due to their limitations in sharing engineering information. You will need rules and workflow support for documentation, design reviews, change management boards, and so on.

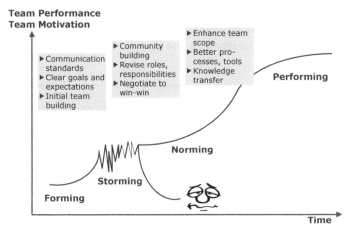

Figure 21.5   Build and maintain effective virtual teams.

We strongly recommend addressing team performance and motivation in virtual teams from the very beginning. Figure 21.5 shows phases of virtual teams and actions to be taken to mitigate motivation and thus performance risks. Problems and defects will be addressed more quickly, and the "throwing over the fence" mentality is reduced.

Staff turnover. This is a specific risk especially in Asian countries due to abundant job opportunities in the respective economies. It is a generic risk whenever outsourcing/offshoring has no clear integration with an organization's overall engineering strategy and career paths, such as having a nearshore maintenance organization within a software company.

Regarding attrition, we have to apply two parallel mitigation strategies. First, it is clear that attrition in certain places of the world is higher than, say in Western Europe. So we have to cope with it and prepare to learn and live and deal with attrition in advance. This means advanced planning of buffers, long-term retention mechanisms such as loyalty bonuses, and so on. Buffers could be foreseen if engineers' unavailability exceeds certain thresholds. Note though that such buffers immediately impact the bottom line and should be carefully pooled to serve several projects.

Second, we should measure attrition and its impact factors in order to control and limit staff turnover. We recommend conducting periodic employee engagement studies from which we can learn and improve the working environment, which shall limit attrition to manageable levels. Based on surveys we then look into specific incentives to keep people, even in times where stock options are not the preferred instrument. For instance, international career paths and excellent individual development skills reduce attrition.

Poor supplier services. One frequent risk with third-party suppliers is not meeting the expectations in terms of quality and delivery schedule. SLAs won't help because once this point is reached, even escalation will not help much, because it will take too long and the product or service quality is already hampered.

The primary mechanism for risk mitigation related to insufficient supplier services is to carefully evaluate one's own processes and those of potential suppliers—before engaging into global software engineering and IT.

As a client you should always consider the golden rule of supplier management: You pay for what you get.

Don't get trapped in contracts that look "cheap," but later incur extra cost due to weak processes and insufficient delivery quality. Preconditions of any successful supplier management are good processes on both sides, that is, for the client and the supplier. Insufficient client processes cannot be externalized. They will not scale up from a single site to several sites. Often those low-maturity processes can be handled in localized development without many overheads due to colocated teams, but will fail with globalization. From our experiences we recommend having a CMMI (development and acquisition) maturity level 3 on both sides, for all impacted engineering and sourcing processes. Additionally, for companies in the IT service domain, COBIT and ITIL are helpful regarding basic service processes and risk management.

When still in preparation mode, negotiate for a fixed project cost, where price is fixed and linked to deliverables with specific quality targets, often including penalty clauses. A fixed price project will make the supplier proactive for performance as payment is linked to quality deliveries and not time spent. Though generally fixed price is at higher cost compared to time and material at the contract negotiation stage, our lesson learned is at the end of the project, it turns out to be generally 10%–15% less costly than comparable time and material projects.

Supplier management includes clarification on non-disclosure and related agreements before starting negotiation. Establish clear acceptance and liability rules following contracting and legal schemes of your headquarter base. For maintenance projects they also include clear SLA in terms of response time, solution time, percentage of return failures, and so on. Set up clear and measurable service level agreements. Ensure that this SLA contains all that matters for you in the contract. Insist on periodic reporting according to the SLA. From the beginning, define thresholds that establish when and how insufficient performance will be escalated. Measure supplier capability or demand such measurement based on industry standards, such as CMMI. Relate value you receive from suppliers to the risk and cost of the delivered services or components. Implement contract evaluation after each single project.

Consider sufficient time and budget (resources) for training the supplier on your processes. A very strong training tool is the scrum process with short team meetings every day where recent results and next steps are briefly reviewed. Any uncertainty should be brought up in such reviews, which should take not more than 15–30 minutes and can be conducted even by telephone conference across sites. Build a supplier program management to handle the necessary review and decision processes. Agree with your supplier review and acceptance processes to assure the right quality level. Installing such processes after the contract signature will create the perception of policing the supplier. You can ask third parties in case of questions or needs for escalation.

Instability with overly high change rate. Frequent changes create extra cost. Often, being present in different markets with individual engineering teams means that each of the teams examine the needs of the local market. When products and features are assembled, inconsistencies appear which cause late requirements changes. Global development amplifies such requirements engineering weaknesses that have, in most companies, long been present but could be camouflaged due to colocated teams. If specifications are insufficient, a remote team will either misunderstand or not accept them.

As a mitigation, outsourcing/offshoring demands more reliable requirements and change requests. We recommend enforcing a rigid roadmapping process that provides sufficiently early insight into feature evolution and release planning. Teams will appreciate it with more anticipation and design for change. Global development demands more communication than colocated development. Specifications and documents must be carefully reviewed, because engineers on the other side trust to what is written. Establish for all distributed work packages a baseline and configuration management based on defined and proven quality entry criteria. The expectations and deliverables in terms of effort, deadline, duration, and quality levels are to be clearly documented and agreed.

We observed that the number of changes to the requirements are highly (negatively) correlated to the content adherence, defined as percentage of features delivered at the end of the project to that of original required features at the start of the project. The correlation coefficient which we use as an early risk indicator and thus lead indicator for risk mitigation actions is -0.99 for a set of around fifty projects in the years of 2004–2007. A possible way to mitigate the risk of uncontrolled requirement changes is to closely monitor the requirement change index (number of changes to the features divided by total number of features required at the start of project, expressed as percentage). Figure 21.6 shows how content adherence is related to requirement change index over years.

Insufficient competencies. This is a risk in each development project; however it is amplified by the bigger dependencies given the globally distributed team combined with less visibility on resource planning and skills availability.

For mitigation we recommend assuring global competence management and resource planning (e.g., with a multi-project management tool such as Primavera or similar) and a skills management on the level of detailed technical skills necessary for the projects. Note that competence management is not the same as above mentioned attrition management. It is, however, a necessary condition to reduce attrition.

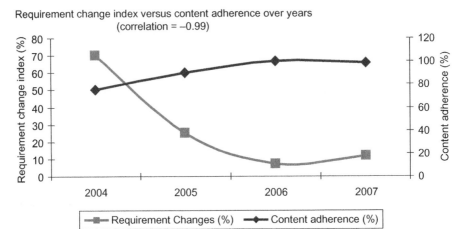

Figure 21.6   Improved content adherence when managing risks and uncertainties with requirements.

We recommend managing competency needs in parallel to technical and project roadmapping. It is a strategic task in the hands of engineering management, not HR. Organizations spend huge effort in training employees but often does not correlate whether the training and improved skills reflect the business needs.

In our case study we have converted the overall team's competences and skills range into a single measurable number by linking available competences and skills and normalizing with required business needs. This single index is monitored for improvement. A direct consequence of skill management is enhanced retention of employees. We observed a strong negative correlation between skill index computed during one year and that of team's lead attrition, that is, attrition of the teams in next year. Figure 21.7 shows the strong influence of team skill index measured at end of 2006 with that of full year attrition in 2007. The correlation factor within a community of close to 1000 engineers is −0.85.

Wage and cost inflation. With the global fight for software engineering talent, wage inflation is a major global software engineering and IT risk. For instance, salaries in India have increased by a double-digit percentage per year during the past ten years. The annual increase in most Asian countries is around 10% [McKinsey08, BCG09, Worldbank11].

The primary mitigation is to carefully consider which regions to utilize and to make a profound business case and cash flow planning taking into consideration expected wage increases in different regions of the world. Where external suppliers are involved, evaluate upfront their business models and past cost evolution. Determine upfront which supplier size fits best to your own company size and

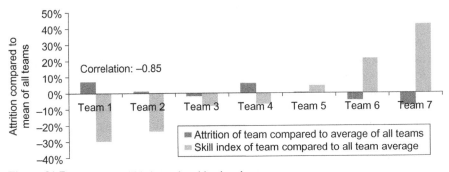

Figure 21.7 Achieved skill index and attrition in subsequent year.

structure. A big supplier with a small enterprise won't fit, because the SME will not have the chance to make corrections once the contract is settled. Evaluate offers during the tender of a supplier contract with dedicated estimation tools such as QSM SLIM to compare and judge feasibility [Ebert07a].

Lock-in. With outsourcing/offshoring supplier competition on a global market, external suppliers often start with rather low rates, and, once the projects are sufficiently large, clients might be forced to lock-in with them due to progress of product development and knowledge transition. In the least we may have to face increasing cost inflation.

The primary risk mitigation is to have multiple partners and distribute critical knowledge on two sources. Each one shall know that we have a choice to make and that will make the external suppliers to remain competitive. To improve efficiency and reduce effects of lock-in, global teams must use the same tools, methods, and processes. It is worth the extra money for tools licenses, although in a low cost country the additional load on engineering cost can be 10%–20% for the necessary design tools. Our recommendation is to avoid supplier-specific and ad hoc tools as they won't scale up and can bring substantial issues if backups cannot be restored or contents are corrupted. Process improvements and best practices gained over years of experience in one engineering team need to be replicated quickly, in other engineering teams. Common processes and tools across engineering teams will benefit quick spread of lessons learned/defect prevention actions across teams.

Lock-in goes beyond suppliers. Do not forget about risks related to certain regions of the world, where you might currently be locked-in. We also recommend maintaining flexibility in where you work and with which supplier. Instabilities can be caused by political turmoil as well as earthquakes, civil war, or terrorist attacks. Don't put all your global development into one single site. Consider distributed hosting of infrastructure and backups. Periodically test the restore mechanisms to a different new site.

Inadequate IPR management. Intellectual property rights are a key success factor in software development. Mostly, software is not patented and copyrights are not enforced equally in all regions of the world. Further risks are related to improper use of external software (e.g., OSS) and careless handling of confidential information (e.g., leaving contracts at printing shops).

As mitigation, make sure that the intellectual property is well-secured. Divide key assets into pieces and provide only fragments to each global team. Share according to strategic relevance. Reinforce copyright protection for external sources. A GPL-protected component included with your product might force you to fully disclose all the software of the product. This can be handled both on policy and architectural levels. Most relevant, however, is that your teams get trained in copyrights and specifically on the traps related to open source software. Install and enforce effective policies for confidentiality, copyright protection and intellectual property handling and train all software engineers and managers on it. Rigorously punish wrong-doing and unprofessional behaviors in this critical domain.

At the same time, do not underestimate the potential of new teams to explore innovation. Creating awareness of how to identify IPR and potential patentable ideas, on-line forums to share ideas, and voluntary moderators to guide raw ideas into potential patents is something that is not to be ignored.

Figure 21.8 shows how distributed teams have generated the patent proposals after awareness training and workshops are conducted in 2006 and 2007, respectively. The correlation between training and workshop timing and the number of idea generation can be seen as quite strong; indicating the huge effect such awareness has on protecting IPR in global software engineering and IT.

Not all of the above risks and suggested mitigation actions may be applicable to all organizations and scenarios. Wage and cost escalation will not be an issue for growing teams, as generally new recruits are at a less cost than existing average and per head cost will come down, even if wage cost is going up. Professional training like certification of project managers increases the risk of attrition due to better sell-

Number of patentable ideas generated over 2006 & 2007

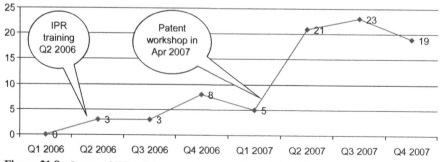

Figure 21.8   Impact of IPR training on patent generation and thus IPR protection.

able skill level in market. Long-term retention methods for attrition management will itself contribute to the risk of wage escalation. Similarly, the strong correlation observed between skill development and attrition might not be a universal phenomena, or there might be other overlying attributes impacting attrition more strongly. We recommend that organizations make an internal analysis to fine tune their approach.

Risk mitigation happens all along the life-cycle. It is not enough to once identify risks and then keep an eye on the repository. Risks are dynamic by nature, and so must be their mitigation.

As a general rule for risk identification in a specific environment, we recommend setting up undesired scenarios, evaluate their probability to occur and decide for some 10–20 of those scenarios to take dedicated mitigation action. A majority is mitigated inside the global development project (e.g., common tools), while only a few must be part of the corporate risk strategy (e.g., handling supplier defection). Organizations should not worry about the number of 10–20 scenarios. They repeat in each of the organization's respective projects and will build a kind of checklist with dedicated and organization-specific mitigation strategies that are reused in each new project. Figure 21.9 shows typical checklists as they are used throughout the life-cycle to re-assess risks and to follow their mitigation.

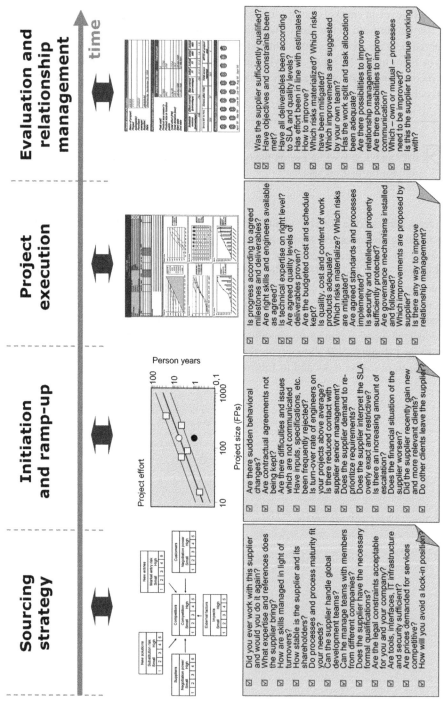

Sourcing strategy

- Did you ever work with this supplier and would you do it again?
- What expertise and references does the supplier bring?
- How are skills managed in light of turnovers?
- How stable is the supplier and its shareholders?
- Do processes and process maturity fit your needs?
- Can the supplier handle global development teams?
- Can he manage teams with members from different companies?
- Does the supplier have the necessary formal qualifications?
- Are the legal constraints acceptable for you and your company?
- Are tools, interfaces, IT infrastructure and security sufficient?
- Are prices demanded for services competitive?
- How will you avoid a lock-in position?

Initiation and ramp-up

Project effort

Person years

Project size (FPs)

- Are there sudden behavioral changes?
- Are contractual agreements not being kept?
- Are there difficulties and issues which are not communicated
- Have inputs, specifications, etc. been frequently rejected?
- Is turn-over rate of engineers on your projects above average?
- Is there reduced contact with supplier senior management?
- Does the supplier demand to re-prioritize requirements?
- Does the supplier interpret the SLA overly exact and restrictive?
- Is there an increasing amount of escalation?
- Does the financial situation of the supplier worsen?
- Did the supplier recently gain new and more relevant clients?
- Do other clients leave the supplier?

Project execution

- Is progress according to agreed milestones and deliverables?
- Are right skills and engineers available as agreed?
- Is technical expertise on right level?
- Are agreed quality levels of deliverables proven?
- Are the budgeted cost and schedule kept?
- Is quality, cost and content of work products adequate?
- Which risks materialize? Which risks are mitigated?
- Are agreed standards and processes implemented?
- Is security and intellectual property sufficiently protected?
- Are governance mechanisms installed and followed?
- Which improvements are proposed by supplier?
- Is there any way to improve relationship management?

Evaluation and relationship management

time

- Was the supplier sufficiently qualified?
- Have objectives and constraints been met?
- Have all deliverables been according to SLA and quality levels?
- Has effort been in line with estimates?
- How to improve?
- Which risks materialized? Which risks have been mitigated?
- Which improvements are suggested by your own team?
- Has the work split and task allocation been adequate?
- Are there possibilities to improve relationship management?
- Are there possibilities to improve communication?
- Which – own or mutual – processes need to be improved?
- Is this the supplier to continue working with?

Figure 21.9 Risk management across the life-cycle.

Chapter 22

Practice: Risk Assessment in Globally Distributed Projects

Adailton Lima and Alberto Avritzer, Siemens

Summary: In this case study we present a technique used to assess schedule risk in globally distributed industrial software projects. To support the case study we analyzed two and a half years of quantitative project data and we obtained team productivity measurements as a function of project site and feature applicability domain. We supplement the quantitative data with a questionnaire that was used to generate qualitative data. The qualitative data is useful, as it helps to identify communication delay and domain knowledge as some of the factors that could explain the observed differences in site productivity.

BACKGROUND

To support our analysis about the main aspects related to project risks, we performed a systematic literature review of project practices and lessons learned from globally distributed projects. The analyzed project was distributed over five sites, two in the United States, two in Europe, and one in India, had more than three thousands requirements and nearly one hundred and fifty developers. Each site has one or more development teams, and the project has 11 teams in total. Our data set contained nine short project releases, spanning twelve months of software development and software integration testing.

Several studies on global software engineering have identified some common aspects that can affect product schedule, such as [Alberts08, Ebert06, Hillegersberg07, Hussey08]:

- Cultural differences
- Many distributed sites
- Different knowledge expertise and domains

Global Software and IT: A Guide to Distributed Development, Projects, and Outsourcing,
First Edition. Christof Ebert.
© 2012 the Institute of Electrical and Electronics Engineers, Inc. Published 2012 by
John Wiley & Sons, Inc.

- Many communication dependencies
- Time zone differences
- Loss of internal knowledge or innovation
- Potential breach of security
- Potential for poorer quality
- Quality deficiencies that are not recognized on time
- Lack of management availability to address project issues.

 Global software development characteristics have a significant impact on software cost, product quality, project schedule, and developers' productivity.

We have extracted quantitative data from the project management database of the large globally distributed software development project under study. We have also interviewed project leaders and developers to balance quantitative and qualitative data in our analysis.

The project management database contained feature productivity data per project site, and feature domain of applicability. The extracted information we used as an input to the feature productivity model were:

- Requirements list
- Expertise of the involved people
- Relationship between features and requirements
- Sites/teams location
- Estimated time required for feature development.

Four members of one of the U.S. teams were also interviewed. One member was the project manager, the second member was the lead project architect, and two other members were integration testers. They all worked at the U.S. site throughout the project. The two testers worked as part of the integration test team, responsible for testing components delivered by different teams from around the world.

According to the interviewers of the testing team, their work was heavily impacted by the different knowledge expertise and the many communication dependencies they had with the different development teams they interacted. It was also reported that these problems were closely related to the project schedule and the quality of the delivered products.

We have conducted a systematic review with the goal of investigating general heuristics that are usually applied to globally distributed software development projects. This information was useful to help the definition of the heuristics implemented on our schedule risk assessment model.

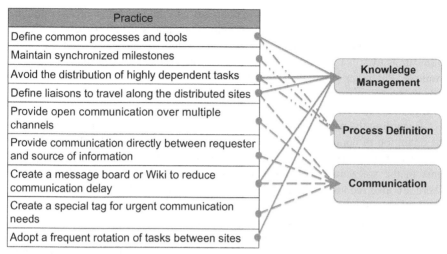

Practice
Define common processes and tools
Maintain synchronized milestones
Avoid the distribution of highly dependent tasks
Define liaisons to travel along the distributed sites
Provide open communication over multiple channels
Provide communication directly between requester and source of information
Create a message board or Wiki to reduce communication delay
Create a special tag for urgent communication needs
Adopt a frequent rotation of tasks between sites

Knowledge Management

Process Definition

Communication

Figure 22.1   Risk domains and project heuristics in global software and IT context.

The systematic review followed the process defined by the Kitchenham [Kitchenham04]. We defined a query string to formally search for the bibliography related to our research goals. We applied the following query to the IEEE database:

*(Project AND (Management OR Assessment OR Control OR Monitoring)) AND
("Global Software Development" OR "Global Software Engineering" OR
"Distributed Software Development" OR "Decentralized Software Development")
AND (Practice OR Lesson OR Heuristic OR Recommendation).*

We obtained an initial result of 205 publications. We filtered each result by first reading the study abstract and then reading the full text of the studies that passed the first reading step. After reading the full text we selected 17 studies for this study.

Figure 22.1 shows the relationship among the risk domains and the main heuristics extracted from the reference studies. These three risk domains (knowledge management, process definition, and communication) were obtained from the data retrieved by our studies.

As an example of knowledge management studies, DeSouza [Desouza06] proposed a classification of different distributed knowledge management models, trying to help organizations decide on the best way to manage knowledge over different sites. The study by Boden and Avram [Boden09] quotes one particular case in which two teams worked together for 6 years without distance being an issue for the project. The authors reasoned that the basic problems of expertise search and remote communication were not critical to these teams because the teams knew each other.

An interesting study by Nguyen [Nguyen08] analyzes a case in which communication was not considered a big issue for the project because project members made good use of collaboration technologies to support distributed work. This practice insight corroborates with the statement of Herbsleb [Herbsleb05] that projects should not have bottlenecks for communication and that direct communication should be made available between the producer and the consumer of information. As reported by Gotel [Gotel08], direct communication is necessary, especially on the integration phase in which developers and testers should have intensive communication to solve the inevitable problems introduced by code integration. For example, Phalnikar [Phalnikar09] reports that the creation of a message board or wiki to share similar questions can improve project communication and avoid basic problems.

Regarding the process definition studies, the most common strategy reported is the definition of common processes and tools over the different development sites. Project managers applied this strategy when faced with global coordination problems in the software development process [Ebert08, Mikulovic06, Herbsleb05]. There are also recommendations related to the execution of project activities, like the definition of strategies to conduct remote meetings and the practices to be used for configuration management of the shared project workspace.

Global software development projects must rely on decentralized control mechanisms to provide adequate support for the remote coordination among sites [Hillegersberg07]. Source code measurements can be collected and analyzed to provide an overview of the software development status [Kuipers03, Kuipers07]. A manager can use these measurements to support project management decisions based on development and testing information processed by their tool.

Project risks can be assessed based on positive and negative project risks drivers [Alberts08]. Risks drivers are collected on the target project and a risk assessment algorithm is applied to calculate project risk. The main contribution of this methodology consists of the risk drivers that can be added to support globally distributed software development projects.

We are not aware of any tool support to automatically perform risk assessment of globally distributed projects using statistical project management data. In addition, project factors such as communication and coordination requirements may have strong impact on globally distributed projects.

We have adopted a simulation approach for the risk assessment of schedule risk. This approach allowed for the creation of a high-level simulation model for the assessment of project behavior as a function of the following parameters: software development process, team productivity, and communication requirements. The simulation tool was used in the following two steps of our investigation methodology: first, we ran general simulations to look for project schedule bottlenecks; second, we reduced the search space selecting specific points to compute the project schedule risk measurement.

Domain knowledge variability and team communication are important factors to consider in schedule risk assessment models of globally distributed software development projects, where features are outsourced to sites that may have less knowledge about the applicability domain. The experimental study was conducted by a series of stochastic simulations based on a model designed using the Tan gram-II tool [Silva06]. This tool allows the creation of event-based models, where the interval between events is determined by stochastic data. Figure 22.2 shows the graphical representation of the simulation model, representing the feature allocation

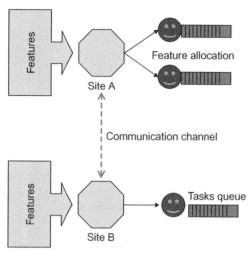

Figure 22.2   Simulation model with global view.

to sites, the communication among sites, and the queuing of features for development resources.

We have extracted quantitative data from the project management database of the large globally distributed software development project under study. We have also interviewed project leaders and developers to balance quantitative and qualitative data in our analysis. The project management database contained feature productivity data per project site, and feature domain of applicability, for nine short project releases.

The simulation model was designed to represent an abstraction of a group of development sites interacting during the software development process. Each site has its own domain knowledge capabilities and a set of features that have been allocated to the site.

The simulation model was based on the characteristics listed above, and contains the following features: feature request at each globally distributed site, feature development time at each globally distributed site, domain knowledge per global site, queuing for development resources, estimation of reduced team productivity due to queuing and communication overhead, and estimation of the project schedule risk. The stochastic model makes assumptions about the probability distribution of factors that are easier to obtain, like the time to develop a feature, the communication pattern between sites, and the pattern of feature allocation to sites.

Our simulation model computes the reduced team productivity due to the communications overhead and queuing for development resources. The project schedule risk is computed by executing the simulation model and extracting statistics about the number of times the simulation resulted in project delay. For example, if we run the simulation one hundred times and obtain as a result that the project was delayed ten times, we define the schedule risk as 10%.

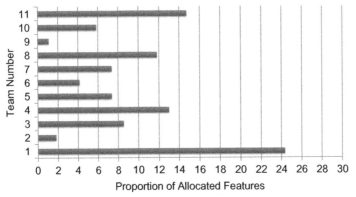

Figure 22.3   Fraction of features allocated to each site for the eleven development teams.

The main assumption in our approach is that the arrival of features to sites, and the probability distribution of the time required to develop a feature at a certain site, can be approximated using stochastic methods with sufficient accuracy to support project management planning tools.

We extracted the following statistical information from the project database: feature domains, feature allocation, team productivity, and productivity by feature domain. Figure 22.3 shows the fraction of features that were allocated to each site, for the eleven development teams involved in the project.

We can observe that team number one was responsible for over 24% of the total number of features. We considered this team as critical for the evaluation of project schedule risk. The software development process used by the analyzed project is composed by a series of development tasks and one integration test task at the end of the software development process. One team that is responsible for testing the product integration and functionality executes this final task.

The testers of the studied project have reported that the centralization of project testing and integration became a bottleneck resource for the project, because of communication and synchronization problems. Therefore, it is very important for project managers to assess how the testing centralization may impact project schedule risk.

The main goal of the experiment is to analyze how the project schedule risk can be minimized. The simulation model has the following parameters that can be varied to analyze their impact on schedule risk behavior: total project time, development productivity for each site, test productivity for each site, communication probability, and feature allocation rate.

We ran simulation experiments to analyze different ranges of values for each analyzed characteristic following the first step of the experimental methodology described earlier. For example, Figure 22.4 represents the result of a series of simula-

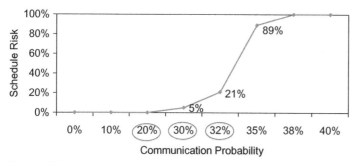

Figure 22.4   Relation between communication probability and schedule risk.

tion runs to evaluate the schedule risk behavior along a range of different probabilities of communication. We observed that the schedule risk increased as the value for the parameter communication probability was increased from 30% to 35%. When the communication probability parameter reached the value of 38%, the schedule risk was evaluated as 100%.

 Schedule risk in distributed development mostly occurs due to coordination and communication bottlenecks on critical steps of the development process.

We have also evaluated critical values for the test team productivity and the productivity of team one (quoted as the main development team on Figure 22.3). For each one of these cases, we obtained three critical values to be evaluated on the second step of the experimental methodology.

We have structured the initial simulation results using the Latin squares technique for experimental design. This approach allowed us to reduce the total number of combinations derived from the three experimental results from nine to three experiments (3 experiments × 3 critical points = 9 new experiments). We reduced the search space by applying a 3×3 Latin square matrix, and then we derived the design of three experiments represented in Figure 22.5.

RESULTS

The successful conclusion of a software development project depends on different management practices that should be applied during the software development process. Our simulation approach derives the project structure and statistics from the project database to generate a stochastic simulation model. The simulation model predicts expected project behavior based on the management practices represented in the model.

Based on our empirical studies, we have identified communications probability and test team productivity as important factors impacting the schedule risk in the

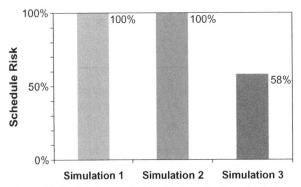

Figure 22.5   Three simulations based on the critical values from the evaluated parameters.

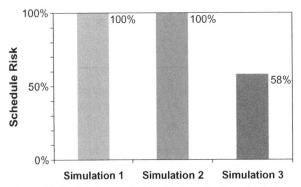

Figure 22.6   Results on schedule risk from the three simulations.

context of the analyzed project. According to the results presented on Figure 22.6 (where the schedule risk is 56% and the communication probability is 30% for simulation three), we can affirm that the communication probability is the most important factor affecting the project performance. The main result obtained from the experimental design was the assessment of the impact of the analyzed parameters on project schedule risk. We can see from Figures 22.5 and 22.6 that the combination that produced the best result included the lowest communication probability (30%) and the highest test team productivity (76 features/week). This is explained by the software development process used, for which the centralization of the test team represents a bottleneck for the project under study.

The common practices on communication management represented in Figure 22.1 can be applied to minimize schedule risk and provide effective communication.

The final simulation results provide support for the published recommendations for management decisions related to amount of remote communication and test team productivity. One of the recommendations for management decisions is to create a message board or wiki to reduce communication delay [Cataldo06, Phalnikar09].

Another recommendation would be to provide open communication over multiple channels [Avram07, Avritzer08b, Boden09, Ebert01, Ebert08, Herbsleb05, Gotel08, Sureshchandra08] to make the communication possible when required.

Recommendations to adopt a frequent rotation of tasks between sites [Sureshchandra08] and to avoid the distribution of highly dependent tasks [Phalnikar09, Prikladnicki08] can impact the test team productivity and reduce the communication requests between remote sites during the project. According to our simulation results and the experience of the testers we have interviewed, both recommendations are expected to have significant positive impact on the developer productivity.

TAKE-AWAY TIPS

We have presented an approach for schedule risk assessment that was based on data analysis from a large globally distributed industrial software system. We have observed the productivity variability per site and per release and we have noticed a variability of about 40% between the most productive and least productive sites and releases. Because of this large variability between development sites, we recommend that project managers apply actual historic data for each site to predict project behavior and assess schedule risk. We applied a simulation model to incorporate the important global software development parameters, site communication and domain knowledge, into our schedule risk model to be able to predict the schedule risk at a finer level of granularity, when aggregated feature productivity data is not yet available to project managers.

One important lesson learned from this empirical study is that a high-level simulation model can provide useful insights to identify project management related bottlenecks for globally distributed projects. The simulation model was used to derive a plot of project schedule risk as a function of communication probability.

 In simulations we showed that project schedule risk is more sensitive to communication than to team productivity.

The process followed by this experimental study can be used by project managers for assessing schedule risk while defining project management policies and planning new project releases. The first step is to define which project management aspects are going to be analyzed and then create variables to capture the targeted behavior on the simulation model. The simulations setup must evaluate measurements that are related to the organization business (e.g., schedule risk) and that are important for the organizational business success.

For project managers that do not have a simulation model for their projects, it is also useful to combine project management historic data and interviews of project members in their analysis. In this case, short pilot projects can be very useful to assess the actual impact of improvement practices that are candidates for the project.

Chapter 23

Intellectual Property and Information Security

Summary: Global software engineering demands a huge amount of knowledge being shared across physical sites. This means a variety of information security risks associated with development practices, infrastructure, and operations that can lead–if not managed adequately–to severe business impacts as well as affect commercial image of the organization resulting in loss of customer confidence and trust. We will provide some guidance on managing intellectual property and mitigating IPR related risks.

Global development, independent of the underlying internal engineering center business model or outsourcing, has raised concerns toward assuring the security of the information and intellectual property being shared across sites. In colocated development on a single campus, today's technology of firewalls and infrastructure protection has sufficient means to protect information security. Hackers and other malicious attacks (often even performed by employees to assure loopholes for their own needs) continuously challenge even this supposedly simple scenario. In the globalized, and thus distributed, site approach, assuring security is much more difficult. Networks must be protected as well as physical infrastructure in different countries with different attitudes to intellectual property and security. Confidential and critical client information needs to be secured in a manner that ensures the client's information security policy.

Security risks in global development are manifold, and we can only name a few which create the biggest exposure to the users, such as access to confidential information by any person who is not entitled to have such visibility, insufficient disaster recovery in case of security breaches or failing operations, lack of adequate management of external intellectual property (e.g., downloading of open source software and polluting own designs), exposure to external security breaches (e.g., hacking, denial of service, implantation of Trojan horses), malicious engineers creating loopholes or other damages, or insecure applications implanted by own workforce on the network.

Global Software and IT: A Guide to Distributed Development, Projects, and Outsourcing,
First Edition. Christof Ebert.
© 2012 the Institute of Electrical and Electronics Engineers, Inc. Published 2012 by
John Wiley & Sons, Inc.

An often neglected security risk is with otherwise trusted parties, such as accidents due to insufficient processes or wrong attitude of own engineers or of supplier engineers. This is where mechanisms of workflow management and restrictive processes come into the picture. The same holds for parties with agendas differing from your own corporate agenda as a user of global engineering.

Imagine a supplier that will lock you in a contract and then restrict the access and transfer of your own intellectual property (e.g., code, designs) that the supplier had created for you. Or it could be an engineering center in some part of the world that is not exactly following WTO rules and pays only lip service to protecting your own intellectual property (take the example of Cisco code and technical documentation which was, a few years ago, being used in the routers of a competitor from a low cost country). Several countries in the world are of that type and should never ever have full visibility to your own design, so that even if something leaks through, nobody could re-engineer what is valuable for your company.

Typically, a layered approach is taken to assure security:

- On the physical level, networks, devices, and connections are secured with encrypted data transfer, shared zones, firewalls, secured remote login procedures, and so on. As an example, one can imagine a collaboration environment, isolated from other tools, where suppliers can access design documents and remotely make engineering changes or review documents. Any shared tool which is accessed from remote or from a third party, must be protected the same way.

- On the information (content) level, it is crucial to manage access rights on both a role and need basis. For instance, many change-management and configuration-management tools provide full access to all stored information once a person is logged on to the tool itself. Only recently have major tools suppliers started protecting work on the information level with shared access to change requests or archives. These security mechanisms apply to basically all repositories, whether it is document management, code archives, change tracking systems, or project management tools. The more critical the information, the more it should be fragmented and individually protected.

- On the process level, policies must be established which enforce robust and secure workflows, even in stress situations where engineers want to achieve fast firefighting results. This includes role-based access rights that distinguish information needs or origin of the engineer.

- On the corporate level, governance and audits come into the picture. Though they do not directly assure security, they help in enforcing policies and assuring accountability. Information security governance (which is often legally demanded by security standards) provides the policies and reporting mechanisms to check application of policies to educate people and establish additional tools and processes as needed. An independent audit function will routinely look into the application of the policies and escalate when risks are not adequately mitigated.

A fragmented approach to security monitoring and management leads to security breaches and accidents as we often see in companies which just start with global development. It might be wise to not give all engineers (even in the same company) full access rights to all repositories. As an example, take a consultant from a third party (external supplier) who works on campus. He will often get temporary access rights to the servers and thus could easily exploit and access design information not relevant for his role but interesting to know.

A successful security framework provides a robust process structure tolerable to adverse inputs, mature and skilled workforce adaptive to a changing environment, and the right combination of different control mechanisms.

From an outsourcing perspective, suppliers of engineering services must assure the continuity of their applications and the surrounding security mechanisms based on the system business impact information, and provide necessary system continuity mechanisms. Specifically, suppliers must confirm to a variety of different legislative rules, depending on region and application domain.

Here is some concrete guidance toward implementing security protection and risk mitigation in global engineering scenarios:

- Copyrights are always created by real persons and must be immediately transferred explicitly to your company as the legal owner. Assure that this copyright tansfer is part of each single employee contract on worldwide basis. Be explicit as to the physical site (country) to which the copyrights are transferred to avoid their resting with your company at the wrong (e.g., not future-safe) legal place.

- Include within each single employee contract formal rules about when and how to work with competitors after the end of a contract with your company. Explicitly mention the policies for security and intellectual property protection in each single contract. Renew contracts in worst case if they have loopholes or if policies had changed. Do not rely on corporate policies as sufficient; as in some countries it is only the personal signed contract that is the policy for the individual employee.

- When working with suppliers or with frame contracts of an external supplier, enforce that these suppliers do the same as in the previous bullets for each single contract of their workforce working with you. Demand a signed list of all persons working for you or having access to information related to your company (e.g., administrators in the back office) to assure nobody will have uncontrolled access.

- Always register trademarks and copyrights in countries where you operate. File for local patents as much as is feasible.
- Establish clear governance rules on visibility and sharing of information. Audit the enforcement of security and backup policies. Check access rights on a routine basis. Many tools and applications (or operating systems) come with defaults that bear high risks.
- Agree on specific security contracts locally. If necessary, include insurances even if they appear expensive.
- Use all available security mechanisms for electronic communication. Establish visibility ranges, role-based identity management or firewalls. Communicate with VPN. Do not allow ftp or messaging.
- Never communicate confidential information on regular phone or e-mail services. Always encrypt contents with a strong authentication key.
- When working with local enterprises for collaborative development, establish replicated documentation and protected shared collaboration zones to avoid direct access to own enterprise intranet.
- Demand good document management from any external supplier to assure that you still have full access to all your critical design documents in case the supplier defects, suddenly disappears, or wants to lock you.
- Audit access rights and security policies at your remote sites and your external suppliers. Consider even the most obvious defenses, such as fire protection or distributed backup. Test your recovery plans and simulate accidents routinely. Restore critical information at least on a weekly basis to avoid surprises in case of accidents.
- Mirror critical knowledge across different physical sites in different parts of the world. Do not locate critical knowledge only in one part that might suddenly become victim of a civil war or an earthquake. Never entrust intellectual property to single persons if there is no skilled second source. Replicate critical skills and manage skills development accordingly.
- Assure that any tools and libraries you are using are covered by necessary global licensing schemes. Not all floating licenses are valid on a global basis. Some suppliers exclude distinct countries from their license schemes. Use license management tools to assure clean and auditable license management.
- Establish policies with respect to reuse of external code (e.g., Open Source Software). Demand explicit electronic signatures upon check-in of new code or technical documents into your document management system to enforce all engineers accepting the rules.
- Demand that your suppliers follow the information security laws and policies of your home base (or any other country if yours is not strong enough).

Chapter 24

Practice: Global Software Engineering in Avionics

Werner Burger, Diehl Aerospace

Summary: This chapter provides a case study from Diehl Aerospace and shows experiences from globally distributed software projects in the aerospace industry. It addresses embedded and safety-critical software where skills are usually deeply embedded into the home company, thus making outsourcing rather difficult. So it will also address cultural issues. The case study highlights relevant themes and guidance from previous chapters in a concrete project context. It offers valuable insights into how to do things in your own company.

BACKGROUND

We started offshoring as part of our software development some years ago. There were two main drivers at that time for starting offshoring. The first one, and at this stage the most important, was that we didn't find enough engineers in Germany or the rest of Europe (we expanded our search for engineers also to France and the United Kingdom), and, second, there was a cost issue. But let me speak first about the engineering shortage.

For that, we discussed, at first internally, whether to ask Indian engineers to work at our sites in Germany. During the discussion we realized there was a need of 50–80 engineers over a period of 18 months, and it would not be possible to do this work onsite in Germany. What else was there to do? The only alternative would be to send this work offshore, but no one in the company had done it before. So there were no experienced people available who could give support for managing entrance into offshore business. The result was that we would have to manage it on our own.

At first we started to think about what would be the greatest obstacles within our company. We saw two of them very quickly. First, we realized we had to set up

Global Software and IT: A Guide to Distributed Development, Projects, and Outsourcing,
First Edition. Christof Ebert.
© 2012 the Institute of Electrical and Electronics Engineers, Inc. Published 2012 by
John Wiley & Sons, Inc.

a process for subcontracting, and for this part of software development we wanted to send it offshore. This was easy to manage because we knew what and how to do software development, how to do subcontracting (we had to write it down and to bring it in process notation) so that everybody would understand it. But second, we saw we needed the support from and also the team spirit of our engineers, which would be the greatest challenge at all.

How to convince your engineers to support work being given away? There is only one answer: show them their personal advantage. The most important advantage for an engineer will be that even in the case of offshoring, he will not lose his technical competence and his chance at further personal technical development. This has to be taken into account when offshoring software development. Second, we have to show the engineers that work being taken away from them also avoids their being overloaded. It is also very important that they keep the more challenging and interesting work for themselves.

After we had set up this strategy, we started realization of the project. We selected three engineers who were well accepted by the team not only because of their technical skills and experience, but also because of their social integration. These engineers developed the process, the way to manage it, and also how to communicate the pros and cons. We flew them to Bangalore, India, to meet with their Indian colleagues—we brought the people together. For the engineers, offshoring was set up by themselves; they had been integrated from the beginning. It was not only a management decision.

Engineering management, which doesn't see advantages for itself, can form an obstacle. Those in management fear the loss of power and influence in the company, as their staff will not increase accordingly. There are always management people who want to have a maximum number of engineers working for them to define their own importance for themselves in the company. This very critical issue can be solved only by the top-level management, which has to support the people responsible for offshoring.

EMBEDDED AVIONIC SOFTWARE DEVELOPMENT

Software development for IT applications and software development for embedded systems: these are two worlds of engineering. Many engineers believe they understand embedded software, but only once you've done it in a project do you have the know-how and the experience to do it successfully. But we are speaking about embedded avionics software development. And avionics has some additional characteristics, a set of standards and directives that has to be followed. A well-structured development process and an independent quality assurance department have to be part of the company processes. Conformity has to be shown regularly. Generally, almost all Indian companies have reached IT or software certification level (like ISO 9001, CMMI, COBIT, ITIL) during the last years, and can demonstrate that without any constraints. Therefore, these processes are established and engineers are trained and familiar with them. Also, the available experience in avionics software development will help to accomplish the tasks and projects in a better, more self-contained manner.

Management and lead engineers should have a multicultural working background. This is necessary to understand how the project requirements of the purchaser can be met. Some experience in working in external, non-Indian projects, for example, in the United States, Australia, or Europe, would be most helpful.

Yet there are some hard facts that have to be assessed, such as the size of the company, organizational structure, team stability, and number of experienced avionics software engineers. The financial background is very important. In the recent past, one of the big players had serious problems, which have influenced contracted project stability and progress.

The hourly rate or cost scheme offered is the required basis for the commercial benchmark, but this has to be associated with productivity, because considering and selecting the company with the lowest rate may not result in the most cost-effective subcontractor, and consequently may not result in the best cost-saving cooperation. Table 24.1 shows an example of an assessment table for use in evaluating potential outsourcing suppliers.

All these facts have to be verified by an assessment list combined with interviews. Only direct personal communication gives a complete picture. An additional company walk-through, accompanied by personal communication and practical inspection, can give an indication of the company's capabilities and strengths. Very often, only demonstrated hard facts are considered, but the possibilities should also be put into consideration.

Finally, at the end of the selection process, a 3-year roadmap with well-defined objectives (measurable) to be reached should be set up. Defined project milestones and a performance indicator will give a good view about the scope of performance and measures to be made to improve it. Non-performance of two milestones allows for cancellation of the contract. This 3-year roadmap should lead to a 3-year contract with well-defined commercial and performance criteria.

 Do the work at the location, where productivity multiplied by cost structure multiplied by dynamic of adoption to new requirements gives the best result.

How do you get the best cost/performance ratio for your software project? First, you have to define which work will be done onsite and which work will be done offsite. What is the guideline for that decision?

All steps where you need expertise and domain know-how should be done onsite. Also, any steps where your customer requirements are very weak or where you know or feel that coding requirements may change very often should be done onsite. On the other hand, many development steps that can be performed in a very structured way, such as coding according to detailed design, all validation activities, and unit testing, are candidates for offshoring.

Table 24.1 Supplier Skills and Potential Assessment

	Criteria	Weight	Points	Sum	Points	Sum	Partner . . .	Points	Sum	Points	Sum
1	Know-how Embedded C Software	10									
2	Know-how embedded Software	5									
3	Tools compatibility (DOORS, Rhapsody . . .)	9									
4	Processes	10									
5	Technical Equipment	10									
6	Quality Management System	10									
7	Potential for increase of technical staff	10									
8	Own capability for team ramp up	9									
9	Training	8									
10	Expereinces in global engineering (Europe)	8									
11	Expereinces in global engineering (US)	10									
12	Langugae skill	10									
13	Fluctuation rate	10									
14	Number of employees	9									
16	Avionic expertise	8									
18	Culture	9									

196

How do you get the best performance from your offshoring partner? Set up a well-defined development process, define a checklist as a basis for the work to be performed, set up a training plan for your offshore partner, define key performance indicators and also improvement figures on a time scale, and set challenges.

How do you get the best cost structure? Take care that your offshore team has senior engineers but also young ones, so that you have a mixed team where seniority is also available. Be cautious: if you have negotiated very low hourly rates your team might have beginners only. Finally, you have to set up a process to handle efficient requirement changes.

Following these guidelines will help you to define which work is done where, onsite or offsite; this, combined with well-defined key performance indicators, can help you reach a very good cost/performance ratio.

OFFSHORE PARTNER SELECTION

Selecting an offshore partner should be done according an evaluation list as described in the following. Table 24.1 distinguishes hard and soft facts. The hard facts (assessment, financial) and the soft facts (experience, culture) give an almost complete picture of the capabilities of the companies under selection, and should lead to a good choice. Last but not least, a personal management obligation given by the CEO of the selected supplier should be given.

The preparation for the assessment and the assessment itself have to be done very carefully. We always did the assessment based on real facts: we looked into source codes that had been done, and we asked staff who we planned to assign to our projects directly about their experience and let them describe in detail the projects they had worked on. We also checked technical details and asked or checked why alternative solutions had not been chosen. By this we got a very good impression of their capabilities; we overcame any inhibitions (mainly those of the Indians), and we got very good information we could use for our assessment and for our selection. We didn't pay too much attention to the marketing people; we focused on the engineering staff.

RESULTS

Implementing offshoring for the first time is like a journey in a dangerous jungle. You don't know the foreign culture, you don't know the foreign people. While the engineers at your company may feel they are the best in world (which is exactly what you told them before), they may wonder why you would want to take work away from them.

You have to win them over; you have to guide your engineers to manage global working. How can you win people over for anything new? In principle it is simple: make your story theirs, make your approach theirs, and make your intention theirs.

It is like a boat ride on a dangerous river. Put courageous people in your boat, start the ride, show them how to manage the first pitfalls, and, after some time, hand over control step by step to your team. When they see that have control of the ride and that they can manage it, they will become proud of it.

What does that mean for our offshore project? Don't start with the most difficult challenges, start with the trivial ones, but incorporate all points, all obstacles, which have to be managed. Set up a pilot project.

THE PILOT PROJECT

Before starting the first "real" project, a forerunner should be done, a pilot project. As mentioned before, we want to test all major issues that will be important for the project's success. At the beginning of the first project you need to decide what should be evaluated by such a pilot. You know your requirements very well, your needs for offshoring, and all the activities that need to be done. Define the pilot, keeping in mind the capabilities of your offshoring partner, think about how you will manage your pilot, and then define your interfaces—such as the project interface, the way to exchange data, the IT interface—and define very well the way the work has to be done and to be controlled, the methods and procedures for monitoring and control, all the roles you will have, the responsibilities within your team, and also the escalation procedure that is to be followed. Finally, define how to measure performance and productivity.

An example from my first pilot project highlights the challenges in their variety. We had planned a pilot project, had built a team with our engineers, and had taken two people on the first trip to India. Have you ever arrived at Bangalore airport at midnight? In those days they had only two international gates in a city of eight million people. Have you ever arrived in India during the monsoon? It was another world. My colleagues were very impressed and, at times, depressed. We passed the heavy traffic, arrived at our client's gate (a building like in Western Europe or the United States), and met with the highly-skilled, friendly engineers. My colleagues were again impressed and they were very open-minded when technical discussion started. At this point, our team and the Indian team started to define the first common project: the pilot project.

The main objectives of the pilot project should be a test of the following:

- Capabilities of the potential subcontractor company
- Project interface
- IT interface
- Methods and procedures for monitoring and control
- Performance and productivity

In any case, the pilot project should have as many similarities as possible to the first foreseen "real" project. An adequate duration should be chosen, such as a small project for 10 to 12 weeks. This allows some critical or complex tasks to be tested and performed. It is very important to very clearly define the objective of the pilot project, both internally and externally. The management levels of both companies have to be incorporated. Methods and procedures for monitoring and control have to be discussed, and, after being reviewed with management, they have to be written down and communicated.

All internal important stakeholders have to be incorporated. "Important" stakeholder means, first and foremost, the "spin doctors" who have to be won to support the offshore project. During the project, these stakeholders should be continuously informed about the results reached and problems coming up. Also at the beginning, the evaluation criteria should be defined and set up.

Another important factor is for you to select two people, one for technical management and one for project management. These two people have to become the internal and external supporters and have to have the required hard skills and experience. The soft skills can be attained by training measures. Performing a pilot project with several potential subcontractor companies can allow a comparison of competence, productivity, and capabilities. This gives a good overview and a broad area of understanding and learning. This information should be considered carefully in future projects. The number of the subcontractor companies under competition will be limited by the available assessment staff. At the end of the pilot project, a lessons-learned process, internally and externally, should be done, wherein all positive and negative results are shown and discussed with all stakeholders. During the first project, measures how to mitigate the "negatives" have to be set up in written form.

STARTING THE FIRST REAL PROJECT

At the beginning, we always very carefully selected the lead technical person and trained him in intercultural issues, mainly in Indo/German specifics. But only real life and real experience can advance intercultural understanding. We asked our technical person to invite an Indian colleague to visit towns and historic sites together, as well as to do something together with their families. This brought forward an understanding of personalities as well as working styles. Most of the later problems were solved without management interaction.

The first real project with the selected subcontractor was started with a defined budget, defined quality and results to be delivered, and defined time schedule. At first, a suitable cooperation model was chosen from three possible types:

- Time and material
- Work packages
- Statement of work

Time and material means that engineers will be selected by the subcontractor company according their skills. These engineers build a team guided by the purchaser company. The task to be done is defined; results to be reached and to be delivered are also defined. If problems arise, either the team has to be expanded or the schedule has to be extended. The disadvantages are that there is no real budget control possible and that the subcontractor company does not have the project responsibility, which remains with the purchaser; therefore, the subcontractor will not learn to take responsibility. Nevertheless, engineering departments at the purchaser's side tend to prefer this model, as they do not have to fix standards to be followed. Requirements should be unique and stable in advance of the project's start. From a budget point of view, the time and material business model cannot be recommended.

An adequate model is the "work package description" model. Here, measurements to be reached will be defined by the two companies. Also, all the procedures and processes to be followed by purchaser and by the subcontractor have to set up and have to be understood mainly on the subcontractor side. This can be reached by several weeks of training on the job at the purchaser site, accompanied by a lessons-learned process. Having a checklist that has to be followed can also be very helpful. This checklist can be used in a "cookbook" manner.

 The work package approach should be used specifically for new relationships because it allows a win-win positioning of both client and supplier.

The following guidance may be given:

- During training, take care of sufficient technical support to answer all upcoming questions immediately.
- Build up personal relationships during training and try to understand the way in which your partner is working.
- Have feedback measures in place so you know when work has been done or when it has not.
- Set up a common checklist, to assure that all items that have to handed over at the start of the project will be.
- Define together performance figures and also objectives as to how to improve productivity and within which time frame.
- Finally, let your partner write a "handbook" for the specific tasks to be performed. This will ensure that the partner has understood what and how the work has to be done. This can be used for all further work.

For the first project, some "higher" measurements should be used, but for the next project, the measurements may have to be adjusted. Contracting work package descriptions becomes simple, as only a brief task description is needed. Costs are calculated on basis of past measurements. Milestones and delivery schedule are part of the work package description.

To define the work to be subcontracted by a statement of work (SoW) is very common. The statement of work defines all tasks to be done, all responsibilities on each side, inputs to be provided by the purchaser results, and outputs to be delivered. Also, reviews, milestones, and acceptance criteria are well specified. The statement of work has to be communicated and negotiated in detail; this is often very time-consuming. The statement of work for big packages, for example, a five-man work team for a minimum of 6 months, is an appropriate model.

IT Infrastructure. Working on common projects, where part of the project is done by a low-cost offshore company, a unique IT structure has to be defined and set up. The amount for definitions, coordination, and installation is often underesti-mated. Some points that have to be considered are addressed here. The first recom-mendation is to define the identical toolset that is in use at the supplier's as well as at the purchaser's site. This toolset should be installed with separate hardware, sepa-rated from the supplier's network, fulfilling adequate security and safety standards. It is self-evident that encrypted data transfer software has to be used. Common access to a shared database is necessary. Access rights can be easily installed, but the way of interaction with respect to elapsed time because of the far distance has to be specified, and, if necessary, adequate separate hardware should be installed.

A common direct line would be the best solution, but this is very expensive. In any case, sufficient time for installation and testing should be planned and some hardware cost for improvement of the access time should also be planned for. Figure 24.1 shows a typical IT infrastructure layout for outsourcing.

Roles and Responsibilities. Another important issue is the definition and set-up of the project interface. Very often, this factor is critical to success or failure. In our case, Indian development and management cultures differ significantly from those

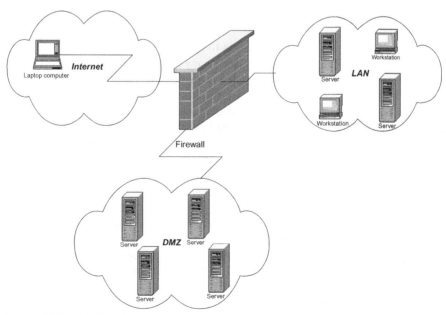

Figure 24.1 IT infrastructure.

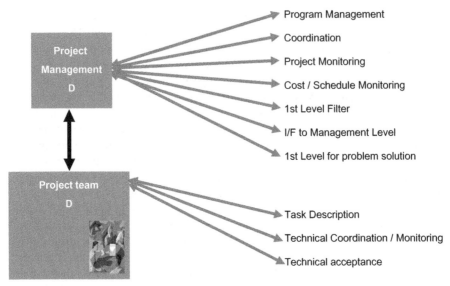

Figure 24.2   Project interfaces and responsibilities.

that we as Europeans know. So these had to be taken into account. Figure 24.2 shows how project management and project teams are split in their responsibilities.

Setting up technical management, with a technical project manager at each side, is the simplest, but most important, issue. Additionally, two program managers should be installed. At least one of them should be trained in the culture of the other, but it is preferable if both are trained in the purchaser's "world" as well as the and supplier's "world."

The program manager will be the first to address for questions; he should take the function of a first filter level. Very often, very simple questions are asked. And very often, the reason for that simple question is that one item was communicated poorly. The first level address avoids disturbances at the project level and, in consequence, to the project progress. The program manager should be an experienced engineer, preferably with expert knowledge in some technical areas. Special attention should be given to the selection of these persons, accompanied with training courses in advance.

Monitoring and control of the project progress is always critical, particularly if the supplier is far away, works in a different time zone, and lives in a different culture. We will focus on some points that need continuous observation. First, there is monitoring technical progress with a hard look at completeness at milestones, and monitoring all commercial progress. Usually, this is covered by procedures already in practice in the purchaser's company. But don't forget to look at simple things such as the contractors. Observe the oversized teams and the stability of the teams, in particular the availability of the lead engineers for the complete project duration.

Experience shows that regular meetings should occur: a weekly project meeting, with the responsible technical person and the program manager at the purchase side;

a monthly management meeting, with the heads of the relevant departments; and a quarterly visit by the executive management at the supplier's, accompanied by a walk-through with the project team. These different kinds of meetings allow you to address all critical points to the relevant management level on a regular basis.

 The statement of work approach should be used, if common subcontractor projects have been done in the past and therefore processes and relationship are well established.

The following guidance may be given:

- Set up a template for an SoW for all non-specific project items.
- Put all subjects that may change, such as the schedule, in appendixes. This will simplify maintainability of the SoW.
- Define in detail the tasks to be performed, inputs to be given, results to be delivered.
- Review the task description together with your subcontractor to be sure that there is a common understanding.
- Set up and agree on the acceptance criteria before the work starts. Define the verification and validation strategy, and how it will be practically executed.
- Define the paying milestones in relation to delivery items.

GENERAL PRINCIPLES

Setting up the offshore process in the right manner defines the amount of savings that can be reached. Many companies with experience in offshoring avionic software development have significant differences in project objectives realized in schedule, in quality expected, in supporting effort needed, and therefore in savings reached. This leads to the point of what is necessary to be installed to get the best results.

Software development looks simple. There are standards detailing how things have to be done, which are often supported by examples. There is a set of detailed requirements that have to be understood and coded according coding standards, and everything has to be done in a disciplined manner. But why is offshoring of avionic software so difficult?

At first, a very good, detailed task description has to be made. This task description has to be done in a manner that will yield an understanding of the software task to be done and an understanding of the application function to be realized. Structuring this task description by simplifying it is always very helpful, and this can best reached by filling out common templates. Part of the task description should be to follow checklists, to define the set of standards to be used, and to create an example of how the results should look. After an exchange of the task description, you should perform a common review to get a common view and a common understanding.

Next, the effort for the task should be estimated in a very detailed manner. A high level of detail allows you to check correct understanding at the supplier's side, to see how effort is calculated, and to figure out any kind of misunderstanding. It is always in the common interest of the purchaser and supplier to have a "good" estimation of effort, because this will prevent teams that are too small, which lead to schedule problems, or teams that are too large, which results in cost overrun.

The result of the cost estimation has to be presented and discussed between purchaser and supplier. At this stage, large differences between the purchaser's and the supplier's estimations may be seen. Now the weak points are on the table. The reason for the different effort estimation has to be analyzed and understood from both sides. Often, a first improvement is easily reached by changing or modifying the inputs to the supplier in a way that improves understanding.

But often, at the supplier, there is a new team that is not familiar with standard procedures to be followed and has no experience available in the domain knowledge that has to be used. It is necessary to start to think about how a continuous improvement of productivity can be reached. Give some targets for improvement for the projects contracted to the supplier. Experience shows that the first project will show negative budget results, the second will show balanced results, and from the third one onward, savings can be reached. However, one precondition must be fulfilled: the team has to be stable over the time project.

A well-skilled, experienced, stable team always has very high productivity. To improve the productivity of the offshore team, you have to measure it and you have to analyze the figures you get to see where further improvement is possible.

Another risk for insufficient productivity is the quality of the inputs for the offshore team. Clarification of questions and open points cannot be done as easily if the colleague is sitting next door. Spend some time reviewing them before sending them out.

Always critical for embedded software projects is the availability of sufficient testing resources, for example, evaluation boards. Analyze carefully the testing process at the beginning of the project and define the amount of resources you need. Eventually, the team will have to work in shift to reach maximum project benefit.

Team stability is key for good productivity, specifically in embedded software development. Insist, therefore, on a name list of who is allocated and actually working on the project. To add new team members is not only a matter of training newcomers. Good productivity is the sum of skills, understanding of requirements, domain experience, experience in common cooperation, and understanding of what the colleague expects.

For the measurement, define key performance indicators (KPI) and use them. Give the offshore team feedback about their success reached and about the improvement of productivity reached. Make a monthly report and put the reports on a blackboard for everybody in the purchaser's team to see it. Also, discuss the KPIs and how better KPIs can be reached. All teams want to get better and to show better results; they want to learn and show strong competitiveness.

Work Culture. Today, significant work in global software engineering is being done in Asia and India. The reasons for that are cost structure and the high number of available engineers, who are well-educated, well-trained, and highly motivated. Nevertheless, there is some reduction at avionics companies to subcontract avionics software development to India. It is mainly based on the differences in working culture and not on a lack of understanding of the different behavior or culture.

This obstacle has to be overcome. The working culture of the subcontractor company has to be understood and methods and means have to be set up and installed. The best way is a very simple one. Start a project and do it. And think about the fact that people will work together in a team if there is a communication culture available, and communication between engineers is much simpler if technical problems have to be solved commonly.

Think about how important daily floor communication in your company is when all the project work is done in your own offices. Doing projects far away means that there will no longer be any kind of floor communication. So you have to install other means to allow information to flow. Set up a "structured" communication to allow fast answering of questions, understanding of technical problems, and a way to solve cultural differences.

Very often this can be done by installing either an onsite engineer at the supplier's site, or a representative from the subcontractor's company at the purchaser's site. However, technical communication has to be simplified, and the right technical people have to communicate on a personal relationship basis.

After communication is set up, you may begin to see that you have one team instead of two fighting against each other. Technical problems may be solved, required quality will be reached, and tough schedules may be kept. These are the key factors for project success.

Ramp-up/ramp-down. Another point that supports project success is described in the following. The nature of avionics projects shows that during integration and testing, problems will be found that have to be solved and incorporated into a new software version—without any delay to or and influence on the project schedule. This means very fast ramp-ups and ramp-downs have to be realized (see Fig. 24.3). A ramp-up of about 50 engineers for 2 months within one project has to be managed. Indian dynamics support that. The precondition for that is to have well-trained engineers available and an excellent team structure that allows for adding new colleagues to the team. Again, special attention has to be given to the project management, preparation of planning, and reaction to project changes. Cultural dynamics and the motivation of engineering teams will provide the basis for that.

Change of project requirements. Unfortunately, there is another weak point that must be solved to reach project success. In general, there are two different kinds

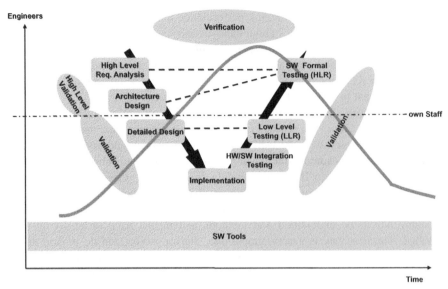

Figure 24.3 Resource evolution along the product life-cycle.

of development. On the one hand, there are mostly very repetitive activities such as validation and verification activities. These can be done in a very structured matter, along a well-defined process, which is very detailed. This can be realized in some "simple" way.

On the other hand, there are "problem solving" activities, such as design, coding, and high-level testing activities. This means understanding the function to be realized. The offshore team members have to make their own design decisions and are responsible for the solution they reach. This can be reached only if they are trained continuously in understanding the tasks that have to be done.

With regard to global software engineering, this is a big challenge. An example should make that clear. During the development cycle, project progress is reached at both sites, at the purchaser's and the supplier's. Problems always occur, solutions are found, and technical interfaces are changed. Often this is done only in a very small manner. But there is often an influence to the part developed at the partner's development team, and they have to be informed about that and a common solution has to be defined. This also means problems have been transferred to solutions. These solutions are realized by some differences to the architecture and software interfaces that are defined before, and those light modifications have to be communicated—in both directions.

At first the teams have to be encouraged to communicate. And for that, the attention of the project manager is a must. The project manager has to be trained in intercultural project management; he has to encourage both teams to move forward in a straight line and to stay within the required schedule. This kind of attention can be given by means of regular project teleconferences.

SUCCESS FACTORS

How do you reach the optimum of savings? This is the key to success, to get a competitive advantage. Hard and soft facts have to be addressed. Excellent management of the soft facts is the basis for any project success. Motivation and continuous feedback are a must. Within the area of avionics, motivation is not too difficult to reach. Everybody likes to be part of the large number of engineers who have successfully developed an aircraft. Giving feedback and giving it continuously is very often unusual, but it is essential for the team working for you. Do everything that the best engineers in the company want working for your project.

But hard facts have to be seriously considered in detail. Following the common practice for project teams in Europe and the United States, the hard facts to be used will be described. Set up a detailed statement of work that consists of separate work packages, with specification of inputs to be delivered from the purchaser's and results provided by the supplier according to a detailed schedule. Define the quality standards to be followed. Identify for each of the work packages the amount of effort you will accept. Define measurements that have to be followed and present those to the responsible lead engineers. Agree on the facts you want to see. Install an intensive coordination and communication structure and define responsibilities and actions, such as answering open points within one working day. Find a solution to problems that will not be solved within the agreed time-frame. And control it in a very direct way. Do not wait for questions to be asked. Sometimes there are no questions. For control you will need a project manager with good technical expertise and project management experience.

Next, set up a cost management change process. Your supplier has to track project progress associated with project cost. The offshore company should give an indication if they will run out of project cost. If this tends to happen, the purchaser's manager has to work out a solution with the supplier's lead engineers. Convince them of your point of view with technical facts complemented by technical proposals, for example, on how to proceed. Let your knowledge and your experience flow.

Many engineers at offshore sites are very motivated to learn and will follow the advice given. But sometimes the productivity is not as good as expected and needed. Then, the measurements agreed upon have to be improved, processes have to be simplified, and for the respective work, easy and helpful tools have to be developed and added to the project. Do not hesitate to improve the measurements until you think savings are nearly at a maximum level.

Why is that goal so seldom reached? Very often, the global software engineering project manager does not get enough time to do this very carefully and is not well prepared or experienced enough for this kind of project management.

What effort is actually necessary for control and overheads? A percentage of 15% of the technical manager's time and 10% of the project manager's time in relation to the total amount of project hours should be a sufficient amount to be spent. Usually, this can be reached after the third project, and with an adequate project size this can occur after one year of cooperation.

TAKE-AWAY TIPS

In the future, avionic software projects will become larger and more complex. Time schedules will become shorter because engineering shortage is a daily experience. Therefore, global software engineering will help to solve these challenges.

Here is some practical advice:

- Don't hesitate to transfer responsibility.
- Give the colleagues at the offshore company the awareness that they are responsible to fulfill the task to the satisfaction of their customer.
- Write down your expectations, do counterchecking for understanding, and do your project monitoring and control along these expectations.
- Set up well-defined milestones and share the results of meeting them, give feedback and address incomplete results reached and make proposals for how to improve. Communicate the results.
- Additionally, continuously do your lessons-learned meetings and incorporate those promptly in your project. Only then will your offshoring become a success.

Prepare the task carefully and comprehensively, and do the right IT-tool selection and installation. Define in written form the tasks (SoW), the quality to be reached, (standards) processes to be followed, and expectations you have. Discuss and define measurements to be realized and performance improvement you want to see, and continuously give feedback about the results reached or not reached before making proposals for how to reach them. Do not forget to monitor and control all the targets set. Your project will then be a success.

Chapter 25

Practice: Global Software Engineering in Automotive

Andree Zahir and Satish Seetharam, Bosch

Summary: This chapter provides a case study from Bosch and shows experiences from globally distributed software projects in the automotive industry. It illustrates how Bosch, in the domain of software development for powertrain control, was able to implement a successful cooperation between the central locations in Europe, the regional centers in the United States and Japan, and their development services unit in India. The case study highlights relevant themes and guidance from previous chapters in a concrete project context. It offers valuable insights into how to do things within your own company.

BACKGROUND

Global distributed software development has become the mandate in the automotive industry for various reasons. To mention just a few:

- All players in the industry need to pursue growth opportunities worldwide.
- Not having access to the globally available engineering resources is prohibitive considering demographic as well as educational trends in the developed world.
- Customers worldwide demand competent development teams which they can easily access rather than being serviced from headquarters many time zones away.
- Suppliers need operations in cultural proximity to important customers to fully understand their strategies and requirements.
- Taking advantage of the vastly different cost structures of operations around the world is essential to stay competitive.

Global Software and IT: A Guide to Distributed Development, Projects, and Outsourcing,
First Edition. Christof Ebert.
© 2012 the Institute of Electrical and Electronics Engineers, Inc. Published 2012 by
John Wiley & Sons, Inc.

Consequently, global software engineering is no longer an optional approach that needs to be balanced against the efficiency advantages of colocated teams. Instead it is a mandatory concept that must be managed in the best possible way.

As the global market leader in fuel injection equipment (FIE), Bosch has the need for an effective worldwide software development organization for engine control units. The lead development locations are based in Stuttgart, Vienna, and Paris with regional development locations being established around Detroit and Tokyo. These locations are referred to as onsite locations. They are supported from the development services organization in India, residing in Bangalore and Coimbatore, collectively called offshore locations.

In order to characterize the nature of work, we distinguish between platform developments (defined as a variety of functionalities being used across several customers) and customer specific development.[1] Product generations are updated every 5–6 years, which is mainly driven by emission legislation. Tighter limits for pollutants and fuel efficiency[2] lead to more complex engine control functions, which in turn require advanced hardware (higher performance microcontrollers with increasing I/O channels), software architecture, and development tools.

Software development projects in the automotive embedded control domain exhibit some unique qualities. Compared with the well-established business application development and IT-services projects typically executed in India, a knowledge cluster in automotive controls is just emerging. Therefore, a lot of training is required in-house to build up required competence levels. Some of the specific challenges are:

- The complex real-time computations required for engine controls.
- Knowledge retention over many years since the product lifecycle, including service periods, easily exceeds 10 years.
- System knowledge on vehicle and engine related topics in the mechanical and hydraulic domain in order to understand customer requirements.
- Specialized and costly test equipment like vehicle simulators, cars, and test benches are essential to validate the embedded control functions.

Offshoring in development organizations is generally understood as outsourcing of certain development activities to locations with a considerably lower cost structure. This case study contemplates offshoring of development work from the above mentioned onsite locations (i.e., high-cost locations [HCL]) to the offshore locations in India (i.e., low-cost locations [LCL]).

The typical problems of such cooperation depends on the specific countries involved but are more closely linked to the different cost structures and cultures of these locations. Henceforth, the lessons we learned from the cooperation between locations in WEU and India can be applied, to a good extent, for situations when offshoring from the United States or Japan to LCL like China or Eastern Europe.

---

[1] The additional variant of customer platforms which cover common functionalities across various projects for a particular customer is not covered here.

[2] CO_2 emissions can only be reduced by improving fuel efficiency of vehicles.

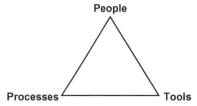

Figure 25.1   Three dimensions in offshoring challenges.

Typical problems related to offshoring are assigned to the categories as in Figure 25.1.

The people part is by far the dominating one and also includes the strategic and intercultural issues related to working in virtual teams. Processes summarize administrative topics of the cooperation together with concerns regarding the development process. Tool related topics are mentioned briefly because that part has good coverage in literature about development environments. The same three categories are used when presenting the approaches chosen to build successful virtual team cooperation with the offshore location.

At the bottom of most of the people related problems when offshoring gets established, lies the basic fear of losing the job. Asking someone to transfer parts of his tasks and responsibilities to a LCL will inadvertently trigger suspiciousness and anxiety. In case people with much lower salaries are able to fulfill the same responsibilities, the positions in the HCL start becoming insecure. The offshoring strategy of the organization becomes a crucial part for either mitigating or fostering this fear.

In case the offshoring strategy is only vaguely defined or not properly communicated within the organization, the associates involved will become concerned about their jobs. Additionally, it is important that the offshoring strategy highlights a long-term perspective for the people at the HCL. The management should not just open a new development center in China, India, or Vietnam and let the information float around with associates guessing what it is all about. Rather, it should be made transparent how the reduced cost structures on a global level relate to the competitiveness and future growth of the organization.

Reluctance to transfer core knowledge: Engineers typically consider their knowledge a personal asset which defines their individual "market value" and/or position within the company. Hence, asking them to transfer their knowledge to somebody else, particularly to a colleague in an LCL such as India, and thus losing some kind of uniqueness is anything but appreciated. For engineers the question is as simple as: "Why should I educate that fellow engineer in India on how to take over my tasks and, eventually, my job?"

Lack of understanding different cultures: The key of most of the problems in virtual teams goes down to a lack of understanding and sensitivity of intercultural topics. Usually, people expect the professional behavior they are used to at home from their colleagues overseas. This assumption does not work in virtual teams as people come from very different backgrounds. Simple statements like "Yes, I can do that task" may have very different meanings in different cultures.

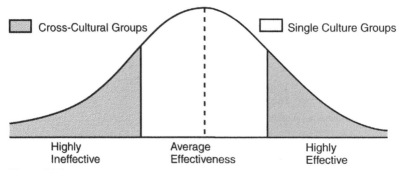

Figure 25.2   The performance dilemma of multicultural groups.

The only way of making an intercultural team effective is for the management to be open and understanding of all the cultural differences affecting work, and to adjust the cooperation accordingly. Typically, project reporting, tracking, quality assessments, and communication styles need to be addressed. It is also important that colleagues from both parties know each other personally. A reasonable amount of travel should always be planned between the locations even though the continuous rise in bandwidth allows high performance video conferencing worldwide. N.J. Adler showed how dominating the intercultural aspects on team efficiency are [Adler91]. Unfortunately, multicultural teams tend toward the extremes regarding efficiency compared to single cultural groups. They are either highly effective or well below the average effectiveness of single cultural teams (see Fig. 25.2).

Inadequate rewards for offshoring: This issue typically results from the diverging motivational factors of development engineers and their management. All the critical areas mentioned affect the engineering staff involved in distributed development. But the rewards for successful offshoring are typically attributed to their managers only. Typical goals for international managers are the reduction of total development costs or balancing the worldwide distribution of development capacity. For engineers or team leaders in software development, goal setting related to technology, increased competence, or efficiency is more usual. Unfortunately, none of these goals becomes easier to achieve in case development work starts getting distributed. Most likely all project managers around the globe would prefer to have their team located in the same place.

In short, the persons struggling with the difficulties related to distributed software development don't earn the rewards of making virtual teams successful. Only their superiors do and this commonly causes lack of motivation.

Limited offshore team stability: Throughout the years prior to the current economic crisis a major complaint concerning India as software development location created the lack of stability within the software teams. People used to switch assignments much faster compared to Europe or the United States for two dominant reasons:

- The tremendous growth in the Indian IT-sector did create plenty of attractive job opportunities for experienced software developers in the market which, in turn, promoted higher attrition numbers across the industry.

- Even growth of the own organization triggers the requirement to put experienced associates in leadership positions or to use them to start new projects, thus removing them from the former project team.

During the highest growth years of the Indian IT industry (2004–2006), attrition rates crossed the 20% mark for many companies. Since these effects are market and growth driven, one needs to find a way to handle operations in such an environment. Preventing attrition from happening is more of a wish than a realistic option.

Replacing experienced associates through fresh recruitment from the job market in India is a setback for the journey to increase the competence level of the organization. Experienced software developers in the automotive embedded domain are difficult to hire because the domestic automotive industry is still in nascent stage with respect to electronic controls. Since the knowledge levels of graduates from colleges and universities vary significantly, we have a much higher demand for training programs in the company compared to Western Europe or the United States.

Under the process topic we will cover issues related to the development processes as well as the general topics related to coordination of work in distributed teams. Different development processes on each side of the cooperation can be a great cause for misunderstandings and inefficiencies. The worst case scenario would be if the complete cost savings from offshoring could get erased by inadequate processes.

Consider the case a virtual team uses different coding and review guidelines at different locations. Arriving at a common understanding on the status of work products becomes more difficult. A simple example could be the acceptable level of Lint warnings in a particular code. The cooperation between one or more development locations is characterized by a long list of parameters such as project contracting, capacity planning, invoicing, strategic reviews, competence development programs, associate exchange programs, and operational reviews on various management levels to name just a few. Each of these parameters can have a significant impact individually on the overall cooperation. Each organization will typically require a certain learning experience to arrive at the best suited setting for these parameters.

Development tools are the essential backbone of every successful virtual team in software development. Without a multisite configuration management system, distributed workflow tools, and a common project collaboration room, virtual teams can lose effectiveness significantly. Responsible management should ensure that distributed project teams work with a state-of-the-art development environment.

RESULTS

We introduced three dominating sources of cooperation related problems in virtual teams involving offshore development sites. We will follow the same order and briefly highlight how the software development units for engine controls in Bosch were able to define and implement practical approaches to make the cooperation successful.

Success Factors: People. We mentioned above that offshoring inevitably triggers the fear of job losses for the concerned persons. Therefore, the management has to create a win-win situation for both sides of the cooperation. Since the receiving side of development work will always be considered as benefiting[3] the focus needs to be put on advantages for the HCL which is prompted to shift work to the LCL.

In principle, there are three different scenarios that enable work transfer to the offshore location without triggering job security fears.

- The work transfer is not mandated by a manager but self-initiated.

- The transferred work is not appreciated by the engineers, but considered a burden. Hence, offshoring creates a "relief" for the concerned persons.

- The work transfer goes hand-in-hand with offering substitute tasks and responsibilities to the person that are considered more interesting. In this case offshoring is perceived as "opportunity" by the affected people.

In case management is not able to create at least one of these three scenarios, offshoring will be perceived as mandated by leadership and not pursued wholeheartedly by the engineering teams. At Bosch we used a combination of all options to motivate people for offshoring.

The first option is realized by limiting development headcount at the HCL so that additional and interesting projects can only be executed when involving the engineering services center in India. Second, by transferring a lot of maintenance work and projects using older generation architectures, developers were relieved from their legacy burden. They proactively helped their offshore colleagues to work independently in those areas in order to focus their time more and more on the latest product generations. The third option is more related to the work split between locations. Initial topics to be moved offshore in many corporations are coding and testing. After the cooperation has matured, higher responsibilities, like complete projects or variant products, get shifted too.

Combining options two and three allowed for the moving of a significant number of developers at the HCL into higher responsibility roles for project management, customer relations, global technology coordination, or new innovation proj-

---

[3] Due to the fact that transferring work and know-how secures employment at the receiving, i.e., offshore site

ects. Consequently, offshoring started to be perceived as enriching rather than just threatening.

The strategy for the offshore center in India clearly reflects that approach. In addition to supporting development projects worldwide, the responsibility of the LCL in India is defined as handling mature generation projects as well as complete projects for local customers in various emerging markets. To complement the global setup, the long-term responsibility of the HCL is defined for strategy development and new innovation projects. People across the organization support this strategy because it offers a compelling vision for both the lead development locations as well as the offshore center. Since this strategy was defined several years ago, sufficient time has passed to reach out through the organization.

Clear commitment of the top-management team at the lead development organization shouldn't be underestimated. It makes a huge difference whether top-managers remain convinced of the offshore approach even in the inevitable situations of operational problems. Statements like "Just make it work together with the offshore team" give a very clear direction. Raising questions about the offshore approach in such situations conveys the message that the strategy is not stable and a rising number of problems could get escalated afterward.

COOPERATION MODEL BETWEEN DEVELOPMENT LOCATIONS

The offshore center implements the simple business model to treat the departments in the lead and regional development locations as customers to service. Since every organization is highly motivated to grow, a strong pull-factor emerges to get development work transferred to the offshore center. At the HCL, the motivation to transfer work is higher in case they are treated as esteemed customers rather than totally equal partners. In India the service sector is well developed and complements this demand. Combined, this approach has proven to be more effective compared to shifting work to India through management pressure at the lead and regional development centers alone.

From the perspective of the lead development locations, full ownership of the supporting development teams in India is encouraged. Team cooperation and performance shows the best results in case people start thinking as one global organization down to department and group level. Once this mindset is achieved, managers start thinking in terms of globally distributed software development rather than shifting work out of their onsite team (see Fig. 25.3). Accepting that kind of global responsibility becomes visible through statements like "I'm in charge for a global development capacity X of which 50% is located offshore in India."

To streamline the interfaces between the development units, the organization in India mirrors the structure of the lead development location. Through this approach we realize a one-to-one relationship between managers on both sides effectively supports a close and sustainable cooperation. In case a manager just needs to call

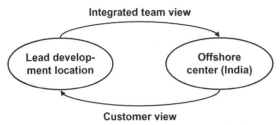

Figure 25.3 Cooperation model between lead development (WEU) and offshore center.

one responsible person in the offshore location to take care of his concerns, a lot of confidence develops and often good personal relationships as well.

INTERCULTURAL ASPECTS

The intercultural part is probably the most complex issue to be addressed. One needs to be aware that any solution requires persistent and repetitive implementation in order to reach down to team and individual associate levels in the organization. Even though many know about the habit in Asian cultures that completing tasks on time is less important and that communicating bad news is avoided until the last moment. But still project managers in the lead development center occasionally repeat the mistake of not following up closely on whether commitments can really be met. On the other side, colleagues in India need to learn that the direct communication common in Germany is not meant to offend, but is just part of their cultural background. Not addressing these issues will result in the virtual team and their project failing to meet the expectations.

 Reduce communication barriers by understanding and mitigating cultural differences. Highly productive distributed teams use a wealth of different communication mechanisms and do not simply send mail back and forth.

Although desirable, it is very difficult to find people who are already exposed to the language and culture of the target country. In order to make the team members aware of the intercultural differences that exist between any two cultures, it is necessary for a formal training.

Covering business aspects, especially the information required for day-to-day work, would make this training very effective. Typical topics in a single-day seminar about a country can include an overview of the history, geography, culture of the people, greetings, and communication tips for telephone, e-mails, face-to-face meetings, and office behavior. Language training can also be an alternate way to under-

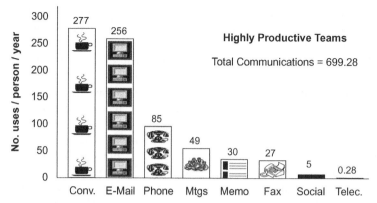

Figure 25.4   Impact of conventional communication on team performance for highly productive teams.

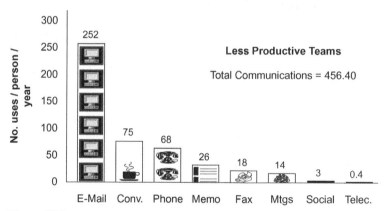

Figure 25.5   Impact of conventional communication on team performance for less productive teams.

stand a foreign culture. Informal or conventional communication (Figs. 25.4 and 25.5) plays a vital role in the success of virtual teams [Gregori09].

The conclusion is that teams with a good spirit (reflected by the informal communication) also work effectively together. Hence, it is important that in distributed teams the key persons visit each other during critical project phases. To get effective teamwork right from the project's start, joint kick-off workshops are encouraged. This allows better bonding of the team members across locations enabling easier understanding of subsequent formal communication. The travel related costs typically pay back through efficiency gains. Alternately, virtual team workshops could also be conducted to increase the understanding between team members using both video and teleconference with the help of a trained moderator.

Offshoring activities in projects normally start with a senior member being associated with the team onsite at the lead development location on a basis of 6–12 months. On return to the offshore center, this person is used as a seed to establish the project at the remote location in a gradual way. Associate exchange programs are utilized in case of a need for a specialized skill at the offshore center. Then the right person, with respect to aspirations and skills, is sent for a travel to Europe in order to learn on the job what is required to transfer the related development activities.

In order to create the awareness of the work environment in Europe, every Indian colleague is sent on a 3-month "orientation visit" to Europe after having worked for roughly one year in the offshore center. After returning to India, these associates know their counterparts in the joint project teams and more fully understand how software engineers work and communicate in Europe. That experience typically leads to good improvement in team efficiency.

REWARDING DISTRIBUTED TEAMS

Reward mechanisms for successfully offshoring projects need to be installed at the right place. This means line management positions from team to department lead need to be addressed rather than top management levels alone. The kinds of incentives that are chosen depends upon the development organization and the overall company culture.

Some incentives, like business growth, are intrinsic for corporate organizations and do not require additional stimuli. Working with a low-cost location, for instance, allows executing more projects within given budget limits. In case this does not motivate team members sufficiently, additional factors can be used:

- Removing the option to engage third-party contractors at the HCL.
- Prescribing certain ratios of development capacity between the high and lowcost locations.

Technical experts can be rewarded for distributing their knowledge to an international expert network. The success can be measured by observing the offshore location performing regional development projects independently from the lead development unit.

OFFSHORE TEAM STABILITY

Attrition depends on the overall labor market situation and can be influenced only to a limited extent. Of course, the offshore center needs to stay competitive within the local software industry regarding compensation, career opportunities, employee benefits, work environment, and so on. For the offshore managers it becomes a key

The primary means to achieve this is to make the offshore operation independent of individual engineers. Since this requires a critical size of operations, it combines well with the growth paradigm of countries like India. Having increased the capacity by nearly a factor of eight in the period from 2002 to 2009, the offshore center, despite operating from two locations, has reached the required level of stability to execute even complex projects. Team sizes and the number of available experts in most of the technical domains allow for a consistent backup plan in order to be prepared for the impact of attrition and job rotations. Additionally, the economic slow-down during 2008/2009 has helped bring attrition levels in the Indian IT industry back to normal. From average rates of 20%-22% in 2006/2007, a reduction to well below 10% percent is observed for 2009.

skill to match aspirations of associates with the situation and goals of the projects. But trying to keep attrition under control in all kinds of market situations would simply become too costly for the company. Hence, the better approach is to manage

 To make distributed development a success, processes and roles should be aligned across all sites. Common development processes, methods, and tools shape the DNA of any global software organization, whereas management processes need to address the regional differences.

the offshore operations in a way that attrition and people rotations affect the project performance in a limited way.

Success Factors: Processes. We integrate the general setup of the international cooperation together with the process related topics. Discussing the processes, we will distinguish between the technical development processes and the managerial part like project planning.

From the technical and quality aspect, it is mandated that the same processes are in place at all locations worldwide. As a global product company serving customers worldwide, it needs to be ensured that products fulfill the same standards no matter where the development location may be. Exactly the same requirements, that is, change, documentation, and configuration management, as well as workflow tools and guidelines regarding software design, coding, and testing, are valid for software developers in all locations. For testing, standard labs with both open- and closed-loop vehicle simulators, oscilloscopes, function generators, and so on, are replicated at the offshore center in India.

Furthermore, exactly the same role definitions within a project apply for all locations. This is essential to make all developers speak the same language in order to facilitate support and assistance within the virtual team. Additionally, the rotation of developers between locations is much easier when using a globally harmonized development approach. Consequently, process harmonization between the locations has become a key initiative for the worldwide organization.

As management processes, we refer to competence management, training, human resources development in general, and project management. For such processes, a need for regional or cultural adaptations is essential. Considering attrition rates in India, as mentioned above, the human resources related processes cannot be a copy of the German version. Similarly, the training system needs alignment to the local education system and the growth rates. The offshore center in India recruited several hundreds of engineers annually. A number that none of the lead development locations would have been able to induct.

The general cooperation part covers administrative topics like capacity planning, invoicing, joint meeting structures, and procedures for communication and information exchange. From an administrative perspective, the Indian offshore center is treated in exactly the same way as a department of the lead development location in Europe. Ordering and invoicing is required on top since the offshore center delivers services across national borders.

We already explained that the captive offshore center in India treats all other development locations as their customers. Consequently, a customer satisfaction survey is conducted for all departments that receive development services from India once or twice a year. After analyzing the feedback, the offshore center publishes the results and their improvement plans to showcase that the results of the survey are taken seriously.

Dedicated planning and reporting of critical issues is very important for the success of a global cooperation. Review meetings are conducted with defined cycles on all management levels. The top management team of both sides reviews the strategic and general setup of the cooperation twice a year. On a department head level, cooperation issues are discussed on a monthly basis and the cockpit chart about the cooperation is reviewed. Every project reviews the progress on a weekly basis.

Another success factor of the cooperation is treating the offshore center as an equal partner with respect to communication and information flow. Important mail distribution lists reflect the global setup of the organization. All relevant meetings are scheduled at times when international participants have the opportunity to join. All these meetings are effectively conducted as teleconferences with international participation. This approach supports significantly to maintain team spirit in the worldwide organization.

Success Factors: Tools. The development environment and network bandwidth are the key means to support seamless cooperation in virtual teams. It is important that all team members work within the tool environment to remove misunderstandings and facilitate effective support between all members. All relevant work products need to be globally accessible with reasonable response times. Hence, multisite configuration management and workflow tools for collaboration form the backbone of the distributed development environment.

Network bandwidth between the collaborating locations remains a critical parameter for efficiency. Since the related costs have come down significantly over the past few years, high bandwidth connections have become the standard today.

In software development, quality is probably the most important parameter. We measure the number of software defects detected after a particular software release is integrated and labeled in the configuration management system divided by the person's years of project effort for that release. For normalization, the defect density of 2006 is defined as one. The capacity growth of the offshore center from 2006 to 2009 brought the defect density down much by roughly a factor of 2 much faster than the absolute number of defects injected. Defect density data of 2009 shows an improvement of more than 65% compared with 2006 (Fig. 25.6).

However, due to growing international teams and increasing data traffic caused by exchanging more complex work products, the network needs constant load supervision and regular updates.

Performance indicators. In order to judge whether all suggested measures lead to a successful international development organization, we compare some key performance indicators (KPIs) with available benchmark data on offshoring.

The defect performance is difficult to compare with industry benchmarks because the numbers highly depend on the technical domain, the development process, and tools. What is possible to state is that the quality of delivered software

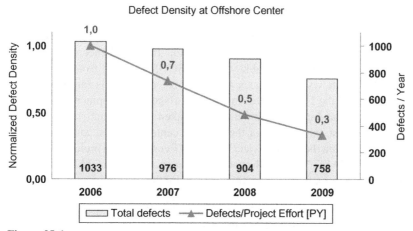

Figure 25.6   Quality improvement in the captive offshore center.

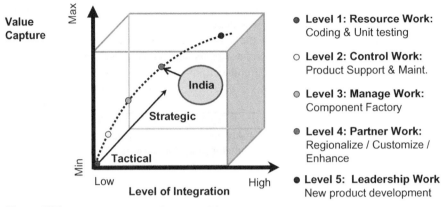

Figure 25.7   The value capture reference model.

from the offshore center is, in the meantime, on par with software developed at the lead development locations.

Another important parameter to judge the capability of an offshore center is the so-called value capture [OI05]. Figure 25.7 depicts the value capture model and explains the different kinds of typical work content for captive offshore development center in India on a scale from 1 (resource work) to 5 (leadership work). We rate our Indian operations on level 4 since complete engine control development projects for the emerging markets are executed there. Such projects are highly cost efficient since no additional coordination effort from the lead development is required. Still, the larger share of development work happens on the lower value capture levels and the current output can be considered as roughly 70% at levels 1 and 2 combined, 20% at level three, and 10% at level 4. Complete new product development, which would qualify for level 5, has not yet started in the offshore center. Although this distribution does not look impressive, it is in fact quite ahead of most captive development centers in India.

Finally, offshoring of development work to an LCL such as India is, to a large extent, about cost savings. Consequently, the cost savings achieved in a particular cooperation can be used as a performance indicator. Industry benchmark data on offshore operations in India is available with NASSCOM. A study from 2006 (refer to [NASSCOM06]) shows that between 40% and 50% of the costs can be saved in India compared with the United States in spite of offshore development being considered less efficient and coordination efforts are taken into account.

Although our cost calculation for the offshore center includes, additionally, all travel expenses between the locations and the extra IT costs to run a multisite location (not mentioned in [NASSCOM06]) the cost advantage is more than 50% in 2009. Our forecast for 2010 shows a further reduction of costs for the offshore center driven by:

- Better utilization of the existing offshore engineering capacity.
- Higher efficiency of the engineering team through gained experience.
- Optimization of the cooperation leading to reduced overhead effort.

TAKE-AWAY TIPS

The software development units in Bosch working on powertrain applications like engine controls started the cooperation with the offshore center in India 20 years ago and made this offshore center an integral part of the global development network. Cooperation models have been adopted over time based on learning and best practices while working in the intercultural context. The chosen approach of fully integrating the international teams while maintaining a customer oriented mindset in the offshore center has proven to lead to excellent results in the cooperation. In the previous chapter we presented data on quality, levels of responsibility, and cost savings achieved in cooperation with the offshore center in India confirming the competitiveness of our distributed team approach.

Selecting the right topics for the Indian service center was essential to achieve broad support for the offshore strategy in the organization. Offshore development should also be used to raise the potential of the lead development locations toward international technology management and innovation. Working successfully in distributed teams needs to be rewarded and building a competent offshore development team an element that supports personal career growth.

Reaffirming the offshore development strategy from top-management is of utmost importance. Establishing distributed development teams across locations with diverse cultural backgrounds is a great challenge and needs continuous management support over many years to be successful. Creating the mindset of being one global organization can only be achieved top-down.

Development environments available in the market address the issues of globally distributed teams and are mature enough for use in professional software development. We experienced that harmonized technical processes and roles significantly help in making virtual teams speak the same "language." Effort spent in setting up the cooperation with respect to meetings, information exchange, escalations, competence development, and other topics are well invested, but dependent on the corporate culture. The goal remains to minimize the impact of cultural differences on the operational aspects of the cooperation.

All efforts regarding processes, methods, and tools will not suffice in case the organization fails to ignite a team spirit across the participating locations. Trainings are essential to make people aware of the intercultural differences and to practice corresponding behavioral patterns. The formal communication approaches required in businesses or project environments are facilitated in case a strong informal communication is already established between the people involved.

Part IV

People and Teams

Chapter 26

Work Organization and Resource Allocation

Summary: Globally distributed software development and IT is highly impacted by work organization and effective work split. Working in a globally distributed environment means overheads for planning and managing people. It means language and cultural barriers. We will provide some practical insights in this chapter on how to best organize work in a global setting.

Clearly, mixed teams with people from different countries, cultures, and, perhaps, companies, stimulate innovation, both in terms of products and technologies, and in terms of more efficient collaboration. Teams that have worked together for a long time, such as departments inside a company, often struggle in identifying really innovative solutions because they are captured within their traditional thinking schemes. As soon as external players are added to such a team there is new stimulus from outside, and it is less easy simply wiping these ideas off the table.

For instance, we have been called in by a client who was in trouble with his product strategy. There were too many products with their own variants which were eating lots of effort but no longer generated enough value. Due to these many variants, there were insufficient resources to start new projects. Several new product launches were repeatedly delayed due to lack of resources. When we arrived it was obvious that one reason was strong departments that did not sufficiently share across boundaries and that rarely worked with external persons in their strategy and development teams. The company, in fact, was of the opinion that even coaching should be done internally by their training center and training experts—not realizing that this makes new stimulus very difficult to obtain. We worked in two steps. First, we opened the silo boundaries and created core teams for products and projects with members from different departments who had full ownership (in an agile sense) for results. Then we brought in external expertise from suppliers that would work for a limited time, such as one year, inside such teams. Suddenly, the teams started with fresh ideas and challenged their way of working. A useful side effect was that knowledge management had to grow in parallel because, due to the mixed teams with members who were no longer available after, say, 1 year, knowledge had to be secured systematically.

Global Software and IT: A Guide to Distributed Development, Projects, and Outsourcing,
First Edition. Christof Ebert.
© 2012 the Institute of Electrical and Electronics Engineers, Inc. Published 2012 by
John Wiley & Sons, Inc.

But the culture and people barriers to global collaboration are not to be underestimated (see Chapter 2) [O'Hara94, Sangwan07, Hussey08]. They range from language barriers to time zone barriers to incompatible technology infrastructures to heterogeneous product line cultures and not-invented-here syndromes. It creates jealousy between the more expensive engineers who are afraid of losing their jobs, while forced to train their much cheaper counterparts. An obvious barrier is the individual profit and loss responsibility that in tough times means primarily focusing on current quarter results and not investing in future infrastructures. Incumbents perceive providing visibility a risk, because they become accountable and more subject to internal competition.

Although there are no patent recipes for global software engineering and IT work allocation, many experiences from previous projects indicate what we might call "typical configurations." Such configurations are shown in Table 26.1.

The first column to the left indicates the "operational scenario" of global product development and operations. It starts with the beginning of the product (solution) life-cycle and moves to installation and operation towards the bottom of the table. The second column shows the most appropriate business model for such an operational scenario. The next column indicates how external suppliers might be included. Obviously, external suppliers do not fit in all scenarios, depending on intellectual property and dependencies exposure, but also related toward risk management of future growth. The learning curve duration and the break even period depend upon these scenarios and are summarized in the subsequent columns. The last column, finally, portrays how many parties (external or internal) are most appropriate. Needless to say, most scenarios are most effectively handled with a small number of contributors–except such cases where the contribution can be well isolated and decoupled from overall project flow and risks (e.g., software components or platforms which are selected and evolve in parallel but without critical dependencies).

Effective work organization and resource allocation is key to successful global software development. There are two options of organizing global assignments, namely virtual teams and colocated teams.

Virtual teams are set up with engineers from different parts of the world with a shared objective for the duration of the assignment. They collaborate inside the team with high functional coherence. Virtual teams are created when skills are distributed and must cooperate toward an engineering product or design. The advantage certainly is the famous "follow the sun" approach of continuous engineering because one part of the team almost always is able to take up the work of another which just finished work hours. Evidently this works not for a setting with engineers in close time zones (e.g., North and South America, Western and Eastern Europe, Western Europe and India).

The drawback of virtual teams is communication difficulties and the lack of team spirit because people do not know each other [Egloff06, Olson00, Herbsleb03, Grinter99]. Virtual teams need precisely allocated work packages and demand an overhead planning. They demand excellent collaboration tools beyond configuration management and document management. Continuous integration of resulting code is a big advantage in virtual teams regardless of whether they work on new designs

Table 26.1 Global Work Allocation and Typical Configurations

Task	Business model	Supplier model	Learning curve	Breakeven period	Number of partners/sites
Definition and analysis of new business models	Preferably onshore; should be collocated	Consultant; preferably own organization	Long	Long	Few
Product definition; platforms and applications for resale	Onshore, close collaboration	Consultant; preferably own organization	Long	Long	Few
Development of internal (ICT) applications	Offshore	Typically outsourcing	Short	Middle	Few-many
Product development (generic)	On-/near-/offshore	Typically outsourcing or own dvmt center	Middle	Middle-long	Few
Product development (embedded; complex)	On-/near-/offshore; single project should be collocated	Typically own development centers	Short	Middle-long	Few
Validation of software	On-/near-/offshore; tasks test and development should be collocated	Typically outsourcing or own test center	Middle	Middle	Few
Maintenance of internal applications	Offshore	Typically outsourcing or own dvmt center	Middle	Middle-long	Many
Maintenance of products	Near-/offshore	Typically outsourcing or own dvmt center	Middle	Long	Few
Selection and installation of software and infrastructure	On-/nearshore, close collaboration	Consultant; preferably own organization	Short	Short-middle	Few
Operation of infrastructure	On-/nearshore	Typically outsourcing or own IT center	Short	Short-middle	Few
Operation of internal applications	On-/near-/offshore	Typically outsourcing or own IT center	Short	Middle	Few

or maintenance tasks. It assures that team members in other places can continue with the same code and be sure it is working when they start.

Colocated teams work at one place with a defined work assignment. They benefit from being together as a team and, thus, from simplified communication. Colocation means that team members should sit in the same building, perhaps the same room. From a mere people management perspective this is of great advantage and can yield productivity gains of 30%-50% [Ebert07a]. Being at one place, they can utilize standard engineering tools for configuration management or their shared documents, thus keeping the setup rather simple.

The difficulty in setting up such teams is that the necessary skills are not always available at one place. Often such teams suffer from interface inconsistencies with their fellow teams working on different assignments in different places. Competition between teams could impact integration negatively. It is of benefit for colocated teams to establish clear quality gates and quality control activities (e.g., reviews, inspections, unit test with defined exit criteria) to assure the right quality level when resulting work products are passed on to other places in the world.

Both virtual teams and colocated teams need a distributed project management due to the distributed nature of assignments, even if they are functionally split. The dilemma with distributed teams is that they need more intensive communication while their nature reduces the possibilities to effectively communicate. We have a few recommendations of how to improve communication in distributed teams:

- Cope with distance and diversity. Use different communication channels to address audiences that are less familiar with each other. Apply some "remote team building" by having non-technical discussions or events by telephone or video. Remote games could be helpful to build such virtual teams.

- Distributed management demands more effort which must be budgeted both in terms of effort as well as skills. As a rule you should plan some 5%–10% of overhead for managing these teams. In the worst-case scenario, with highly fragmented tasks and loss of escalation to resolve conflicts, the overhead can grow to 20%–40% as we experienced in some cases.

- Consider sending managers and staff to remote sites. Rotate middle management across sites so they won't get into the "us versus them" mode. Assure that managers feel obliged to live for some time in offshore countries. Not only is it worth living close to your engineers in the global sites, but it also helps adjusting one's perspective by living as a foreigner for some years. Offshore managers should have many years of experience with living in different countries.

- Agree on concrete team KPIs which would only provide a benefit if the entire team succeeds. Often, the local line management in Europe or North America would dominate teams even if they operated in several countries. This is the tradition of Anglo-Saxon and western line management. Reduce the impacts of these lines dramatically. As long as local line management influences decisions and bonuses, engineers will never care for global teaming. Literally speaking, local management has to act as "hotel managers," providing the best possible infrastructure, but never interfering with actual assignments.

- Agree on some communication protocols with the teams. This might include the various communication channels, as well as when and how to use them most effectively. For instance, it seems a normal pattern for many engineers to send e-mails if they don't know other people in person. Stop this and demand that your engineers also call unknown persons by phone. Have a common project portal for all project-related information.

- Plan for sufficient training. A common failure in global software engineering is the lack of necessary technical or process skills, and thus, delays. Assure that skills and competences ramp-up in due time before they are needed in the project. Adapt training mechanisms to the variety of cultures and preferred communication means. Mix different formats, such as classroom (can be remote and virtual), live webinars, or e-learning of predigested contents. Force departments, team leaders, and project managers to periodically assess skills and skill needs of their teams. Demand training plans for each single engineer. Always remember that sufficient training and the right skills are some of the best motivational instruments.

Independent of the team structure (i.e., virtual or colocated) we recommend using fully allocated team members and coherent assignments.

Coherence means that the work is split during development according to feature content, which allows assembling a team that can implement a set of related functionality. The more coherence the work assignment has, the less dependencies and interactions occur with other teams that might work in different settings or even different places and time zones. Projects are at their kick-off already split into pieces of coherent functionality that will be delivered in increments to a continuous build. Coherent functional entities are allocated to development teams, which can be based in different locations. Architecture decisions, decision reviews at major milestones, and tests should be done at one place. Experts from countries with minority contribution will be relocated for the time the team needs. This allows effective project management, independent of how the project is globally allocated.

Full allocation implies that engineers working on a project should not be distracted by different tasks in other projects. The more allocation to a single task and shared objective within one team, the fewer engineers are distracted by disturbances and, thus, context switches. Full allocation does not mean 100% but should certainly be higher than 60%. If tasks are too small, related tasks should be allocated to the team. The difficulties usually start with very heterogeneous assignments, such as working on two different products. In such cases, the context switching from one to the other product is highly dysfunctional and causes dramatic productivity loss.

These working principles directly impact productivity. Team members must communicate whenever necessary, and without long planning and preparation, to make the team efficient [DeMarco99]. Alcatel-Lucent, for instance, evaluated projects over five years and could distinguish, according to the factor of collocation and allocation, degree [Ebert01b]. Colocated teams achieve an efficiency improvement of over 50% percent during initial validation activities. This means that with the same amount of defects in design and code, those teams, which sit in the same place, need less than half the time for defect detection. Allocation directly impacts overall project efficiency. It was found in the same long-term study that small projects with highly scattered resources would show less than half the productivity compared to projects with fully allocated staff. Cycle time is similarly impacted. People switching between tasks need time to adjust to the new job. In that same study Alcatel-Lucent found an impact of a factor 2 to 3 compared with what is necessary if resources are allocated to one job during a window of one week upward.

 Ensure that people work on few tasks or work packages with the highest possible allocation. More tasks means more interruptions, and thus more defects and longer response time and, ultimately, reduced motivation.

Here are few guidelines for effective allocation:

- Ensure that allocation of the majority of persons who contribute to the project (i.e., the engineering role) is almost full-time. This is measured with the scatter factor that relates the persons contributing to a task to the total effort of the task. This scatter factor should be around 1.5 with a clear tendency to further reduce.

- Ensure that allocation is reliable, which implies agreements on beginning and end dates. Having time fixed means that with clear quality and cost targets, the only variable factor is content. Content thus serves as a buffer to mitigate unexpected overruns, and is facilitated by incremental development and continuous build.

- Ensure that teams are colocated, even if the project is distributed across sites. Teams that are assigned across several locations cannot effectively work as a team and thus deliver their work products with reduced efficiency.

- Distinguish development (i.e., new functionality) from maintenance activities (i.e., defect correction). Organize both as separate projects, where the maintenance project due to the unpredictable workload would combine many markets.

In some companies, such changes in allocation mean a big cultural change with the clear target of replacing isolated expertise with skill broadening and effective teamwork. This implies a clear individual responsibility for overall project results. Such simple, yet effective, rules demand a sufficiently detailed project plan at the start of project that breaks down resource needs to skills and duration, and provides a feature development breakdown to teams and increments.

Enriching jobs in the way described above means also more training and coaching needs. We saw, however, in our own experiences over the past ten years, that coaching pays off. Looking only at cost of non-quality, that is, time to detect and correct defects, we found [Ebert01b, Ebert01a] that projects with intensive coaching (ca. 1%–2% of accumulated phase effort) could reduce the cost of non-quality in the phase by over 20%. A break-even point is typically reached at ca. 5% coaching effort. This means that there are natural limits toward involving too many inexperienced engineers.

The higher the allocation, the more motivation and ownership you will gain from your global development teams.

Consider the following case study from an ICT company [Ebert01a]. With an overly high fragmentation of tasks around the world in over ten different development centers, engineers increasingly lost visibility of how their own contribution affects the overall project. Several project post mortems indicated that activities and work product quality were seen as extremely isolated. The effect was that whenever we tried to build the complete product or iteration, a huge overhead was necessary to bring the pieces together. This holds as well for individual work products which were not sufficiently validated as for an entire activity, which was not seen as an entity, but only as pieces. Due to not having a product perspective, work products were handled inefficiently. Results were forwarded to the next in the chain, and cost of non-quality as well as delays accumulated. For instance, inspections typically did not follow the defined process, involving checkers, an inspection leader, and a maximum reading speed. Many inspections were considered finished when the respective milestone date appeared, instead of applying reasonable exit criteria, before continuing the defect detection with the next and more expensive activity. Tests were conducted with a rather static set of test cases that were not dynamically filtered and adjusted to reliability growth models. The root causes were obvious, but so deeply embedded in the culture that a complete reengineering process was necessary to facilitate global development at competitive cost.

The major changes for a team moving to global development are concurrent engineering and teamwork. They need to be supported by the respective workflow techniques. We assemble cross-functional teams especially at the beginning of the project. Even before project kick-off, a first expert team is called to ensure a complete impact analysis that is a prerequisite to defining increments. Concurrent engineering means that, for instance, a tester is also part of the team, as experience shows that designers and testers look at the same problem very differently. Testability can only be ensured with a focus on test strategy and the potential impacts of design decisions already made during the initial phases of the project.

Teamwork is reinforced to the degree that a team has sole responsibility for realizing a set of customer requirements. This means that no longer would a designer leave the team when his work product is coded. He would stay to test the work products in the context of those changes provided by other team members. Feature-orientation clearly dominates artificial architectural splits [McConnell98]. The targets of the team are based on project targets and are shared by all team members. They are followed up on the basis of delivered value, that is, feature content. Periodic

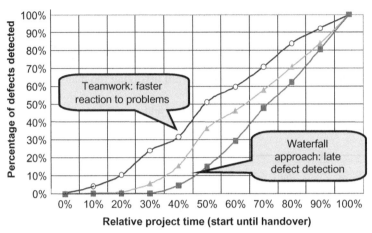

Figure 26.1   Effective team management scales directly up to faster reaction time.

reviews of team progress with the project lead are necessary to follow up and help in case of risks that cannot be mitigated inside the team.

The effects of this reengineered team process were carefully evaluated over several years. There were two major effects. Response time, and thus overall cycle time, is reduced as defect correction happens in the team (Fig. 26.1). Cost of non-quality in the overall project and field defects were reduced significantly[1] due to earlier defect detection.

Let us also spend a few words on architecture and work breakdown organization. Global development impacts product development heavily toward fewer and simpler threads of design variants. We recommend a strong product line–oriented approach for variant management and evolution. The product line concept is based on a few core releases that are further customized according to specific market requirements around the world. The structuring of a system into product families allows the sharing of design effort within a product family and, as such, counters the impact of ever growing complexity.

Based on a mapping of customer requirements to architectural units (i.e., modules, databases, subsystems, and production tools), global engineering activities can be treated according to their impact on architectural entities:

- Small independent architectural units that could be fairly well separated and left out from any customization. Typically, they are subject to moving into separate servers. Development is colocated at one place.
- Big chunks that would be impacted in any project and thus need a global focus to facilitate simple customization (e.g., different signaling types can be captured with generic protocol descriptions and translation mechanisms).

---

[1] Both hypotheses were tested in a set of 68 projects over 4 years (i.e., before and after the change). As a result we can accept with a significance level of >95% in a T-test that the change toward feature-oriented development impacts both cycle time and cost positively.

Development happens in multi-skilled teams. These skills are replicated in almost all locations.

- Market-specific or customer-specific functional clusters that would be defined based on the requirement analysis and, ultimately, form the project team responsible for a customer project. This type of requirement must be the exception and asks for a dedicated pricing strategy as it creates the most overheads, but could be the most interesting for our customers to differentiate.

Such separation of architectural units is the necessary pre-condition for splitting a global project into teams that can be individually colocated.

Chapter 27

Roles and Responsibilities

Summary: Global software engineering and IT must start with a strategic view, top-down, which is implemented in the lower levels of the organization down to the actual development, or engineering projects that translate requirements and work packages into responsibilities across sites. We will show here some of the roles and responsibilities, such as a project manager or an offshoring manager, and how they collaborate in global projects.

Global software and IT impact the entire enterprise (see Fig. 27.1). It should be set-up and managed top-down starting with clear business needs and addressing the overall strategy. Repeatedly, global software engineering and IT failed in the past due to an overly isolated or bottom-up approach with the spirit to work in another location because it is cheaper or has the right skills. Later, the product manager or sales representative might detect that quality decreases and customers defect as a consequence. Outsourcing, rightshoring, and global development must have a clear focus considering enterprise strategy, product portfolio, core competences, market perception, customer satisfaction, and the long-term health of the enterprise.

 An essential factor in managing a global project is to achieve accountability for results. We often faced, in the past, a situation where distributed projects were heavily impacted by the functional line organization or even some local legacy organization. However, nobody felt responsible for achieving results. The result was poor productivity and unpredictable delivery accuracy. The availability and empowerment of key stakeholders must, therefore, be ensured throughout the product life-cycle.

The key roles facilitating global development are the following:

The Core Competence role of highly experienced senior developers deciding on the architecture evolution, specifying features, and reviewing critical design decisions in the entire product line. They influence architecture design decisions and are involved in setting up a concrete project.

Global Software and IT: A Guide to Distributed Development, Projects, and Outsourcing,
First Edition. Christof Ebert.
© 2012 the Institute of Electrical and Electronics Engineers, Inc. Published 2012 by
John Wiley & Sons, Inc.

Figure 27.1   Globalized software development and IT impact the entire enterprise.

An Engineering role with the majority of resources is responsible for designing and integrating new functionality for all software. This involves detailed design, coding, inspections, module test, and unit testing until the functionality is integrated, but also testers who maintain a continuous build.

A Service role that serves on specific functions for a group of projects, including industrialization and maintenance activities. Often distinct skills are necessary shortly or repeatedly, but not at a high allocation need. Examples include customer documentation or production. For better visibility, this group of engineers is assigned to serve on a need-basis, however, this is still following basic estimation guidelines.

These roles are then allocated to various development teams, which constitute a project. They are not necessarily colocated according to these three functions. In fact, service and engineering are often split across sites.

A project is managed by a **project manager** and has various teams responsible for developing specific features.

Project management must be adjusted to outsourcing/offshoring. If teams are distributed across sites, project management must be more restrictive than with a colocated team. Management by walk-around will not work anymore and many managers have to learn new ways to monitor and be present, even if it is only virtually. As a first step, the project objectives must be very explicit and clear. Each team member must commit to the project and feel it in their bonuses if the objectives are not reached. Project and team managers must follow up milestones very closely. Showing insufficient care when a milestone is passed without results will be immediately translated to weak management. Flexibility must be used very carefully because it can be misinterpreted. If you are flexible, explain why. As a rule, you need to push for results. Techniques, such as earned value, are certainly better than

Home engineering center

External supplier
(or captive site)

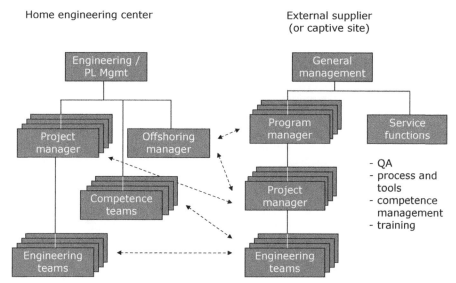

Figure 27.2   An organization structure template for global software development.

weak work package tracking. Incremental development is a strong practice for managing global projects as we have seen earlier.

Teams should get sufficient autonomy and empowerment to deliver results. The project manager is unable to manage details—and it would not be appreciated in many cultures anyway. It is better if teams have clear objectives and an agenda that is followed, rather than their individual team management.

If you have many global development activities, we recommend installing an **"offshoring manager"** role to coordinate the various activities specific to global software engineering and IT, such as infrastructure management, security management, and mobility management (see Fig. 27.2). A skilled offshoring manager can guide the many team leads and project managers that are exposed for the first time to global software engineering and IT. He can help foreign engineers to network and find the right contacts. And he should be able to maintain major supplier interfaces in case of offshore outsourcing. This offshoring manager is measured at the success of all running global software projects. He is measured on delivery accuracy (schedule, quality, cost), productivity, and SLA adherence.

Chapter 28

Soft Skills

Summary: Soft management skills such as communication, team management, and project management are core competences of any person involved in a globalized software or IT project. Specifically, for persons with leadership roles, such as a project manager, it is crucial to develop these soft skills before the assignment starts. Often, they need to both grow their own soft skills and also adopt existing soft skills to the different cultures present in the global project. We will emphasize in this chapter some soft skills and provide many useful hints for how to improve specific soft skills for international projects and work-slit.

Soft skills revolve around relationships and the ability to communicate and influence, rather than technical expertise. Relational issues are impacted by the values and norms that underlie each national culture. Thus, global team leaders must learn how to manage cultural diversity without physically being there. Cultural sensitivity and strong interpersonal and communication skills are critical to motivating members of globally dispersed teams and engaging them to be active members of the project. Language competences must be addressed before the start of a distributed project.

 In growing soft skills in the team and in practicing them consistently, a manager will immediately be highly recognized as somebody who tries to understand first before pushing to be understood.

Not all soft skills are equally valued in different cultures. A project manager might be successful in his own home turf, while not succeeding in working across time zones and cultures. Sometimes it is a matter of distance, such as for managers

Global Software and IT: A Guide to Distributed Development, Projects, and Outsourcing,
First Edition. Christof Ebert.
© 2012 the Institute of Electrical and Electronics Engineers, Inc. Published 2012 by
John Wiley & Sons, Inc.

who like to meet and greet their team members continuously, which is obviously not feasible in a distributed project. At times, it is a mere misunderstanding of different behaviors.

For instance, while leading an international team, one of my project managers from Europe complained that some managers from China would not reply to e-mails. We looked into it and found that they were never formally introduced to this European manager. Both their social status and the still rather infant impersonal communication approach did not allow them to just answer as people are used to in the Western hemisphere.

Most persons from a more remote location want to first be formally introduced to their counterparts and also "socialize" a bit before engaging in project work. Simply sending an assignment might even be considered embarrassing as they do not have the means to adequately reply without losing face in one way or the other.

Here are some examples of how to better manage distributed team members, and thus to improve culture and feelings in such a project:

- Be aware of cultural differences even if people are working in the same country. Be sensitive to their feelings, background, and past experiences.
- Be aware that your priorities are initially not necessarily theirs. Maybe they have just observed a project crash or some political or natural crisis that impacts their perceptions.
- Build trust at the beginning. Hold direct meetings at least one, if feasible. If it is not feasible, travel as the manager to all sites and hold a video conference with the entire distributed team each time so that they see you there.
- Hold more project meetings than you are used to from a colocated project. Use techniques such as scrum to engage all team members in brief status reviews and high visibility.
- Allow some time in each meeting or review to reflect learning, feelings, and behavior. Have team members work together and interact socially. There are lots of techniques and games to facilitate remote socializing.
- When socializing and planning for team events, be aware of the different cultural backgrounds, as they might create negative perceptions from events considered normal somewhere else.
- Facilitate continuous interaction of all team members.
- Set clear expectations for tasks, assignments, and projects.
- Educate all stakeholders that the meaning of what one writes or says in the project's shared language might be perceived and understood differently by different persons, whether a native speaker or not.

- Work with stakeholders to create common terminology with clear definitions. Write a glossary for key terms and maintain it across the entire program. Note that you might know a lot about the product, but not necessarily about the supplier or foreign new team member.

- Communicate expectations clearly and in the way the different persons normally "receive" such expectations. This could mean to write and then telephone or to have an intermediate local manager to communicate such expectations.

- Jointly review expectations and targets. Develop project plans based on these reviews to assure each member's commitment.

- Have people commit themselves personally, such as in a round-table, where each person repeats his role and responsibility, and articulates his commitment.

- Define roles and responsibilities. Write them on an intranet forum with access to all stakeholders. Review roles and responsibilities before allocating names.

- Build relationships with different channels. Often the meet and greet informal relationship-building is not feasible. Investigate which method of relationship building and meeting each other is most promising. Be creative in formats to use and always consider how people might perceive it.

- Send critical information, documents, and materials to all team members at the same time. Agree ways to efficiently inform everyone about changing requirements or project plans.

- Make all relevant information accessible from a single intranet repository, wiki, or document management system.

- Set up communication policies for the different channels to be used. For instance, emphasize not to send mail as ping pong, but rather pick up the phone and talk. Foster in these policies the use of different communication means in parallel.

- Vary the timing of meetings and telephone conferences across different time slots to accommodate all involved time zones.

- Allow sufficient time for members to digest and respond to shared information. Do not push hard for a decision when people have not yet understood whether it is possible for them and for their own management. Allow typically for one day between the information and the decision-making. It is worth the extra step, and ensures lasting commitments.

- Develop and distribute written records of all meetings independent of format and channel. Write minutes with a collaboration tool while conducting the meeting so that all persons can immediately see what is written. Encourage your team members to do so as well.

- Never shoot immediately. Take advantage of time zone differences and your perceived invisibility to all persons at the same time to first prepare an answer thoroughly before communicating it.

Often it is claimed that outsourcing or offshoring suppliers or even employees in captive development centers are not as motivated as developers in the home country. Perceived reasons are different salaries, less possibilities to develop new things in the low-cost country, or insufficient opportunities for career or sharing the benefits from growing business. This perception is questionable and, to our experience, mostly wrong. We heard in several interviews with engineers from India and other low-cost countries that they observe higher motivation in their own teams compared to the engineers at their clients' sites. One manager said, "We seemingly are eager to grow and learn new things. In the United States and Western Europe I sometimes have the feeling that people are saturated and doing so well that they cannot imagine improvement. They work to get work done, but not to personally grow." While this is an opinion, it is still thought-provoking in terms of how we are perceived from people in low-cost countries, and how much we are able and capable of motivating our people in high-cost countries every day, again and again.

Chapter 29

Training and Coaching

Summary: Continuous technical training and coaching seems natural for any engineering activity given the fast pace of technology evolution. Looking into post mortem studies of finished projects, we found that training has profound impact on the success of global development. There are big differences in productivity, and even success rates, of teams and projects that you can trace back to skills and competences. Competence management with appropriate formats, therefore, is a success factor in outsourcing/offshoring projects that deserves special attention. This chapter highlights how to practically improve skills and competences.

Competence management has several dimensions. First, there is the basic ramp-up of engineers to a specific technology and responsibility with related functional and social skills. Second, there is also the more specific coaching in front of a new assignment or start of a new development activity.

Basic skills ramp-up follows the responsibilities and roles and is provided by means of competence grids (mapping specific technology and behavioral needs to visible skills). Engineers will typically follow some introductory classes when starting with a new responsibility. Competence grids are used to find weak spots or skill gaps which would be eventually closed by training. Training can be delivered in various formats, where in the case of global software engineering and IT, it is mostly remote formats such as e-learning or video-based training. More general purpose training will be supplied by local trainers who will come on campus or offer classroom training in the region of the development site. To assure effectiveness of these training formats, we recommend good planning (so that engineers will actually join the training) and feedback surveys after one week and, again, after a few months. Only if the training has lasting impact after a few months is it sufficient and the gap can be considered closed. A good practice in performance management and people management is to make individual reviews with each employee by his line manager (in the same site) and identify, on a quarterly or half-yearly basis, the program's strengths and weaknesses and update the training program. Strengths should be captured in a skills management database to allow fast and efficient mapping of available skills to needs in the next period.

Global Software and IT: A Guide to Distributed Development, Projects, and Outsourcing,
First Edition. Christof Ebert.
© 2012 the Institute of Electrical and Electronics Engineers, Inc. Published 2012 by
John Wiley & Sons, Inc.

English skills must be rigorously improved in any global software engineering set-up. Implement a policy that all (and this means *all*) documents are written in English. Do not allow exceptions or you will see a flood of translation trials with huge overheads. Push increasingly that English is used also for all e-mails. It doesn't hurt anything and it improves everyone's English skills. While this is a no-brainer for North Americans, the British, or Indians, it is fairly difficult in the bigger European countries where the local languages are considered such an important cultural heritage that using them justifies severe economic drawbacks. The frictions resulting from these local legacy languages are tremendous. English is the lingua franca and must be taught and enforced in order to have effective global working.

 Assure that team members have possibilities offered to improve their English skills.

We had, for instance, good success in several places in fast ramp-up of English simply by offering a mandatory English class each morning from 7 to 8 o'clock. People were free to select any weekday but they had go to the class each week for 6 months.

Coaching prior to a new assignment or activity, such as a validation step, has a direct impact on engineering performance. This coaching is less standardized in terms of content, duration, and format than the basic skills ramp-up. Coaching comes on top of regular technical training and happens entirely on the job by means of allocating experienced engineers to teams of less-experienced engineers. We found big differences in terms of phase-specific training that involves both technical and process aspects. Some project managers focus heavily on providing all necessary technical and process information at respective phase kick-off meetings (e.g., start of detailed design or start of test), while others just present some rudimentary technical information and do not bother further with ongoing coaching. Effective coaching considers the main learning effects from past projects and relates them to available process expertise of the respective teams being coached. Given the strong impact of coaching on global team success, we will look to an example about contents. Our example is the coaching for more effective verification of a distributed design team. The chosen format is a coach who would provide verification support to all engineering teams worldwide. This assures consistency. He would be on-site for introduction and question and answer sessions for large teams that need a lot of training. Otherwise, the coaching would be done via video conferencing. In any case, it is always specific to needs, assuring focus and immediate value for participants. The coaching contains the following elements:

- General availability of a review or inspection leader: Only a trained and internally certified inspection leader is allowed to plan and perform inspections to ensure adherence to the formal rules and achievement of efficiency targets. The number of certified inspection leaders and their availability limits the number of performed inspections for a particular project. The coaching for this part looks into the dedicated skills of a review leader and assures availability of sufficient number of such trainers.

- Planning details to prepare verification activities. For instance, the actual design effort per component (i.e., class or module) provides an estimate of how much code will be new or changed. This indicates the effort that will be necessary for reviews and inspections. Based on the program language and historic experiences in previous projects, the optimal checking rate determines the necessary effort to be planned. Relating to the checking rate the total amount of the target size to be inspected defines the necessary effort.

- Expertise of the reviewer. If specific knowledge is necessary to check particular parts of the software, the availability of correspondingly skilled persons will have an impact on the planning of code reviews and code inspections. An example is security for which reviewers need to look to certain design guidelines, review checklists, and common errors that might impact security of a component or product.

- Quality targets: The coaching will help to set the right quality targets depending on criticality of a component and impact of errors. Quality targets balance the cost-benefit trade-off of review activities: The intention is to apply code inspections on heavily changed modules first to optimize payback of the additional effort that has to be spent compared to the lower effort for code reading. We recommend code reading to be performed by the author himself for very small changes with a checking time shorter than 2 hours in order to profit from a good efficiency of code reading. The effort for knowledge transfer to another designer can be saved. If high-risk areas are identified (e.g., unexpected changes to previously stable components or unstable inputs from a previous project) exhaustive inspections must be considered.

- Achieving the entry criteria: The inspection or review can start earliest if entry criteria for these procedures can be matched. Typically, at least error-free compilable sources have to be available.

During several global development projects, we found that providing a certain level of coaching within the project reduces cost of non-quality [Ebert01b]. We compared a set of projects within one culture (i.e., Europe) and similar skill background (i.e., engineers had sufficient technical knowledge of the software package) that received a coaching effort of ca. 1%-2% of total project budget with a second set of projects that received no coaching. Intensive coaching will reduce the cost of non-quality in the project by over 20%. We found that for our own process and defect detection cost a break-even point would be reached at ca. 5% coaching effort. Obviously, this is much more than what we usually consider necessary. This also means that there are quantifiable limits to involving too many inexperienced engineers in one project.

Often, coaching of engineers during the projects is reduced due to assumed negative impacts on total cost and duration. However, we found the opposite. Reduced coaching harms overall project performance. Assure that you also coach your expatriates. They need even more support because they often have a huge load of responsibility (managing a project or a team in a remote site), while being exposed to a different culture, language, and work environment.

Chapter 30

Practice: People Factors in Globally Distributed Projects

Bikram Sengupta, IBM

Summary: This chapter provides a case study from IBM and shows how to manage people in globally distributed software projects. The case study highlights relevant themes and guidance from the previous chapters on people and soft factors in global software and IT in a concrete project context. It offers valuable insights toward how to do things in your own company.

BACKGROUND

As a "globally integrated enterprise" [Palmisano09] IBM Corporation has been an early adopter of the practice of locating tasks anywhere in the world based on the right skill, cost, and environment. This practice has been applied to both its internal functions and associated re-organization and also to how it develops solutions for its customers throughout the world.

For example, IBM operates an integrated network of global delivery centers in more than three dozen countries, providing clients with business process, infrastructure, consulting, and application services, utilizing best-of-breed tools, processes and automation technologies–many of which have been developed in close collaboration with IBM Research, itself a globally integrated enterprise that operates eight labs in six countries worldwide with each lab engaged in several cross-site projects at any time. Software development projects within IBM thus generally involve globally distributed teams who bring in unique skills and local perspectives to deliver innovation through highly collaborative engagements. Several years of experience in distributed projects has helped IBM to develop deep insights into the challenges of global software development and delivery as well as build company-wide core competence in tools, methodologies, and education in this area.

At IBM Research, we have been studying the phenomenon of distributed software delivery, working closely with our colleagues in the application services domain. In particular, IBM Research–India has the advantage of proximity to development teams who are heavily involved in offshore delivery. IBM has six global delivery locations in India and this has allowed us to closely observe the challenges these teams face, as well as the best practices they have developed to address the same. We have also interacted with onsite team members in client-facing roles to obtain a more comprehensive view of the delivery process. Many of the technical challenges that we observed have been documented earlier in [Sengupta06]. In this article, we will focus on another equally important aspect of global development, one that is often the main deciding factor between a distributed project's success and failure – the people factor. We will draw upon our interactions with practitioners of distributed delivery in IBM's application services line of business to discuss how this factor has implications for team composition, collaborative work and project management.

RESULTS

Our interactions with practitioners engaged in distributed software delivery provided us with many interesting insights as to how such teams start working together, how their relationship evolves over time, the challenges that may arise, and how to address the same. Several anecdotes and best practices shared by the team members helped us derive these insights. One of the first things we discovered was that selection of team members for global software development projects has to be based on factors that go much beyond the usual requirements for colocated software projects (e.g., specific technical skills or relevant years of experience). We have found good communication skills (generally in English) to feature very high in the list of desired attributes of global team members. A number of offshore team members reported that they have taken (and benefited from) courses on communication skills (including listening skills and skills for effective telephonic conversations). Such teams often develop their own best practices to foster effective communication.

For example, e-mails from offshore teams to customers may be peer-reviewed prior to sending. One project followed a practice of weekly 1-hour sessions, where everybody had to take turns speaking on some topic. Some team members put a different perspective on communication by pointing out that in distributed projects, those who are shy and not communicative may not be adequately recognized in spite of hard work, and, in fact, keeping quiet during team phone calls is often perceived as lack of interest or understanding. As a result, people who are more articulate are often the first to be recognized.

Apart from communication skills, some of the other sought-after characteristics of global team members include: ability to work independently with limited direction from other sites, good coordination and time management skills, flexibility (e.g., with respect to working hours and travel), respect for each other's point of view, and a general appreciation of cultures.

Select team members for global projects carefully look out for strong communication and coordination skills, ability to work independently and deliver work in a timely fashion, and keep an open mind to various viewpoints and cultures.

A kick-off meeting is arranged at the start of a project it should be conducted over the phone if travel budget is not available. During this meeting, team members generally engage in informal interactions to get to know each other better. In one project, we found that a shared folder containing photographs of team members (and subsequently, team parties and outings) was maintained, and team members felt that this helped in creating a spirit of "one-team" in spite of being geographically distributed. A key element that needs to be constantly fostered in cross-site relationship is trust. We have found that trust in global teams builds up over a period of time. Most team members we spoke to observed that timely deliverables and high-quality work products automatically lead to more trust. As one offshore manager said: "Trust is not a short-term phenomenon, it takes time to develop…it is good to show incremental results periodically to build trust." The same view was echoed by a developer: "At the start of a project, there can be very close monitoring, but if you show ownership, trust automatically develops." Face-to-face interactions also lead to more trust. An offshore team member had this to say: "When you speak to someone over the phone you tend to visualize the individual in a particular way, for example, a customer team-member used to sound like an army general over the phone, but when we met face-to-face, I found him to be actually soft-spoken."

In a successful case, remote teams are frequently encouraged to ask questions freely in order to understand requirements because common understanding increases the trust level. Trust also develops where there is transparency. For example, a team-member facing a technical issue that he is unable to solve should raise it during team meetings instead of keeping quiet about it and delaying resolution (which can impact other sites). As one developer said, "As long as sincerity is reflected in your activities, you can be open with your customers and team members…if something cannot be done, then say so." However, trust between remote teams can also be fragile and disturbed by incidents that may be handled with relative ease in colocated settings, where developers share informal camaraderie. For example, as some developers pointed out to us, incidents like over-riding code changes without adequate discussions can disturb team dynamics significantly when participants are in different geographies and seldom meet face-to-face.

Global team members have to be sensitive to such issues, and project managers may help by clearly defining roles and responsibilities, and ensuring transparency and accountability.

Encourage open, responsible, and transparent communication between team members, as well as informal interactions whenever possible. Occasional face-to-face meetings can go a long way in developing comfort levels within the team. At the same time, a focus on technical work and quality deliverables is what will sustain trust in the long run.

Another issue that has a bearing on cross-site relationship is cultural differences that are bound to exist in multi-site projects. These can stem from differences in local customs, language, accent, attitude, working practices, and even differences in corporate cultures between organizations in the same geographic location.

To give a simple linguistic example, an India-based developer pointed out that when Indians have a question, they frequently say they have a "doubt," whereas, in many places like the United States, the word may be interpreted as expressing lack of confidence. This can create misunderstandings when the question involves the work or skills of a team-member. To give another example involving more generalized cultural notions, in a distributed IBM development project involving the Netherlands and India that we studied, a Dutch developer observed that Dutch people were more direct and less process-oriented than their Indian colleagues.

To address such issues, the usual practice is to give at least some informal cultural training to new or junior team members. Sometimes, more formal training is provided by sharing documents on the culture of the different geographies involved. If possible, early face-to-face meetings are arranged, so that differences in culture can be observed first-hand and seen in the proper context. In fact, some successful multi-site projects in IBM have had as much as 8 weeks of face-to-face contact for training of key team members. The other advantage of face-to-face meetings is that when developers return to their own sites, they may be able to act as contact people or liaisons. Team members at both sites use the help of these liaisons to initiate contact with the remote site, or to find out answers to a wide variety of questions regarding the remote site. This naturally imposes a significant cost on the liaisons, particularly in projects that have only a few people with cross-site experience. Thus, some IBM managers invest their best people in liaison roles. It is especially useful if the liaison is knowledgeable about local cultures of the sites he is trying to bridge. For example, we found that the U.S. site of an IBM global project, which frequently needed to collaborate with developers from Taiwan, used a Taiwan-born technical liaison, who understood the cultures of both sides of the world.

Cultural differences are a reality in distributed projects, so be prepared for them. The primary spoken language will frequently differ across sites, a common language can be spoken and interpreted with subtle differences. Working styles can genuinely differ across geographies and companies. Arrange for training, spend some time together, and seek out liaisons when possible.

In addition to cultural understanding, a few simple, but effective, practices may also be followed to promote the notion of "one team" and support cross-site work.

> For example, some projects maintain a glossary of common terms to facilitate shared knowledge and more effective communication between team members. Given that remote meetings are almost an everyday feature in distributed projects, we found that teams follow a routine that try to ensure meaningful participation from all sites. Compared with colocated meetings on the same topic, when scheduling remote discussions, additional time is often reserved in advance for effective summarization and wrap-up.

To get around unsatisfactory web meeting experiences due to poor bandwidth and connectivity issues that may plague some remote sites, presentation materials for a meeting are usually circulated to the whole team in advance. Again, when remote employees are not able to attend a meeting due to time-zone issues, minutes of the meeting and follow-up actions are shared with them over follow-up e-mail. In some projects, measurements are collected for ascertaining how the whole team is working together. In one of the projects we studied, the simple measurement of frequency of contributions and interactions is used as a measure of overall project progress and team morale. In another project, respondents had to provide answers to questions on personal work, teamwork, knowledge work, and so on. This process is subjective, but if the same set of people is interviewed periodically, then the changes in response may serve as an indicator of the change in project health and status.

While measurements and disciplined team practices like the ones above are helpful, software development, at its very core, is a creative activity that benefits from rich, informal interactions between team members, which familiarize them with the working styles of each other, allow them to brainstorm and have awareness of each other's activities, and, in general, foster team spirit. It is thus difficult to completely separate people factors in global software development from technology: the communication media that connects remote sub-teams in to a virtual whole, and keeps them engaged and motivated. IBM distributed projects make extensive use of tools in aid of communication (e-mail, chat, phone calls, web meetings etc.), document/status sharing (team rooms, wikis, etc.) and software development (tools for various life-cycle activities).

The choice of communication medium depends on the context and personal preference. In general, text-based communication introduces more overhead, but practitioners prefer it for discussions that need to be recorded. A far-reaching impact of distributed development in IBM has been on tools for software development. As reported in [Sengupta06], SDLC tools for requirements, design, coding, testing, and so on traditionally have not provided built-in support for collaboration. Remote practitioners had to hold all discussions related to these activities outside the tools over standard communication media. As a result, we observed that they experienced significant context switch, and many important discussions on SDLC artifacts were never preserved, leading to gaps in understanding over time. In addition, support for formal collaboration (e.g., awareness of changes) was limited, leading to coordination problems in global projects. Distributed development thus presented a compelling case for making software development tools and environments more collaborative [Booch03]. A product strategy around collaborative application lifecycle management was established that resulted in IBM Rational Jazz,[1] which is a new technology platform that transforms how people work together to build software and has been uniquely designed keeping the needs of globally distributed teams in mind.

One of the most crucial factors that determine the success of a multi-site software project is the role played by the managers. They have to perform both people management and project management duties across remote sites. In the successful projects we studied, the management of the primary team provided robust leadership and set overall directions, but also ensured that the participating groups felt equal and valued.

For example, there were projects where initially the primary team (usually the onsite client-facing team) assigned work directly to individual remote team members and monitored progress, but this sometimes led to friction. Subsequently, remote teams were allowed to partition work between their members, which led to smoother execution. Many team members also felt that the best source of motivation for them comes from the quality of work that is assigned. Hence it is important for managers to distribute work in an equitable manner and promote technical leadership in remote sites. Working-out of hours is a normal occurrence in multi-site projects. Some remote teams observed that hardships due to time-zone differences needed to be shared better, and pointed out that the situation can be particularly challenging for women professionals in offshore locations.

In general, the social life of team members in distributed projects (particularly in offshore locations) is adversely impacted, and managers have to be sensitive to this and allow more flexibility and provide personal support whenever required. In case of cross-site reporting, managers need to ensure that career progression of remote employees is not neglected, strong individual development programs are put in place, and appraisals and remuneration are fair. Good managers provide timely communication that is transparent and widespread, keeping remote teams in the loop all the time. They also try to make provision for periodic face-to-face meetings of team members (even in the face of travel budget restrictions) to create strong rapport between them, and schedule these meetings in a way that makes the time spent together very productive.

---

[1] http://www-01.ibm.com/software/rational/jazz/

A partially de-centralized leadership model works well in distributed projects. A primary site is needed for overall planning management, but you must do nurture leadership in remote sites. Allow them to operate autonomously on local issues and encourage their participation in project planning and decision-making. Focus on remote employees, their development needs, career progression, and work–life balance.

TAKE-AWAY TIPS

People, factors, and teaming issues have always been recognized in software development, a discipline that has a strong social aspect to it. However, they have never been more important than in today's world of globally distributed projects, where many of the observed challenges in practice can be traced back to inadequate communication between team members separated by distance as well as cultural and time-zone differences.

Here are our recommendations—drawn from our experiences described above—for those who manage or participate in global projects:

- Select well-rounded, responsible individuals with good communication and coordination skills, who can work independently and manage their time well.
- Encourage informal interactions across the team and open sharing of thoughts, ideas, and concerns. Ensure that formal communication is timely, transparent, and widespread.
- Foster cultural awareness and sensitivity, through direct contact when possible, or through the required level of training and the help of liaisons.
- Share the hardship of time-zone differences; prepare and circulate discussion materials ahead of time, leave sufficient time for going round the table to summarize and wrap up, and share important minutes and follow-up actions.
- Select collaboration tools judiciously, and use them extensively for both informal and formal collaboration around project tasks; these tools keep team members coordinated and engaged with the virtual team.
- Actively encourage technical leadership and local decision-making in remote sites and focus on the development needs and career progression of remote engineers.

As our experiences with IBM practitioners indicates, the industry is cognizant of these challenges and is combining the best practices for building and sustaining remote teams with the next generation of collaboration technology and sensitive people management to ensure that distributed software development stays viable and its many benefits continue to be realized.

Chapter 31

Practice: Requirements Engineering in Global Teams

Daniela Damian, Sabrina Marczak, and Irwin Kwan,
University of Victoria

Summary: This chapter provides a case study from different companies and shows how to manage requirements in globally distributed software projects. It indicates organic patterns of collaboration involving considerable cross-site interaction, in which communication of changes was the most predominant reason for collaboration. Although the developers' awareness of remote team members who work on the same requirements did not seem to be affected by distance, our case study identifies challenges in maintaining the awareness of remote colleagues' accessibility in collaboration. We discuss implications for knowledge sharing and coordination of work on a requirement in distributed teams, and propose directions for the design of collaboration tools that support awareness in distributed requirements engineering.

BACKGROUND

Global software development (GSD), driven by growing business opportunities and advanced communication technologies, has created challenges in coordination and collaboration. The increase in distance between project team members brings about problems in awareness of progress that affects one's work [Cataldo06, Herbsleb99, Ehrlich06].

Requirements engineering (RE), in particular, is a key issue in GSD. Due to its intense collaborative needs, requirements engineering is a challenge in global software development. How do distributed teams manage the development of requirements in environments that require significant cross-site collaboration and coordination? In this chapter, we report a case study of collaboration and awareness among team members during requirements engineering in an industrial distributed software team. Using the lens of requirements to group team members who work on a particular requirement, we used social networks to investigate requirements-

Global Software and IT: A Guide to Distributed Development, Projects, and Outsourcing,
First Edition. Christof Ebert.

centric collaborations in a project, and to examine aspects of awareness of requirements changes within these requirements-centered networks.

Contribution from many stakeholder roles is needed throughout the software development life-cycle to define, develop, and test requirements. Up-to-date information about requirements and their evolution in changing environments is critical. Changes to requirements and design specifications, frequent in large software projects [Cataldo06], need to be communicated promptly to team members to avoid negative impacts on quality and team productivity.

However, not only does GSD introduce delays in project communication [Herbsleb01], but distributed software teams have to coordinate work across diverse organizational settings, cultural backgrounds, and time zone differences [Damian03b, Herbsleb01]. Consequently, developers have difficulty coordinating requirements development. There is little support for monitoring progress of requirements or identifying team members who are knowledgeable of certain features [Herbsleb99]. While some collaborative tools aiming at supporting RE in distributed teams [Sinha06] rely on teams self-subscribing to communication about a particular requirement, we found that teams that have relevant knowledge and work related to particular requirements have dynamic membership with unpredictable patterns [Damian07]. These teams evolve over time and are affected by factors of geographical distance, organizational structure, and RE process. What we still do not know is how distributed teams manage requirements evolution and change information, nor do we know what gaps in communication and awareness need to be identified in order to avoid loss of critical knowledge within these requirements-centered networks.

This case study was conducted at the Brazilian software development center of one large international IT manufacturing company. The project we selected for study had significant interaction between the Brazilian location and the United States headquarters location. The project was an infrastructure maintenance project to an application developed in the United States over the past 7 years. The project team consisted of 10 members (7 in Brazil and 3 in the United States); more specifically, 6 developers, 1 system architect, 1 test leader, and 2 technical leaders (one of them also acted as a business analyst).

RESULTS

The traditional definition of a team in software engineering presents an image of a strict hierarchical structure in which team members work on related components. However, studies of current practice [Ehrlich06, Herbsleb01] reveal that team members are often working on multiple requirements within cross-functional teams that may contain developers, testers, and technical writers. A study of requirements-engineering process improvement in a medium-size organization [Damian06] indicates the positive impact of collaboration within cross-functional teams during requirements-management processes. These teams, composed of designers, developers, and testers used collaborative activities during the analysis of requirements to maintain awareness of requirements and their changes throughout the project life-cycle, reducing rework and risk while increasing developer productivity.

In our case study we used the concept of a requirements-centered team (RCT) as a cross-functional team in which each member is involved in a particular stage of a requirements' development (e.g., design, code, or test). A team member may belong to more than one RCT at one time, and a project has as many RCTs as the number of requirements. By relating the team members who work on the same requirements, we can gain a better understanding of how people collaborate and coordinate based on the requirements-related tasks that they complete.

RCTs, in addition to encompassing members from different teams, have a changing membership. As the development of a requirement evolves, more people are involved in contributing to the corresponding RCT. Our own empirical studies indicate that the group of people who work on a common feature is continually expanding [Herbsleb01] as a result of expertise seeking and management of inter-dependencies between requirements. Ehrlich and Chang also found that team members often go outside of their established team boundaries when seeking information about their work [Ehrlich06]. When a member of an RCT collaborates with a person who was not initially allocated to work on a specific requirement in order to help develop this requirement, this person is considered as an add-on, or an emergent team member, to the RCT.

We represented relationships among team members in a RCT using a social network. We thus defined a requirement-centered social network (RCSN) as a social network that represents an RCT. Each connection between the members in an RCSN represents a communication line between two team members in which the partici-pants communicate about the requirement. We used the RCSN to study the collabo-ration among team members relevant to the design, development, and testing of a requirement, as well as any awareness problems they experience in distributed interaction.

To better understand the dynamic nature of an RCT and how we can support effective collaboration within cross-functional distributed teams, we used an RCSN to study the evolution of the RCT over time. By deriving an RCSN from project plan data (such as task assignment based on a work breakdown structure), we gener-ated a planned RCSN that indicates who should be communicating with whom in the project. We then compared this to an actual RCSN generated using actual com-munication data collected through a questionnaire during the project, and identified the differences between the planned RCSN and the actual RCSN.

The RCSN, with its emphasis on communication lines between team members, was a useful tool when studying interaction in distributed teams. We observed com-munication among the colocated as well as distributed team members, and studied effects due to distance and availability. We were particularly interested in using the RCSNs to examine how a distributed development team in the industry propagates information to make every team member aware of the state of the requirements and their changes, and manages the collaboration around them.

Who is involved in actual RCSNs? We were able to study and characterize the distributed collaboration within social networks associated with 13 requirements that we identified in the Software Requirement Specification document. We found that each requirement's RCSN was extremely dynamic and included important cross-site interactions. More people collaborated during the development of each requirement than was originally planned, and about one third of interactions in the team were with emergent team members. Whereas in our previous work [Damian07] we identified that teams working on same requirement are dynamic, here we bring further insights about this trend: all 13 RCSNs consistently had emergent interactions.[1] In particular, a developer was most likely to be added to an RCSN, though technical leaders and testers were added as well. Interestingly, the tester was not involved in any planned RCSN, but appeared in every actual RCSN, suggesting that the tester was always involved in the requirements work for this project.

We obtained these insights by analyzing the 13 planned and actual RCSNs. Each planned RCSN included a subset of the 10 team members who were assigned to the project. To build each corresponding actual RCSN, we identified, from questionnaire data, all project members that the respondents identified as communicating about the requirement, in addition to those we listed from the planned RCSN. Analyzing these 13 actual RCSNs, we identified a total of 38 emergent team members (adds) across all RCSNs; these are non-unique, that is, there are duplicates across RCSNs.

By way of illustration, see Table 31.1, which shows details of the planned and actual RCSN of requirement 6 (R6), as well as the distribution of team members across all RCSNs. On average, there are a total of 2.9 emergent people per network, 2.3 of them (79.3%) are from Brazil and 0.6 (20.7%) are from the United States. This indicates that, on average, about one third of the team members in the project are emergent in an RCSN.

A further analysis of the emergent team members and their project roles within the 13 dynamic RCSNs shows that 19 out of 38 (50%) of roles involved in emergent interactions are Developers, 13 (34.2%) are Testers, and 6 (15.8%) are Technical Leaders. Table 31.2 shows the data across all RCSNs and the total of people in each role; data is shown across all RCSNs. Note that none of the planned RCSNs included a Tester.

Table 31.1   Distribution of Team Members

Requirement	Team members in planned RCSN		Team members in actual RCSN		Emergent people in the actual RCSN (adds)	
	BR	US	BR	US	BR	US
R6	3	1	4	2	1	1
Total across all requirements	41	22	71	30	30	8
Average	3.2	1.7	5.5	2.3	2.3	0.6

[1] See Appendix at http://segal.uvic.ca/collaborationpatterns.

Table 31.2 Distribution of Team Members by Requirement-Centered Social Network per Role

Role	Team members in planned RCSN		Team members in actual RCSN		Emergent people in the actual RCSN (adds)	
	BR	US	BR	US	BR	US
Developer	15	1	32	3	17	2
Tester	0	0	13	0	13	0
System Arch	0	13	0	13	0	0
Test Lead	13	0	13	0	0	0
Tech Lead	13	8	13	14	0	6
Total	41	22	71	30	30	8

What interactions and information exchange can be found in RCSNs? To identify patterns of collaboration and information exchange within RCSNs, we identified, from questionnaire data, who talked to whom and what information they exchanged within each RCSN.

Overall, project members mostly communicated about changes in their work. However, although requirements changes were the predominant reason for communication within and across sites, and two thirds of the respondents believed that they did not receive requirements changes in a timely fashion.

As a project developer told us, he worked on implementing a requirement for about three days until he heard the Brazilian development leader by chance, in a project meeting, negotiating a new delivery date with the project manager in the United States for the requirements changes that the developer was not even aware of: "Because I was having difficulties developing a solution that would interface with previous component specifications, I asked the development leader for help. He was in a hurry to attend a management meeting, then he invited me to follow him. I sat in the meeting thinking that I needed to get back to work. Suddenly I hear the project manager asking if the new data was feasible to implement the changes to the requirement I was working on. If it wasn't for my presence there, the development leader was going to take about one more day to tell me that I was trying to implement a solution for an obsolete requirement. He knew for about two days that the requirement had changed and did not have the chance to communicate it to me due to things with higher priority he had to take care of."

  Changes are the most predominant reason for interaction in requirements-driven collaboration and thus collaboration tools should support timely propagation of requirements changes information to affected project members.

This highlights an area in which improved change awareness, by increasing its timeliness, may have a strong effect on collaboration. Software projects will benefit from communication processes and tools that provide specific support to the communication of changes, both to improve the timeliness of change notifications and to reduce the communication overhead required to make team members aware of every change.

Similarly, we found that project members communicated frequently with colleagues who were not initially allocated to work on the respective requirements but who became involved in the communication and coordination effort driven by these requirements because of their relevant expertise.

During one of our interviews, the Brazilian development leader told us that because some of the people who conceptualized the system architecture and worked on maintaining the application in the past are still working for the company, the current team seeks their help to clarify requirements, requests, and decisions on how to implement the release requirements This team has been working on maintaining this application for about four years, but sometimes we consult with former members about technical specifications. This application is critical to the company shipping process so we cannot afford to try making changes to the application structure that would risk stopping its operation on the ground. Since we do not have a complete documentation about how the application interfaces with other dependent applications, we would rather ask those who conceptualized the system about the potential impact of the enhancements we are requested to perform in each release. Although they are working in different business areas now, they are open in supporting us from time to time, which makes our lives easier.

 Communication with project members who were not included in the initial project plan accounted for about one third of the entire communication. Thus, being aware of who these emergent, relevant, collaborators is important in effective requirements change management.

We show an example of requirements-centric social network for R6 in Figure 31.1. Each node represents a person, and an edge is an instance of communication between these people regarding the requirement. Each project member is identified by his or her name (fictitious, to protect anonymity), location (BR or US), and role. Project members included in the planned RCSN are identified in parentheses, and emergent people are identified in square brackets. The dotted lines indicate communication lines that were expected from the planned RCSN, and the solid lines indicate the communications reported in the actual RCSN. Details for the other RCSNs can be found online.[2]

---

[2] http://home.segal.uvic.ca/~pubs/pdf/132/2010_GSEBook_Damian.pdf

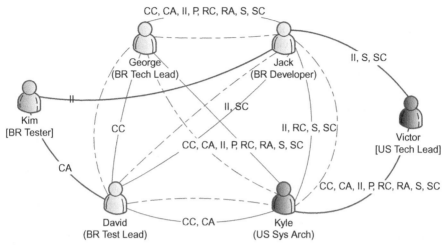

Figure 31.1   Real example of a requirement-centered social network for a single requirement. See text for details.

To characterize the information exchanged within RCSNs, Figure 31.1. also shows an example of communication patterns in information provided by our respondents about the nature of interaction they had with the other project members working on same requirements. The labels on the edges indicate the reasons for communication as provided in the questionnaire: Communication of Changes ("C" in Fig. 31.1), Coordination of Activities (CA), Implementation of Issues (I), Planning (P), Requirement Clarification (RC), Risk Assessment (RA), Support (S), and Synchronization of Code (SC). For example, Kyle reported reasons for interaction with David as Communication of Changes (CC) and Coordination of Activities (CA).

RE involves information acquisition and expertise seeking, as well as coordination across multiple teams. Geographical distance is known to negatively affect communication among stakeholders [Herbsleb01]. Awareness, which is defined as an understanding of the activities of others, which in turn provides a context for one's own activities, is linked to issues related to coordinating team effort. Communication is a main means to distribute awareness information, so we expect that a developer's awareness of who else is working on his requirements and whether they are available for contact is affected in GSD. In our study we were interested in how aware team members in a GSD project are, and what influences that awareness.

We also investigated *general* awareness, which refers to an individual's knowledge of who has expertise in the project. With respect to requirements work, an individual with good general awareness can readily identify who in the project team can provide help with a particular requirement. We were interested in how a distributed development team, which is limited to remote communication, learns about each other's abilities. *Current* awareness, or *task* awareness, refers to how aware an individual is of another individual's workload [Ehrlich06]. In requirements engineering, this is important because a software developer would benefit from knowing about developers working on related or similar requirements. *Availability* [Ehrlich06] refers to how aware one is of an individual's accessibility for information seeking.

Experiences so far indicate that awareness is significantly affected in distributed teams. Ehrlich, et al [Ehrlich06] found not only that people tend to communicate more frequently with someone about whom they have current or general awareness, but also that both general and current awareness, as well as availability, decrease significantly across sites. Herbsleb reported similar findings, observing that outside scheduled communication, distributed team members rarely communicated with each other [Herbsleb99].

In our case study, we (1) collected information on whether project members maintained awareness of work and changes within RCSNs, and (2) investigated whether current awareness, general awareness, and availability are correlated with communication patterns in the project, as well as whether they are affected by geographical distance. Furthermore, we wanted to obtain insights into whether project members have awareness of members that work on inter-related requirements, so as to further our understanding of coordination needs within requirements-centered social networks.

Overall, we found that a team member generally knew who else was working on the same requirements, regardless of geographical location. This was somehow surprising, given the RCSN's dynamic nature and the significant number of emergent relationships in these networks. We also identified an interesting relationship between distance, communication, and awareness. On the one hand, we noticed a significant decline of general awareness when frequency of communication was lower, indicating that people were more likely to communicate with someone whom they knew could help with the work. We also observed a significant decline of communication frequency and availability over distance. The communication with the remote colleagues was less frequent than with the local ones, and the remote team members were more difficult to reach than the local ones, respectively. Let us present some details of the many aspects of awareness from the responses in our case study.

First, we asked the respondents if they knew who in the project team was working on the same requirements they were allocated on. The answers were positive: almost all members were always or most of time aware of who in the local project team was working on the same requirements, and two thirds of project members were always or most of time aware about the remote team members. Only 12% of the respondents were never aware of who was working on the same requirements in the remote team.

In our 3-month observation sessions we noticed that the awareness in the project came from informal conversations at the coffee-break area or from discussions during lunchtime. It is important to share that Brazilians usually have long lunch breaks (about 90 minutes long) that include eating and socialization. One of the developers told us: "I enjoy how we go out for lunch all together. Not only because I can enjoy some company while eating, but also because I usually learn about what is going on in the project from colleagues that I am working with. We discuss technical difficulties we are having about a certain requirement, and it is common to hear that someone else on the team has knowledge about how to solve the problem."

An important aspect of maintaining awareness of changes that take place within the project is to avoid rework. When asked whether the changes in the project were communicated in time to avoid rework, 75% of respondents believed that always or most of time the changes were communicated in time. Although 25% of respondents believed the alerts were timely "because changes are immediately communicated," 37% still believed that there were some issues about communication of changes ("changes take long to be communicated," or "some project team members are not communicated," or "changes are not communicated at the same time in both locations"). This indicates that, although the respondents believed the alerts were timely, there was still a feeling of gaps in communication.

Knowledge sharing across sites is also a known problem in global teams [Desouza06] as inadequate channeling of information, or incomplete information, is communicated across sites [Damian03b]. We thus asked which information they currently receive when requirements changes are communicated, as well as which additional information they would like to receive to help them better understand which requirements have been changed at the remote site. They could select one or multiple reasons among: requirement identification, justification of the change, schedule changes, or other. Responses included requirement identification (75% of responses), schedule changes (62.5%), and justification of change (37.5%). Among the additional information they would find helpful, respondents indicated requirement identification (50%)—which was an interesting finding since 75% already reported as receiving requirements—schedule changes (75%), and justification of change (75%).

We also observed that project meetings play an important role in bringing awareness to team members. The team meets weekly to discuss development, testing, and management issues. The meetings are held separately by team, and there is a short weekly meeting with the entire team to share progress updates. The U.S. development leader told us over the phone: "This team is quite special. Everyone knows each other personally although the majority of the team is located in Brazil, and this makes working with them easier. We have built trust on each other over the years, thus it is more comfortable to host a meeting to discuss impact of requirements changes and team allocation over the phone. Our meetings go beyond progress report. Any time we need to make an important decision we call on a meeting, and share the responsibility of making decisions. During these meetings we exchange information about the project status, which allows me to be aware of what others are doing and perform my work from a distance."

TAKE-AWAY TIPS

In this analysis of an industrial, distributed software project, we examined collaboration, awareness, and distance in requirements-centered social networks. Our findings indicate organic patterns of collaboration involving considerable cross-site interaction, in which communication of changes was the most predominant reason for interaction. Although the developers' awareness of remote team members who work on the same requirements did not seem to be affected by distance, our case study identifies that distance creates challenges in maintaining awareness of remote colleagues' accessibility for collaboration. Below, we summarize a number of important insights that software practitioners may find useful in guiding the analysis or improvement of requirements-driven collaboration in their own organization.

Requirements networks are dynamic and different from those one would draw from the initial task-allocation plan. Reasons for the dynamic nature of these networks include the fact (1) that the initial project plan may not accurately list all roles and project members responsible for the activities related to a particular requirement and thus does not reflect all members who will be working on the development of the requirement, but also (2) because members who work on related parts of the system may have relevant expertise or interest in contributing to the collaboration, and thus becoming part of this network. This has implications for ways in which collaboration should be supported in colocated and distributed development teams, as discussed below.

Maintaining general and current awareness becomes critical in dynamic, distributed software requirements-centric teams. Requirements engineering is a complex task involving continuous knowledge acquisition and sharing. The spread of technical and domain expertise across multiple individuals creates the need for constant collaboration. Awareness about who has the relevant knowledge about particular requirements, and who is available and accessible for collaboration, becomes the key enabler for effective collaboration in requirements-centric teams. In our case study, although there was not a clear relationship between distances and whether or not a developer was aware of a remote team member who can help him on his requirements, distance did affect the frequency of communication and access to this person. Despite the fact that a developer may know which remote member to contact regarding the requirements he is working on, that person was perceived as being difficult to communicate with.

Collaboration tools must be able to leverage information that is not always electronic in order to maintain awareness in distributed teams. Although expertise seeking and requesting assistance is typically supported by informal communication in colocated teams, distributed teams lack this communication depth and are left with the inability to know who works on the same requirements and to whom changes should be propagated for effective cross-site coordination efforts. Mechanisms that aim at providing awareness information will have to use sources of information such as elements of the project environment (e.g., who created or changed a requirement in the requirements specification, or who tested a requirement) to understand the current status of the project and who the relevant collaborators to avoid failures in the project are.

Collaborative tools should be able to facilitate unplanned collaborative work among software team members, as well as initial contact among team members working on the same and interrelated requirements. Because requirements-centric teams have dynamic membership, they reflect what we called *emerging interactions,* or interactions between members initially allocated to work on the respective requirement and those outside this network but who posses knowledge relevant to the requirement. For effective collaboration, tools must be able to (1) allow expertise finding when and such that these emerging interactions do occur, and (2) maintain current (or activity) awareness among the members of these dynamic requirements-centered social networks, without overloading them.

Tools that create and maintain RCSNs automatically help managers identify gaps in communication and awareness, prompting the need for improvements in process or project communication infrastructure. In our study, the fact that those who communicated more were also more aware, as well as the considerable reliance on verbal communication or local experts (project members kept aware of each other through regular meetings or unplanned interactions), raises important questions for tool development, such as, What type of local or verbal interaction facilitates the maintenance of this awareness? How can an awareness system replicate it in the distributed interaction? Which information from the development environment can be collected by such an awareness system automatically in order to supply it to the project members? With more studies practitioners should also benefit from additional investigation of the impact of other factors such as work (process) or ethnic culture on awareness. While we only sought to correlate awareness with communication in this study, it is also possible that awareness was maintained as a result of certain procedures for knowledge dissemination in project meetings (process), or may have been hindered due to different communication styles across sites.

Chapter 32

Practice: Educating Global Software Engineering

Gopalaswamy Ramesh, Chandrashekar Ramanathan, and Sowmyanarayanan Sadagopan, International Institute of Information Technology, Bangalore (IIIT-B), India

Summary: This chapter provides a case study from India and shows how to train and educate students for globally distributed software projects. The case study highlights relevant themes and guidance from previous chapters in a concrete project context. It offers valuable insights toward how to train people in your own company, and how to utilize university education to grow international awareness and globalization skills.

BACKGROUND

Over the past 15 years or so, there has been a sea change in the Indian IT industry scenario that has had a significant effect on the Software Engineering Education landscape. In this section, we will look at the factors that have changed the software industry in India, the three "waves" of evolution of software industry in India, and the demands that this evolution places on the kind of skills that Indian engineers are expected to possess to succeed in the competitive global marketplace. This section is a case study of the methods adopted by a premier academic institution (IIIT-B) in India to equip the students with these skills and the lessons we learned in this process. Over the past 10 years, IIIT-B has graduated more than 1,100 students who have been successful entrepreneurs or have been successful in large multi-national corporations, working in world-class global software engineering projects and products.

Three factors changed the course of the Indian IT industry in the early-to-mid 1990s. First, Indian companies matured to have effective processes that enabled scalability of operations without compromising quality. This is amply demonstrated by the fact that India has the highest number of CMMI Maturity Level 5 certified organizations in the world. Second, the blossoming of Internet suddenly removed

Global Software and IT: A Guide to Distributed Development, Projects, and Outsourcing,
First Edition. Christof Ebert.
© 2012 the Institute of Electrical and Electronics Engineers, Inc. Published 2012 by
John Wiley & Sons, Inc.

all communication and distance barriers. Teams in India and in several locations across the globe could work collaboratively to produce state-of-the-art software products. Time difference and geographic separation suddenly became non-issues. Third, India, as a local market, started blossoming. Not only did Indian companies start adopting products and solutions like Enterprise Resource Planning (ERP), Customer Relationship Management (CRM) and Supply Chain Management (SCM) to streamline their businesses and provide a competitive edge, but also new markets that encouraged innovation and entrepreneurship started to emerge in India. Indian matrimony (which is of unique Indian ethos) and local cultural, religious, and business opportunities sprang to the forefront, with applications like bharatmatrimony.com, eprarthana.com, and so on. In addition, in areas like mobile telephony, India more than compensated for missing out on earlier parts of the telecom revolution by being one of the most vibrant markets in the world. Thus, the presence of local markets in India spurred new changes in the software scenario which were hitherto unknown in India.

All these changes had significant ramifications of the role that typical Indian engineers played in the global market. During the past 15 years or so, Indian software industry has gone through three "waves" of evolution. In the first wave (that actually started the IT age in India in the 1970s), it was looked at as a source of resources (*Resource Model*) that were to be managed, controlled, and directed by a team in another location; these resources were either "onshore" or "offshore."I In the second wave, it was given the leeway of being able to take on independent management of a downstream activity like programming, testing, and maintenance (*Life-cycle Model*). In the third wave, it graduated to being a peer team to other global teams that were engaged in the entire life-cycle of a product and fully tied into current versions and technologies (*Integrated Team Model*)[Ramesh09].

This change in the nature of engagement of Indian software industry with the global marketplace in these three waves has necessitated some significant transitions that Indian engineers needed to make. Some of these transitions are (Table 32.1):

Dependent → Independent → Interdependent. The work carried out in the first wave was in the "work-to-specs" mode. This placed a complete dependency for the Indian engineer on getting detailed instructions or "specs" from his "Project Lead" in another part of the world. If the specs were not clear, the execution stopped, almost as if it was an automaton. In the second phase, when they started working on independent chunks, for example, on maintenance of an older release of a product or on a life-cycle activity such as testing, they needed to make independent decisions, but still they were not fully integrated into the high-risk, high visibility, mainstream products and releases. In the third phase, the Indian engineers are now expected to work collaboratively as peers in globally distributed teams, working on current versions, technologies and products. This necessitates strong soft skills fostering communication and teamwork as well as being ranked among the best in the world in their respective work areas.

Tool smith → Technology savvy → Customer-oriented. Indian engineers who, in the first wave, were specialists in programming languages (or manual

Table 32.1   Necessary Skills Required for Each of Three Introduction Approaches

Attribute	Wave 1: Resource Model	Wave 2: Life Cycle Model	Wave 3: Integrated Team Model
Independent thinking	Complete dependency on specs	Moderate dependency on specs	Peers required to carry on work without being spoon fed and being able to guide others to think
Management Structure	Dependent resources	Independent Management	Inter-dependent teams
Nature of proficiency	Tool smith; proficiency in a tool or programming language	Familiarity with the entire technology stack or life cycle operations	Awareness of and empathy with customer requirements
Nature of knowledge	Know *how*; purely mechanical	Know *what*; got a more complete idea of the specs, without knowing exactly why the specs are what they are	Know *why*: Understand the rationale for the specs; look at it from customer viewpoint; even conceptualize the product and visualize the product;
Nature of products	Near end-of-life products; low risk	More recent technologies and versions; moderate risk	Most current technologies and products; high risk and visibility

testing), worked in silos of their own modules or programs, had to graduate to knowing the entire technology stack in the second wave. In the third wave, with the advent of collaborative, state-of-the-art work with significant market exposure, the Indian engineers had to develop customer-centricity, being able to visualize the customer needs and being able to map these to the technology landscape.

Know-how → Know-what → Know-why. All the above factors have necessitated the need for an awareness of the bigger picture on the part of the Indian engineer. A clear understanding of why they were doing what they were doing became vital to the success as the "how" and "what" kept changing really quickly with rapid strides in technology. This emphasis on "know why" transformed the Indian engineer to innovate ideas and products, instead of just execution of tasks.

Near end-of-life → "N-1" State → Current Technologies. In the first wave, Indian engineers dealt with low-risk, near-end-of-life products; in the second wave, they took on a more recent product release that was still in widespread use (and thus of higher risk); in the third phase, they worked on the most current leading edge technology and product versions. This required the education system to keep pace with the current technologies.

In this entire quest, Bangalore was becoming the center stage of global software engineering roots in India. Several reputed product companies like Bosch, Siemens, Texas Instruments, Motorola, and Oracle started setting up software development centers in Bangalore. Indian IT majors like Infosys started making Bangalore their home base.

RESULTS

It was in this context that IIIT-Bangalore (IIIT-B) was formed as a government–industry partnership. While the vision and mission for IIIT-B to be a key player in the global IT scenario to focus on global software engineering was very clear, there were some significant challenges and opportunities presented by the Indian IT education scenario. Some of these were generically "India-centric." We will look at these India-centric challenges in engineering education before going into some of the specific issues we faced at IIIT-B.

Large volume. Indian engineering student pool is one of the largest in the world. Just to give you an idea, the neighboring state of Tamil Nadu boasts of being one of the largest sources of engineers, with close to 230 colleges and approximately 60,000 engineers of different disciplines churned out every year. The State of Karnataka (Bangalore is the capital city for the state of Karnataka) has 138 engineering colleges and 55,000 seats. This large volume leads to some scalability issues that are perhaps unheard of in other places.

Lowest common denominator syndrome. One of the issues that the large volume throws up is that not all students are of the same caliber. More importantly, not all colleges or faculty in the colleges are equally competent. The goal of the evaluation pattern was not to identify top talent, but to ensure that no "injustice" is done to the "weaker" sections that were at a disadvantage because of lack of resources. As a result, the emphasis degenerated to encourage mere rote learning.

Low industry-academia collaboration. The industry-academia collaboration which truly was one of the reasons for success in the Western countries was conspicuous by their absence (or at least presence in very limited pockets). This had two effects: First, a majority of the students who came out were not employable, and second, a majority of the faculty did not get exposure to industry practices. This, combined with the lowest common denominator syndrome discussed above, acted as a deterrent for the teachers and students to make their knowledge relevant to industry a very unrewarding experience.

At IIIT-B, we were cognizant of the above generic challenges and made a few strategic decisions upfront:

- We chose to have a presence only in the Masters level, at least to start with. This enabled us to take students with a higher level of maturity and caliber, and thus not concern ourselves with the lowest common denominator syndrome.

- We will restrict the class strength to about 100–120.
- We will have a strong and sustained collaboration with the industry.
- We will provide exposure and expertise in an all-around manner, not just limit ourselves to mere "technical excellence." We decided that exposure to areas like Marketing, Finance, and Soft Skills were absolutely essential for our students to be "industry-ready".

We will now discuss some challenges that we faced (that were unique to the IIIT-B mission and strategy) that we had to overcome for us to achieve our lofty goals. The students who entered the program came from a diversity of engineering backgrounds which included Computer Science and Engineering and Information Technology, as well as other disciplines. This diversity posed some challenges to us. For example, the non-CSE/IT students needed basic grounding in subjects such as data structures, object orientation, and databases, while these subjects were already completed by the students from CSE/IT backgrounds. The course was designed to be a two-year program, with the last semester fully dedicated to an industry internship. This meant that we had only three semesters to cover a variety of subjects to the diverse set of students. Obviously, this placed a heavy burden on both the teaching staff and the students.

In order to ensure that the students achieved both breadth and depth (in a chosen area), we introduced the concept of areas of specialization. In addition to gaining mastery over the basics, each student had to choose an area of specialization.

Getting industry practitioners to teach. The practitioners who were willing to teach were already busy with their deadlines and getting them to visit our campus on a regular basis was not easy. The geographical distribution of the software companies within Bangalore and the distances compounded with road traffic problems did not make it any easier.

Goal of providing all-around exposure. We needed to get the students exposed to the so-called non-technical subjects like Marketing. The mindset of "I am an engineer and why should I learn this?" had to be removed for the students to be motivated enough to get an insight into these areas.

GETTING STUDENTS READY FOR GLOBAL SOFTWARE ENGINEERING

We need to produce well-rounded, industry-ready graduates who become valuable contributors to the global software engineering scenario. In this section, we will describe our approach and some of the specific things we did to achieve this goal.

We realized that global software engineering has two components. First is the *software engineering* component, on top of which comes the *global* component. In order to address the software engineering component, we took the following approach.

Highlighting real-life, all-around activities. Through all the courses, the students got to understand and appreciate the importance of all the different life-cycle phases that make up software engineering and product development. For example:

- Students were encouraged to conceptualize product ideas, rather than being "given" run-of-the-mill projects.

- Students had to understand and apply standards for performing the various software engineering activities. They used standards like the IEEE Standard for documenting requirements [IEEE98a, IEEE98b], got exposure to review mechanisms like Fagan Inspection [Fagan76], and so on. This indoctrinated them to the best practices of global software engineering.

- Students got a solid grounding in foundational and architectural aspects of building a software product. For this, the students had to finish a set of core courses (Table 32.2). The core courses not only had courses related to traditional Computer Science, but also factored in courses on Accounting and Finance, Marketing and Strategy, Industry-oriented software engineering, and Technical Communication. This was in keeping with our strategy and objectives of providing an all-around background.

Table 32.2   Curriculum at IIIT-B: Core and Foundation Courses

Prep-Semester Courses		
Course Number	Course Name	Credits
PS 101	Introductory Programming	1
PS 102	Mathematics	1
PS 103	Information Systems Analysis and Design	1
Core Courses		
Course Number	Course Name	Credits
CS 101	Algorithms	4
DB 101	Data Management	4
SE 101	Object-Oriented Design	4
NC 101	Networking and Communication	4
CS 110	Operating Systems	4
SE 110	Industry-Oriented Software Engineering	4
MG 581	Accounting and Finance	3
MG 582	Marketing and Strategy	3
MG 583	Technical Communication	3

- A systematic approach of product development was encouraged and even mandated. Process disciplines like maintaining a Requirements Traceability Matrix through a project were also experimented.

- Independent testing of students' work was part of the grading criteria [Desikan06]. Just like in a global software engineering environment, we experimented with a team's product being tested independently by another team playing the role of a customer performing acceptance testing.

- The importance of maintenance in real-life software development was stressed by making the students recognize some of the popular models like the Follow the Sun model which leverages India's geographical time zone position to maximize work opportunities [Ramesh06].

Stressing the importance of support activities such as configuration management or software maintenance. Often in academic institutions, students develop small programs, and then, after the assignment or course gets completed, the programs are discarded. This seldom represents what happens in real life. Issues like change control, configuration management, reviews, effective testing, process compliance, and maintenance assume paramount importance in real-life globally distributed teams. Most university curricula in India make, at most, a passing mention about these vital issues; in our program, we emphasize these issues and give opportunities for students to practice some of these tasks.

Consciously having industry people come and teach classes. As mentioned earlier, this is an integral and central part of our strategy. Through interactions with such faculty, students gained a number of advantages that would stand them in good stead in the industry.

- The practitioners were able to bring to the table "state of the art practices" and highlight what works and what does not work in real-life.

- The practitioners provided exposure to the students on the effective use of tools that increase productivity and quality of deliverables

- The students got to "learn by observation" some of the traits like effective presentation from these seasoned practitioners.

Obviously, this did not come without any hardship to the students. In order to accommodate the busy schedules of the visiting industry people, classes were scheduled over the weekends. But this extra effort that the students put in made them cherish the benefits even more.

Going beyond mere comprehension and rote reproduction. Very early in our evolution, we made a conscious decision not to fall prey to just testing rote learning aspects of a course. Mere comprehension and reproduction was not sufficient. In terms of Bloom's taxonomy of learning, we wanted the students to master the higher levels of learning, such as application, analysis, evaluation, and synthesis [Bloom56]. The evaluation pattern for all the courses stressed on these higher level objectives.

For example, instead of asking the students to enumerate different types of black box testing, we would present them with different scenarios and ask them to choose the most appropriate method. This approach stirs the higher level of learning that is necessary to facilitate taking initiative and making decisions without expecting someone to spoon feed micro-instructions to them all the time. In the context of moving to life-cycle model and integrated team model of global software engineering teams, this was a giant step forward.

Emphasizing originality, out-of-the-box thinking, and creativity. A number of our courses expect students to carry out projects that demonstrate the ability to analyze and apply the concepts taught in that course as well as integrate and synthesize the concepts learned in other courses. As mentioned earlier, these self-initiated projects instilled a competitive sense in the students. In the course of a single semester, they were able to conceptualize and design interesting and innovative applications like a complete travel planning and reservation system, project work bench, news aggregator, and so on.

For addressing the *global* component, some of the methods adopted include:

Setting non-negotiable value systems. The objective of the program was not just to get technical excellence, but also to instill some basic value systems into students that will stand them in good stead in the global arena. Some of these were:

- Creativity is rewarded. This was the case whether it was evaluation of tests and exams or in projects.
- Open communication is encouraged. For example, students could give open feedback about the courses
- Ethics is constantly emphasized. We even offered a course on ethics and on issues like emotional intelligence to instill the students with a more humane approach to life

Encouraging teamwork and communication. The courses gave opportunities for fostering teamwork and communication. When the students did group projects, they were made to share with the class what each of them contributed. In order to ensure there was participation from all the members, different team members were made to present different parts of the project.

Simulating real-life environments during courses and projects. We used several novel methods to simulate real-life environments for the students' projects. (See also the inset below). First of all, we made sure the students didn't do "toy" projects, but were able to do projects that have a semblance of reality. We also made sure they understood that projects in the real world aren't done by one-man armies, but by demanding and rewarding teamwork and communication.

In order to emphasize that software engineering practices cut across application domains, students were allowed to do software engineering course projects by choosing projects within their respective areas of specialization (e.g., networking and communication, embedded systems, banking) and guided by domain experts in those areas. This allowed the students to appreciate the fact that software engineering processes and practices are applicable in any type of software development project.

We designed and offered a unique course called "Global Software Project Management," where we went beyond vanilla project management issues such as SDLC or WBS and tried to simulate a team that is run in a globally distributed team. Here, we paired up teams, with one team acting as the "customer" for the other team and vice versa. For example, when the first team produced a SRS document, it was reviewed by the second team who did the design using the SRS. Whenever the second team found any gaps in the SRS, they either had to make some reasonable assumptions or had to ask the SRS team. This way, we short circuited the typical scenario when students don't write proper SRS because they are confident they can make up for it all in the coding stage. We simulated the global environment by forcing the team to communicate only by e-mail and allowing, at most, two phone calls during the course of the semester. No personal contact was allowed in discussion of the project. While we obviously would not be able to enforce this, we evaluated this by looking at how effectively they documented the minutes of such meetings, as well as how well they carried forward action items. We taught them sessions on e-mail etiquette and phone etiquette so that they knew how to write good e-mail and participate meaningfully in phone calls, both essential traits for global software engineering. We also had a course on software testing that included aspects of software maintenance. During this course, we made the students produce studies on popular SDLC tools that support globally distributed environments like the ones from IBM Rational, Borland, and so on. This made them study these tools and made them ready for the real-world global environment. Another innovation we attempt in the software testing course is to encourage the students to contribute to the testing of open source projects. Students get involved with one specific open-source project of their choice. The aim again is to give them a truly global exposure of working in large virtual teams and mentors spread across the world. The success of this experiment is yet to be ascertained as the term is still in progress.

Enhancing soft skills. Soft skills are comprised of attitude, communication, and etiquette [Ramesh10]. By our non-negotiable value systems and by the staff members themselves conforming to the values and being role models, we laid the foundation for good attitudes. We provided many opportunities for students to improve their communication and leadership skills. This included a course on business communication as a part of the core curriculum, and a primer on good e-mail and phone etiquette as a part of the Global Software Project Management course. We also gave them exposure to working under pressure while not slipping on quality or values. There were a number of extra-curricular activities that required the students to develop their initiative and leadership skills. With IIIT-B's emphasis on the all-around learning and not just a mere "teaching shop" approach, there were opportunities for learning yoga and music, playing indoor and outdoor games, as well as sensitizing students to social activities, including visits to orphanages and organizing regular blood donation camps. All this ensured that we were able to sharpen and develop necessary soft skills in the students in order to enable them to compete better in the global software engineering marketplace.

IIIT-B has graduated more than 1,100 students. These students are well placed in reputed MNCs as well as Indian IT majors. There have also been successful entrepreneurs. One of our students, Padmanabhan, who is a co-founder of the startup 8KMiles.com says: "What I learned as a student at IIIT-B in Global Software Engineering and the finer aspects of communication and collaboration and remote project management apart from an understanding about the foundations of requirements engineering, estimation, design, development, and elaborate testing as part of the complete SDLC, has helped me immensely in real life: First, while working on many globally distributed projects with teams spread between U.S., UK, and India; and currently by applying it as a core concept in my own start-up and also while hiring talent for my team, clearly knowing what skills I need to look for in people for projects that are truly global." Another student, Manish Thaper, currently working in GE Healthcare says: "My stay at IIIT-B helped me realize that building a software system is no less than devising a new product in any other engineering branch. Developing software is not just writing algorithms, but needs to address plans, resources, tools, costs, quality measurements, delays, patterns, and much more. We also realized that, in the global scenario, non-functional requirements like performance, scalability, reliability, and security are vitally important to build world-class software and that too with an ever improving delivery speed."

Feedback such as that mentioned above underlines that training on global software and IT competences will effectively build world-class software engineers who are ready to make a significant contributions to global software engineering.

TAKE-AWAY TIPS

Teaching truly global-scale software engineering is highly necessary to prepare students for business needs, but it is challenging. We conclude with brief take-away tips for any educational institution trying to create world-class talent in global software engineering. Any institution chartered with training people to work in the offshore and distributed environment should ensure the following:

- Software engineering should be projected as a discipline rather than a stand-alone course. The principles and practices of software engineering should be interwoven in all the courses.
- Success in distributed environments requires appreciation of communication challenges in such environments. The students will be industry-ready only by being exposed to the use of the soft skills required for such environments
- Evaluation of students should be on the basis of projects which test both the engineering practices as well as the effective use of related processes such as reviews or communication.

- Students will maximize their learning by constant interactions with industry professionals. Having such professionals teach some of the courses, as well as having the students spend an extended duration in the industry as a part of an internship, will have immense benefits to both the industry and students.

We have been constantly refining and fine-tuning our approach because each time we tried to do something new we have learned a lot.

Part V

Advancing Your Own Business

Chapter 33

Key Take-Away Tips

Summary: Managing global software development is not easy and has high-risk exposure to lowering overall productivity. Still, if risks are managed well, the positive impacts dominate. This chapter will summarize major take-away tips from this book, without repeating what was highlighted before.

There are five major lessons from global software engineering and IT, namely right-shoring, establishing and enforcing shared values, improving process maturity, accountability for results, and managing risks. Together, these five building blocks will assure that your global software engineering and IT will not fall to pieces.

RIGHTSHORE ACCORDING TO NEEDS

 Teams working on a coherent task should not be split across sites. A task should be handled in a place with team members being as close as possible.

Colocation of related development drives the necessary informal communication that is the driver of good architecture and improved reuse (i.e., sharing best practices, challenging results in due time). Global software engineering activities should be done in a few rather big development centers rather than many small teams. This assures flexibility of assignment due to a big pool of readily accessible resources. Turnover can be more easily managed in bigger teams and demands fewer buffer needs. Big sites facilitate horizontal mobility. With horizontal mobility you foster engineering flexibility and motivation. Rightshoring drives improved load and pipeline management. Management overheads are reduced with fewer, but larger, offshore centers. If hardware or systems development is coupled with the software engineering, the integration testing activities should always be at the site of the hardware development and prototyping. Software ships more easily than hardware in case of small updates. Rightshoring also implies mixing legacy and innovative products across sites. Having legacy in one center makes that center unattractive with low motivation and increased turnover rates. After a defined period of roughly

Global Software and IT: A Guide to Distributed Development, Projects, and Outsourcing,
First Edition. Christof Ebert.
© 2012 the Institute of Electrical and Electronics Engineers, Inc. Published 2012 by
John Wiley & Sons, Inc.

three years, engineers should be reassigned to a different product in order to keep flexibility on sufficiently high level.

ESTABLISH AND ENFORCE SHARED VALUES

 Agree with the critical stakeholders across sites on a small set of values that would be used to drive target setting, performance monitoring, and so on.

Consider regional, cultural, religious and other behavioral impacts and treat them so that employees understand and feel understood. Where there are clear discrepancies between different value sets of behavioral factors across the involved societies and teams, speak openly about it and find a shared solution. Never sweep those discrepancies under the carpet, as they will haunt you forever!

We found in a company with a captive development center in Asia that different time perception created frustration in teams. For instance, a designer from Asia was allocated to a critical project, but would not appear for telephone conferences. When asked why, he explained that a relative was sick. This happened quite often until we found out that the person was simply not used to keeping such time commitments to the minute. We established some guidelines to avoid misperceptions and frustration in teams (e.g., appear at meetings no more than 5 minutes late or you will pay X amount of money in penalty) which employees have to obey inside the projects or company.

Shared values must be enforced rigorously because they direct behaviors and all operational activities across the teams. If employees find that managers themselves appear late at meetings they will be late as well. If employees find that their managers don't keep commitments or do not follow performance objectives, they themselves won't.

IMPROVE PROCESS MATURITY

 Assure that your processes are in good shape before they are used in a global context.

A CMMI maturity level 3 for different sites and partners helps for successful collaboration in global projects. This can also be achieved by means of COBIT and ITIL, as well as clearly enforcing process discipline. Rigorously enforce using the agreed standard process that relates to a high-maturity organization pattern. Provide an interactive process model based on accepted practices that allows tailoring processes for the specific needs of a project or even a team.

Organizations on CMMI maturity levels 1 or 2 should not expect that global software engineering would yield immediate benefits. Instead, it will reveal major deficiencies in processes and workflow which create all type of difficulties, such as insufficient quality, delays, additional cost, cancelled offshoring contracts, unmotivated workforce in both places (previous and new), and much more. The most viable approach for such low-maturity organizations is to use external support and ramp-up the home processes before proceeding with global software engineering and IT.

On the other hand, we have seen, from previous experiences in ramping-up big internal software teams in Eastern Europe, India, and China, that solid processes not only accelerate introduction of outsourcing/offshoring, but also serve as a safety net to assure the right training, good management practices, and so on.

We did one controlled experiment when setting up Chinese development teams. The building of a distributed team was fastest and most reliable in the case in which the parent organization (product line) was on maturity level 3. We also did it with lower-maturity parent organizations and learned that the maturity level 2 organizations could manage with some external support, while the maturity 1 organization almost failed.I It took us quite some effort to build their processes and train the workforce on the parent side.

HOLD PEOPLE ACCOUNTABLE FOR RESULTS

 Assure that each piece of work always has one defined owner.

Ownership is crucial for engineering tasks and this holds specifically in software development with the many built-in interfaces and dependencies. As soon as a team is responsible with people scattered in different reporting lines or around the world, it is impossible to assure good quality and reliable commitments. Each person in such an endeavor would normally have his own priority setting and not work toward a shared goal. Team building will help, but not solve, the issue because the lack of vision and shared objectives has a deep impact. It is, therefore, absolutely clear that any global development team must have one single agenda and must be measured on mutually shared objectives. Work products must have, for the same reason, a single owner, not a pair of programmers in different sites where one would always wait for the other to do his homework. Ownership assures accountability.

People who know what the piece of work is used for and what it eventually brings toward the customer are much more eager to deliver high quality and assure that commitments are kept. If they feel like a small wheel in a complex organization, they rely on "the others" and on "management" to get conflicts resolved. This creates immediate trouble in global projects and outsourcing. Managers in such situations should refrain from micromanaging and instead split work into meaningful tasks with clear links to global objectives and track the earned value as an externally tangible measurement for each team.

CONTINUOUSLY MANAGE RISKS

 Manage uncertainties and risks on a continuous basis. Don't consider any of your business case assumptions as being stable.

The unexpected happens because we become focused on managing what we can foresee and imagine. However, especially in global software engineering and IT, lots of unexpected events can happen. At the moment where you have settled all project risks and closely collaborated with all stakeholders, you can be sure that a global communications link will break down, some of your key designers will decide to leave, or a civil war or disease will start in one of your offshore centers. Note that outsourcing/offshoring has more and different risks than what you are used to hearing from general folklore. Build trust face-to-face to rely in critical situations on all stakeholders worldwide. With mutual respect and trust, remote execution becomes much easier.

Perform SWOT (strength, weakness, opportunity, threat) analysis on a yearly basis. Control attrition of engineers well in advance. Establish the right set of indicators. Promote your valuable engineers and managers. Assign them technical challenges. Check how critical skills can be replicated without many overheads. Control budget and prepare for changing cost. Relatively low-base labor costs are typically loaded with various additional costs, for example, interface management, translation, necessary managerial levels. Offshore salaries tend to increase much faster than in Europe. Review cost of engineering and project cost structure periodically. Allow, where appropriate, for local contracts with suppliers and tools vendors. Global suppliers (for tools or components) often charge less to Asian local companies.

LESSONS LEARNED ALONG THE LIFE-CYCLE

There are many more lessons learned that we captured in this book together with examples and explanations. As a take-away tip, we will summarize some of the best practices that we have identified over the past years that clearly support global software development.

INITIATION

- **Foster communication.** Provide sufficient communication means, such as video conferencing or shared workspaces and global software libraries. Assure that English is the language for all communication in the company. Provide language training to all exposed engineers. Enforce the use of the English language even in meetings and e-mails. Set up a project homepage for each project that summarizes project content, progress measurements, planning information, and team-specific information.

- **Implement a sound business model.** Decide on a global software engineering and IT business model (e.g., external vs. internal offshoring). Determine a clear business plan (why offshoring, what expectations). Evaluate different alternatives by means of business case (e.g., suppliers, sites, products).

- **Assure stakeholder buy-in.** Agree on strategy and mid-term goals with all impacted stakeholders. Assure that all stakeholders understand and support strategy and goals. This includes sites, projects, and different functions. Visit impacted sites to build relationships. Never globalize only on the basis of low cost. Make offshore labs equal partners.

- **Select the right people.** Establish recruiting strategies if you decide to grow your own team at a new site. An effective recruiting strategy assures that talent is chosen consistently considering a number of criteria, such as cultural awareness, language skills, technical skills, or process and social competences.

- **Carefully ramp-up.** Grow stepwise. Learn from errors. Execute pilot project within defined scope. Carefully analyze lessons learned and use that knowledge for future risk mitigation. Start small and carefully evaluate relationships, results, growth potential, market, and customers.

EXECUTION

- **Enforce specific objectives.** Agree and communicate the respective project targets, such as quality, milestones, content, or resource allocation at a project's start. Similarly, at phases or increments, start team targets are adjusted and communicated to facilitate effective internal team management. Assure that there is always a specification describing *what* has to be done (we call it customer requirements for simplicity) for any task or project or product being developed in a global development mode. Also ensure that there is a second specification which is linked to the first for traceability and consistency reasons describing *how* this will be done by the remote team. Having these two documents enforces understanding of the task at hand and fosters accountability later on.

- **Define interfaces and responsibilities.** Make individual teams responsible for their results. Define which teams are involved and what they are going to do in which location at beginning of projects. This includes a focus on allocation rules such as scattering or collocation.

- **Monitor progress.** Continuously manage risk. Mitigate risks related to contract, people, business, and IPR up-front. Manage projects, risks, and

Table 33.1 Effectively Mitigating Global Software Engineering and IT Risks

Mitigations	Risks								
	Engineers are not available in due time	Insufficient project management	Poor specifications and documents	Quality deficiencies are recognized too late	Frequent changes create extra cost	Inconsistencies and incompatibilities	Intellectual property infringement	Instabilities in a host country	Inadequate supplier management
Rightshoring	x							x	x
Establish and enforce shared values	x	x		x	x	x	x		x
Process maturity		x	x	x	x	x			x
Accountability	x	x		x					
Manage risks	x	x					x	x	x
Foster communication		x	x	x	x	x			x
Implement sound business model		x							x
Assure stakeholder buy-in	x	x							x

	1	2	3	4	5	6	7	8
Select right people	x	x						
Carefully ramp up	x	x						x
Enforce specific objectives	x	x		x			x	
Define interfaces and responsibles								
Monitor progress			x	x	x	x	x	
Train people and enhance competences	x			x		x	x	
Maintain global pool of talent	x			x			x	
Manage configurations			x	x	x	x		x
Use the right tools			x	x				
Rotate management	x						x	

assumptions. Within each project follow-up continuously on the top-ten risks, which, in a global project, are typically less technical than managerial. Always compare against written agreements. Ensure that commitments exist in written and controlled form.

- **Train people and enhance competences.** Plan and provide training and coaching to all levels (engineers and management).

- **Maintain global pool of talent.** Overlook turnover rates of engineers in remote countries. Rates depend on countries and it is the objective of a local site manager to assure that his own turnover rate is in the upper quartile of the respective country. Set up mixed teams from different countries to integrate individual cultural background toward a corporate and project-oriented spirit. While having one project leader who is fully responsible to achieve project targets, assign him a project management team that represents the major cultures within the project.

- **Manage configurations.** Rigorously enforce tools for configuration management and build management rules (e.g., branching, merging, synchronization frequency) and provide the necessary tool support. Synchronize different versions or variants. Install necessary tools for configuration management (defect tracking, change management, build control, product data management, product life-cycle management, etc.).

- **Use suitable tools.** Evidently, remote work needs more tools support than being in one place does. It starts with communication links and includes all types of tools support from basic infrastructure up to collaborative engineering tools. Look into what tools suites offer the best possible interworking (e.g., traceability between different work products or alert mechanisms in case of changes). Secure tools access both internally and externally. Back up decentrally and periodically. Have a tools expert in each site to avoid lengthy and unproductive wait periods. Don't rely on centralized license management and tools installations. If you have central licenses, make sure that engineers can still work even if a link falls down. Avoid vendor lock-in. The first tool to buy is always easy, afterward, however, many mechanisms work that all try to lock you with a single vendor.

- **Rotate management.** Assure that management of different sites knows other locations and cultures to create the necessary awareness for cultural diversity and how to cope with it.

These best practices can be mapped to the risk list which we introduced in Chapter 21. Table 33.1 shows how these global software engineering and IT risks can be mitigated by best practices.

To be successful with globalized software and IT, companies typically demand external support in domains that they are not really familiar with:

- Evaluating and judging the business model and strategy.
- Assessing and mitigating risks before sourcing is started.

- Improving engineering and management processes (ALM, PLM).
- Introducing knowledge management.
- Benchmarking suppliers.
- Setting up appropriate contract and SLA.
- Establishing supplier-management processes.
- Independently reviewing quality and performance.

Chapter 34

Global Software and IT Rules of Thumb

Summary: In order to effectively plan global software engineering and IT, you need your own history database with baselines for estimation, quality planning, and the like. However, you might not have this data available yet, or it may not yet be scalable for global development projects. This chapter will provide facts and rules of thumb from our experiences in global software engineering and IT projects.

Assume that you have a supplier and want to check his estimates and later follow his planning. How much effort is necessary? What overheads have been factored in? Is the supplier offering a low price, but will later fail? Everybody, at some point in time, is in bootstrapping mode with the need for some concrete data. Where do you get such initial data? We started looking into books and conference proceedings, cost estimation tools, and lots of our own project lessons learned. We gradually extracted some simple rules of thumb that we could use even in situations where no historic information was accessible. This is what you will find here. The list is far from complete, and it is certainly not as scientific as one would like, but it is a start. The data stems from our own history databases, as well as from a number of external sources, such as estimation tools or project management literature [Ebert07a, Jones07, Lyu95, McConnell98, Rivard08, Sangwan07].

Project planning is based on size, schedule and productivity. A good predictor is the Putnam formula that states that effort in a project is proportional in size to the power of 3 divided by duration to the power of 4 and divided again by productivity to the power of 3. The minimum project duration in months is 2.5 times effort in person-years to the power of 1/3.

Team size is roughly the square root of effort in person-months. This means that a task with 10 person-months estimated effort should be done with 3 persons. Obviously, high independencies inside the task allow for more persons, and thus, shorter durations. However, most probably, the task was specified too broadly and should first be broken down in smaller tasks, such as 10 tasks with 1 person-month effort, done by 10 persons.

Engineering productivity can be rather easily improved by 5%–10% per year. This is done by means of CMMI or specific improvement activities. More than the 10% are difficult to achieve, but are, in some industries, inevitable due to competitive pressure.

Duration of a task or project (given that all other factors are known) can be improved by up to 25% in one shot by improving productivity. This implies excellent team building and teamwork, strong planning and monitoring on the critical path, strong method and tools support, high parallelism, and early defect removal. Such mechanisms are not sustainable and demand strong follow-up. They bear the risk of high stress levels and attrition of team members if pressure is maintained for too long.

Allocating engineers to several projects in parallel reduces productivity. Experience shows that productivity is reduced in steps depending on the amount of context switching due to the different assignments (e.g., phone calls from the second project while doing design in the first). As a rule of thumb, consider some 30% productivity decrease if you are working on several independent assignments.

Working in several locations, as we do in global development, costs extra effort. We found in many studies, including own experiences, that with two locations you should budget some 20%–30% overhead and for three to four locations, some 30%–40% overhead. This overhead is due to additional interfaces, management, team effort, collaboration support, quality control, reviews, and so on.

Requirements change with 1%–3% per month normalized to the effort originally estimated. For instance, if the requirements are estimated with 1 person-year, you would expect an additional effort or change impact of 1–2 person-weeks per month. This is not peanuts; it needs to be considered in building change review boards and clear rules for change management. Target a freeze point of your requirements in due time by planning backward from a project's (or task's) end.

Cost of non-quality (i.e., defect detection and correction after the activity where the defect was introduced) is around 30%–50% of total engineering (project) effort. It is, by far, the biggest chunk in any project that can be reduced to directly and immediately save cost. For global software engineering projects especially, this cost increases due to interface overheads where code or design would be shipped back and forth until defects are retrieved and removed.

The amount of defects at code completion (i.e., code has been finished for a specific component and has passed compilation) can be estimated in different ways. If size in KStmt or KLOC is known, this can be translated into remaining defects. We found some 10–50 defects per KStmt depending on the maturity level of the respective organization. This is based on new or changed code only and does not include any code that is reused or automatically generated. For such codes, the initial formula has to be extended with percentage of defects found by the already completed verification (or validation) steps. An alternative formula takes estimated function points to the power of 1.25.

Verification pays off. Peer reviews and inspections are the least expensive of all manual defect detection techniques. You need some 1–3 person-hours per defect for inspections and peer reviews. Before starting peer reviews or inspections, all tool-supported techniques, such as static and dynamic checking of source code should be fully exploited., Preferably, fully instrumented unit tests should be done before peer reviews. Unit test, static code analyses, and peer reviews are orthogonal techniques that detect different defect classes. Often, cost per defect in unit test is highest amongst the three techniques due to the manual handling of test stubs, test environments, test cases, and so on.

Each verification or validation step can detect and remove some 30% of the defects. That translates into 30% of defects remaining at a certain point of time that can be found with a distinct defect detection technique. This is a cascading approach, in which each cascade (e.g., static checking, peer review, unit test, integration test, system test, beta test) removes each 30% of defects. It is possible to exceed this number slightly toward 40%–50%, but it comes at dramatically increasing cost per defect.

Remaining defects are estimated from estimated total defects and the different detected defects. This allows for planning of verification and validation and allocating necessary time and budget according to quality needs. If 30% of defects are removed per detection activity, then 70% will remain. Defects that remain at the end of the project equal the amount of defects at code completion times 70% to the power of independent detection activities (e.g., code inspection, module test, integration test, system test).

Release quality of software shows that typically 90% of all initial defects at code completion will reach the customer. Depending on the maturity of the software organization, the following defects at release time can be observed: CMMI maturity level 1: 5–60 defects/KStmt; maturity level 2: 3–12 defects/KStmt; maturity level 3: 2–7 defects/KStmt; maturity level 4: 1–5 defects/KStmt; maturity level five: 0.05–1 defects/KStmt. Don't expect high quality in external components from suppliers on low maturity levels, especially if they are not explicitly contracted. Suppliers with high maturity might have low defect rates, but only if they own the entire product or component. Virtual (globally distributed) development demands more quality control, and thus cost of quality, to achieve the same release quality.

Improving release quality needs time: 5% more defects detected before release time translates into a 10%–15% added duration of the project.

New defects are inserted with changes and corrections, specifically those late in a project and done under pressure. Corrections create some 5%–30% new defects depending on time pressure and underlying tool support. Especially late defect removal on the critical path to release causes many new defects because quality assurance activities are undermined, and engineers are stressed. This must be considered when planning testing/validation or maintenance activities.

Test effort can be planned by estimating the necessary test cases. This is done by a target quality level and coverage criteria to be achieved based on operational scenarios and use cases. Starting during the requirements analysis phase, test effort can be estimated by functionality and translates roughly into 0.3–1 test cases per function point. For procedural languages such as C, this translates into 3–7 test cases per KStmt. This is a very rough formula and should be handled with care. Note that, across projects, at least 30% of all test cases are redundant. Such average holds for both legacy and new projects because engineers have the tendency to add test cases "to be on the safe side," but do not control them by means of coverage or related effectiveness criteria. This is an excellent business case in itself toward applying better test management and test coverage tools. Orthogonal test case arrays help in reducing test redundancies.

Maintenance effort for the last level (engineering effort related to defect removal after the welcome desk, etc., had done their job) amounts to 5%–15% of project effort per year. Make sure that this effort is budgeted and staffed before release or you might end up in difficult times with your customers who expect proper SLA management. New and changed functionality (on top of defect corrections) account for 5%–8% of new functionality per year and 10% of functionality being changed per year. Altogether, this translates to one third of project cost being budgeted for maintenance, especially in the first year after release. It will typically decrease thereafter.

The Pareto principle also holds for software engineering. As a rule of thumb, 20% of all components (subsystems, modules, classes) consume 60%–80% of all resources. Some 20% of all components contain 60% of all effective defects. Some 20% of all defects need 60%–80% of correction effort, and 20% of all enhancements require 60%–80% of all maintenance effort. This looks a bit theoretical because, obviously, one can in most cases find a Pareto distribution. However, there are concrete benefits you can utilize to save on effort. For instance, critical components can be identified in the design by static code analysis and verification activities and can then be focused on those critical components.

Chapter 35

The World Remains Flat

Summary: Global software development is not the target per se, but is rather the result of a conscious business-oriented trade-off. The guiding principle is to optimize the cost of engineering while still achieving the most feasible integration of all R&D centers worldwide. Outsourcing/offshoring is driven by acquisitions, setting up development centers in countries that offer necessary skill and resources at same or higher productivity, and presence in key markets. This chapter will get back to the four drivers for global software and IT and provide an outlook for what to expect next. It will certainly stimulate your own ideas on better utilization of globalization and collaboration.

Global software engineering is the consequence of the rather friction-free economic principles of the entire software industry. Basically, any code can be developed at any place in the world and made visible and accessible to any other place in the world at virtually the same time. There are not many overheads in distribution or industrialization as long as source code is shared. Many companies start global development due to perceived cost differences. Achieved cost reductions are further delivered to customers, which means competitive pressure for those enterprises not yet embarking on global development.

Further advantages appear when intensifying global software engineering and IT, such as more flexible work hours for engineers, and a demand-oriented provisioning of skills. Starting with smaller chunks of work, outsourcing/offshoring intensifies toward globalizing the execution of entire business processes or products. Innovative products are created due to having more capacity and more efficient workflows. Product life-cycles and technology growth will further accelerate due to this increasing innovation driven by global software engineering and IT. The principle, as such, is amplified and will not allow any enterprise to exit.

As we have seen in Chapter 2, there are four drivers of fuel globalization, as shown in Figure 35.1: efficiency, presence, talent, and flexibility.

1. **Presence.** Outsourcing/offshoring is part of companies' growth strategies and keeps them accelerating:
   - Broad base for resources, skills, technology, and innovation.
   - New markets at emerging economy sites.

Global Software and IT: A Guide to Distributed Development, Projects, and Outsourcing,
First Edition. Christof Ebert.
© 2012 the Institute of Electrical and Electronics Engineers, Inc. Published 2012 by
John Wiley & Sons, Inc.

4. **Efficiency**:
   Process
   excellence.
   Speed to profit
   ahead of
   competitors.

1. **Presence**:
   Global growth
   strategy.
   Learn from new
   markets.

3. **Flexibility**:
   JIT networks
   across
   organizations.
   Technology
   expertise that
   depends on
   context.

2. **Talent**: Race
   for skilled
   people.
   Value creation
   happens where
   the skills are.

Figure 35.1   The way ahead: four drivers fuel future globalization.

- Mergers and acquisitions.
- Tax optimization, local R&D funding, governmental support.
- Blue Ocean approach to innovative products and services.
- Learning from non-Western research (e.g., Asian medicine).

     Global growth, therefore, is a self-sustaining force. Understanding local markets and being present will boost these markets (e.g., India and China account for 2.5 billion potential customers), which, in turn, will boost consumption and economic growth, which then further amplifies global software and IT. On top of that, global R&D helps to address global problems (e.g., diseases, green energy, water, nutrition).

2. **Talent.** The race for skilled people will create a global talent marketplace. In turn, talented engineers will work at places they enjoy most so that companies will offer space and labs in those areas. Companies will chase after talent offshore, regardless of cost. Success will be determined by global attractiveness to engineers.

3. **Flexibility.** Networks across organizational boundaries will further grow, just in time. We face them today already with suppliers or community source environments in some areas. The organizational layout will move from task-based offshoring with defined relationships to a flexible business process globalization. There will be JIT networks of processes, suppliers, and services around the world. Collaborative networks (e.g., community source, research broker) will further evolve.

4. **Efficiency.** All these factors will only grow if the machine behind them, that is organizational processes and tools, operates at the highest efficiency. Engineering and management processes must tame two diverging forces:
   - Sharing knowledge and skills for innovative products.
   - Protecting results in order to achieve necessary margins to grow.

Process need to facilitate speed, organization, and collaboration. They must leverage investments quickly because of the ever-growing risk of IP loss. The new product life-cycle is determined by the time it takes to copy, compete, and implement processes that provide agility and efficiency. Companies need to balance time-to-profit with time-to-copy. They need to develop an organizational and management strategy for offshoring, along with an economic business case. Collaboration will further grow across disciplines, cultures, time, distance, organizations. This demands a completely new skill set that is currently not taught at universities (e.g., managerial, teaming, sharing without losing).

Outsourcing/offshoring makes deficiencies more visible and it amplifies weaknesses. These deficiencies are always there, with or without global software engineering and IT, but in a global and distributed context they have more impact. The needs for global engineering must be carefully balanced with additional costs that might be incurred only at a later point. This includes staff turnover rates, which vary greatly across the globe; cost overheads related to traveling, relocation, communication, middle management, or redundant development and test equipment; lack of availability of dedicated tools that allow for globally distribution and work environments; impacts of the learning curve which slow down with as more locations are involved; cultural differences which can impact the work climate; insufficient language skills; different legal constraints related to work time, organization, or participation of unions; and building up redundant skills and resource buffers to be prepared for colocated teams and for unforeseen maintenance activities.

We faced all these obstacles and had to deal with them by means of planning, risk management, and communication. Even the best training cannot substitute for extremely cooperative engineers and highly effective management, both of which are oriented toward overall success and not impacted by legacy behaviors.

In the near future, global engineering will evolve into a standard engineering management method that must be mastered by each R&D manager. Processes and product components will increasingly be managed in a global context. Suppliers from many countries will evolve to ease start-up and operations of global software engineering and IT, even for small and mid-sized enterprises in the high-cost countries. Brokers will emerge to help find partners in different parts of the world and manage the offshoring overhead. Cost per headcount will stay low for few years but will steadily increase due to rising standards of living in the emerging countries that contribute to outsourcing/offshoring. Global software engineering and IT have a strong contribution in improving living conditions around the world. Bridging the divide is best approached by sharing values and understanding cultures. Such increasing standards of living in China, India, and many other low-cost countries will generate hundreds of millions of new middle-class people who will demand more information technology.

Unfortunately (for the expensive Western countries), these changing conditions will not have a sustainable positive impact for today's highly paid software engineers. On the other hand, an increasing number of competing software companies will evolve and further push for global alignment of engineering costs (but this time cutting down the top salaries). What looks healthy from a global perspective may have a negative impact on those of us who do not adjust quickly enough to the new work split.

To be successful in a global market, a company should manage the risks of global software development and utilize the positive aspects as drivers to shape the software engineering processes in detail and the culture in general. The challenge is to continuously improve processes, innovativeness, and productivity. IT and software engineering have low entry barriers and a global resource pool. Engineers will have to assess their own competitive value frequently and change gears and functions opportunistically to stay employable. That is the task of all of us software engineers in the future. Those of us who stagnate will be out of business faster than we might think.

History has shown us time and again that mixing genes is the best thing that can be done in the path of evolution. Or, in the words of Charles Darwin, one of the first truly globally acting scientists, "It is not the strongest of the species that survive, or the most intelligent, but the ones most responsive to change." Globalization is, in fact, about the same thing—an embodiment of Darwin's concept.

Appendices

Appendix A

Checklist/Template: Getting Started

Global software and IT cannot be learned on the job. That would be a very expensive exercise. It is smarter and more cost-effective to start with the best practices and then enhance them according to your own specific needs, culture, and risks. These best practices should then lead to your own processes for the different life-cycle phases of the sourcing or offshoring project. This book provides guidance for finding answers to most problems and risks. Here is a simple checklist and template for beginners so that they don't overlook some critical factors.

No.	Check	Your Status / Comments
	Sourcing strategy	
1	Define and implement a company-wide strategy for guiding offshoring evolution–from support to core competences.	
2	Determine a clear business plan (i.e., why outsourcing/ offshoring, which business model, what type of sourcing or captive engagement, what products, etc.).	
3	Agree on an implementation strategy and operational targets.	
4	Determine and agree on the concrete outsourcing and offshoring business case addressing the costs and benefits across its life-cycle.	
5	Evaluate different alternatives by means of business cases (e.g., suppliers, sites, tasks).	

(Continued)

Global Software and IT: A Guide to Distributed Development, Projects, and Outsourcing,
First Edition. Christof Ebert.
© 2012 the Institute of Electrical and Electronics Engineers, Inc. Published 2012 by
John Wiley & Sons, Inc.

No.	Check	Your Status / Comments
6	Ensure senior management support on objectives and the entire program.	
7	Set clear and measurable objectives of what should be achieved by what date.	
8	Assure internal stakeholders buy-in. Get relevant stakeholders in projects and in the line on board.	
9	Set up and agree on a clear governance policy that addresses major outsourcing-/offshoring aspects and which is mandatory for all stakeholders	
10	Consider external expertise and experiences to successfully manage the outsourcing/offshoring program.	
	Initiation and ramp-up	
11	Determine an experienced project manager with full responsibility for the project (i.e., budget, content, and resources). If there are several such projects, determine a strong manager to be totally responsible for the outsourcing/offshoring program, including supplier management.	
12	Set up an effective steering board for the outsourcing/offshoring program with all its projects.	
13	Standardize and document all relevant processes and interfaces between you and your supplier(s).	
14	Reengineer your engineering processes to master the changing needs toward global collaboration. Adapt your processes in engineering, IT, management and controlling to the changed needs of such an outsourcing/offshoring program.	
15	Carefully evaluate how to protect intellectual property while growing global innovation (time-to-profit vs. time-to-copy).	
16	Make sure that your organization exhibits the necessary process maturity to address outsourcing/offshoring and have the processes been assessed on maturity level two (e.g., CMMI-DEV with distributed development, CMMI-ACQ for outsourcing, A-SPICE for the automotive industry, COBIT, and ITIL for IT companies).	
17	Develop global managers and a global workforce management.	
18	Set up clear evaluation criteria for potential suppliers, covering technical, market, and soft factors. Tailor such lists according to specific project needs and risks. Avoid any bias toward a specific supplier.	

No.	Check	Your Status / Comments
19	Select potential suppliers and evaluate them according to agreed upon and written criteria. Ensure that bias is avoided and risks are considered.	
20	Select a supplier who understands your business; target win-win (contract, SLA). Meet the supplier so he understands your culture, specific market, needs, and technical/environmental constraints and products.	
21	Prepare a formal SLA between you and the supplier addressing your targets, risks, escalation, and measurable objectives.	
22	Review the SLA with legal experts and fine-tune.	
23	Review the SLA with the suppliers on feasibility.	
24	Ensure by means of your own processes and SLA that supplier changes, dual supplier structures and knowledge management are adequately addressed.	
25	Set up a steering board with representatives of the supplier. Determine frequent meetings, specifically during the ramp-up and initiation.	
26	Train relevant stakeholders (employees and managers) on outsourcing/offshoring best practices, risks and management skills.	
27	Prepare your engineering teams for global collaboration (e.g., values, awareness). Train relevant stakeholders (employees and managers) on outsourcing/offshoring on soft skills, cultural aspects, and cross-country communication.	
28	Train relevant stakeholders (employees and managers) on your processes applicable for the outsourcing/ offshoring project and the tools to be used for effective collaboration.	
	Project execution	
29	Set up and execute a pilot project with defined scope.	
30	Establish and maintain a list of relevant risks and appropriate mitigation actions (e.g., contract, people, business, security, IPR). Ensure ownership of each relevant risk, specifically where interfaces are involved. Enforce periodic risk status reviews.	
31	Ensure that each project has its own single source requirements list covering both functional and non-functional requirements and acceptance criteria.	
32	Provide access to the requirements list for impacted suppliers. Provide collaboration mechanisms to exchange requirements.	

(Continued)

No.	Check	Your Status / Comments
33	Ensure that all requirements are formally specified and managed throughout the outsourcing/offshoring project.	
34	Establish and maintain a sufficiently detailed project plan which addresses all relevant activities. Establish clear responsibilities for an efficient work split.	
35	Review and commit to the project plan and requirements with all relevant stakeholders (including suppliers for their parts) so that they agree to deliver necessary resources in due time.	
36	Ensure that the project plan considers all "support activities" such as reviews, configuration management, quality management, training, documentation, etc.	
37	Set up and ensure a continuous monitoring of all processes and deliverables addressing both quantitative and qualitative needs.	
38	Set up a formal control with the supplier which considers cost control, SLA deliverables, and relevant project parameters (e.g., budget, milestones, and quality).	
39	Address deviations from the plan or the SLA immediately and follow up through closure, specifically during the ramp-up and initiation.	
40	Establish and maintain a quality assurance plan covering all relevant activities to ensure the necessary quality.	
41	Ensure that the quality of the delivered software periodically measured and compared against targets (e.g., maintainability, reliability, usability, etc.).	
42	Establish and maintain a single change control board with all impacted stakeholders, including the supplier(s), for their parts.	
43	Establish and maintain a systematic change management process with support tools that are uniformly applicable for all suppliers (e.g., requirements repository, intranet information dashboard, configuration control system, source code control system, test case, defect tracking, etc.).	
44	Make sure that all necessary information on the project and processes is available to all stakeholders across all locations (e.g., quality plans, tools, quality status, configuration baselines, etc.).	
45	Make sure that all necessary tools for efficient collaboration are available and used (e.g., requirements engineering, documentation, project management, team meetings, wikis, etc.).	

No.	Check	Your Status / Comments
46	Train configuration managers on baselining and recovery mechanisms.	
47	Make sure that basic engineering and management tools are used consistently across all sites and projects (e.g., defect tracking, configuration management, project management, workflow management).	
48	Make sure that the available IT infrastructure is sufficient to collaborate across sites and to interface with the suppliers' IT infrastructure (e.g., performance, security, etc.).	
49	Establish and utilize different communication channels (e.g., site visits, video conferencing, telephone calls, online meetings, collaboration tools).	
50	Set up periodic project and technical reviews with stakeholders across sites, functions, projects, and with the supplier.	
	Relationship management	
51	Establish and enforce transparent performance evaluations to periodically assess and improve performance and cost of the existing supplier agreements.	
52	Continuously manage your technology, IPR and competence portfolio and roadmap to identify needs and resolution over time.	
53	Maintain your own critical expertise.	
54	Grow stepwise. Learn from your errors.	

Appendix B

Checklist/Template: Self Assessment

This test gives an impression and brief risk assessment of how good your chances are to successfully implement your global software and IT program. Success means that you will reliably achieve your project objectives (schedule, quality, content, cost, and budget). The test will help you to identify risks, assess them and pinpoint to potential solutions.

It is a strength-weakness profile which creates a starting point for improvements. Due to its short format, it will not substitute a professional risk evaluation.

Answer this test alone and for your own specific current situation. Take relevant current projects or activities in order to obtain a representative response. Answer all questions from the perspective of these chosen projects. Stay realistic. Avoid wrong assumptions and hopes that things will be better.

The test consists of several questions that you evaluate using a numerical scale:

3 points: Yes, fully

2 points: Probably

1 point: Doubtful

0 points: No, not at all

If the outsourcing/offshoring project has just been launched you should anticipate responses to operational issues due to the current plans, company culture, and project experiences.

We use the term "outsourcing/offshoring project" to address different formats to global software and IT projects. This can be an IT outsourcing project or a globally distributed software development at various locations or the use of an open-source its components.

Global Software and IT: A Guide to Distributed Development, Projects, and Outsourcing,
First Edition. Christof Ebert.
© 2012 the Institute of Electrical and Electronics Engineers, Inc. Published 2012 by
John Wiley & Sons, Inc.

EVALUATION

Sum up all given points on the right side of the table and multiply the raw sum by the correction factor (see last page) to get the final result.

If you have less than 120 points, there are substantial risks in the outsourcing/ offshoring project. Between 120 and 160 points means that you have an average situation with average performance which means that you will have some problems that will lead to delays or additional expenses. If you have more than 160 points, you are among the small minority of projects that will achieve the targets with high probability.

Now we address the most important part of this self test. Identify priorities and risks of your outsourcing/offshoring program based on the given answers. What did you learn from the test? What are your biggest risks? Where do you go from here? What priorities will be addressed? How do you implement the solutions to the outsourcing/offshoring program? Identify, based on the content of this book, how to mitigate risks and improve. Create an action list (which you should discuss with employees or supervisors). You need to decide what is important to you before you begin to change.

You can also discuss the test later with colleagues in your company or with your employees.

No.	Check	Your Answer (No = 0 . . . Yes = 3)
1	Does the outsourcing/offshoring project have clear and measurable objectives?	
2	Is senior management fully supportive of the outsourcing/ offshoring program?	
3	Does outsourcing/offshoring project management in your company agree that the objectives are realistic?	
4	Is the entire outsourcing/offshoring program (Engineering/R&D/IT, Finance, Procurement, Operations, etc.) focused on the same objectives?	
5	Is there a clear governance policy which is mandatory for all stakeholders and that addresses major outsourcing/ offshoring aspects?	
6	Is there an experienced project manager with full responsibility for the project (i.e., budget, content, and resources)?	
7	Is there one outsourcing/offshoring sponsor who is held personally accountable for the success of the outsourcing/ offshoring program?	
8	Is there an effective steering board for the outsourcing/ offshoring program?	
9	Have all your employees and managers been sufficiently trained for the outsourcing/offshoring activities?	

No.	Check	Your Answer (No = 0 . . . Yes = 3)
10	Have all employees and managers been sufficiently trained on cultural aspects, cross-country communication, etc.?	
11	Does the outsourcing/offshoring project have a clear business case when addressing the cost and benefits across its life-cycle?	
12	Is there a single requirements list for the outsourcing/offshoring project covering both functional and non-functional requirements and acceptance criteria?	
13	Does the supplier possess the skills and competences (technical and non-technical) demanded for the outsourcing/offshoring program.	
14	Does the supplier know and understand your specific market, needs, and technical/environmental constraints of the products?	
15	Is the selected supplier oriented toward the agreed targets and requirements?	
16	Is there a signed formal SLA between you and the supplier addressing your targets?	
17	Does the supplier consider the SLA to be feasible?	
18	Are the contracts between you and the supplier sufficiently concrete to ensure that outsourced services and processes seamlessly fit with your own processes?	
19	Are all outsourcing and supplier contracts aligned across different projects and suppliers? Are they managed by a single sourcing manager?	
20	Are later changes of suppliers or providers prepared and feasible based on the agreed upon contracts? Are lock-ins effectively avoided?	
21	Are deviations from the plan or the SLA immediately addressed and followed through to closure?	
22	Do your processes for development, provisioning, management, and controlling fit with your supplier and the needs of the outsourcing/offshoring project?	
23	Are all relevant processes and interfaces between you and your supplier(s) sufficiently standardized?	
24	Have your processes in engineering, IT, management, and controlling been adapted to the changed needs of such outsourcing/offshoring programs?	
25	Does your organization exhibit the necessary process maturity to address outsourcing/offshoring and have the processes been assessed on maturity level two (e.g., CMMI-DEV with distributed development, CMMI-ACQ for outsourcing, A-SPICE for the automotive industry, COBIT and ITIL for IT companies)?	

(Continued)

No.	Check	Your Answer (No = 0 . . . Yes = 3)
26	Are all requirements formally specified and managed throughout the outsourcing/offshoring project addressing all impacted stakeholders?	
27	Is there a sufficiently detailed project plan which addresses all relevant activities?	
28	Has the project plan been reviewed and agreed upon by all relevant stakeholders so they agree to deliver necessary resources in due time?	
29	Is the project plan built upon clearly defined work packages which are either open (0% complete) or closed (100% complete) and which are owned by a single person?	
30	Is there a continuous monitoring of all processes and deliverables addressing both quantitative and qualitative needs?	
31	Is the current progress compared to the committed plan known by all relevant stakeholders?	
32	Have all requirements been systematically estimated by impacted stakeholders so they commit to the overall planning?	
33	Does the project plan consider all "support activities," such as reviews, configuration management, quality management, training, documentation, etc.?	
34	Has a formal control been agreed upon with the supplier which considers cost control, SLA deliverables, and relevant project parameters (e.g., budget, milestones, and quality)?	
35	Are your customer requirements traceable to the requirements and test cases and are those relationships maintained through the project?	
36	Is there a quality assurance plan covering all relevant activities to ensure the necessary quality?	
37	Is the quality of the delivered software periodically measured and compared against targets (e.g., maintainability, reliability, usability, etc.)?	
38	Are project plans realistic and considered feasible by all impacted stakeholders (e.g., looking to availability, skills, holidays, turnover, trainings, etc.)?	
39	Are all external interfaces of your project known and managed (e.g., to your clients)?	
40	Is there a written plan on all activities related to changes to requirements to your suppliers?	
41	Is there a systematic change management installed for all suppliers (e.g., change control board, configuration baselines) which is followed across the project?	

No.	Check	Your Answer (No = 0 . . . Yes = 3)
42	Is all necessary information on the project and processes available to all stakeholders across all locations (e.g., quality plans, tools, quality status, configuration baselines, etc.)?	
43	Are all necessary tools for efficient collaboration available and used (e.g., requirements engineering, documentation, project management, team meetings, wikis, etc.)?	
44	Is the source code under formal configuration control as of project start to allow, at each moment, an automatic build and/or fall-back?	
45	Are the basic engineering and management tools being used across the sites and projects (e.g., defect tracking, configuration management, project management, workflow management)?	
46	Is the available IT infrastructure sufficient to collaborate across sites and to interface with the suppliers' IT infrastructure?	
47	Is the bandwidth sufficient for tools, video conferencing, backups, etc. to work and collaborate across sites?	
48	Are the backup and recovery policies and tools sufficient for fast recovery? Are they periodically tested in real life?	
49	Are different communication channels effectively and efficiently used (e.g., site visits, video conferencing, telephone calls, online meetings, collaboration tools)?	
50	Is there a maintained list of relevant risks and appropriate mitigation actions?	
51	Are there periodic reviews with stakeholders across sites, functions, projects, and with the supplier?	
52	Are transparent performance evaluations used to periodically assess and improve performance and cost of the existing supplier agreements?	
53	Are there sufficiently skilled people available in due time to avoid overtime?	
54	Are risks and problems detected and resolved in due time across sites, suppliers, projects, and processes?	
55	Are the supplier employees fully allocated to your outsourcing/offshoring program?	
56	Is the employee turnover rate of the supplier below 10%?	
57	Do you believe that all impacted stakeholders actively support the outsourcing/offshoring program?	
58	Do you believe that all impacted stakeholders want a sustainable partnership with the selected supplier(s)?	

(Continued)

No.	Check	Your Answer (No = 0 . . . Yes = 3)
59	Do you believe that all relevant risks of the outsourcing/ offshoring project are sufficiently mitigated?	
60	Do you have sufficient external expertise and experiences available and used for preparation and training to successfully manage the outsourcing/offshoring program?	
	Initial sum	
	Multiplication factor: 1.5 if your organization is experienced with outsourcing/ offshoring projects with the selected supplier. 1.25 if your organization is experienced with previous home outsourcing/offshoring activities?' Otherwise 1.0.	
	Sum (= initial sum x multiplication factor)	

Appendix C

Checklist/Template: Risk Management

Global software and IT pose lots of risks and challenges which are not so relevant in regular colocated projects. These risks must be identified, assessed, and managed, otherwise global software and IT might be a very expensive exercise. It is certainly helpful to start with the best practices and then enhance them according to your own specific needs, culture, and risks. This book provides guidance for finding answers to most problems and risks. Here is a simple checklist and template which summarizes typical risks.

Risk	Mitigation Actions
Project delivery failures	Professionally train all project managers. Apply best practices from the CMMI (DEV + ACQ), COBIT, ITIL for IT companies frameworks. Implement CMMI maturity level three on supplier and customer side. Maintain an organization risk repository. Use lessons learned and root cause analysis reports from previous projects to avoid repetition of problems.
Insufficient quality	Establish and use quality indicators. Systematically follow quality gates at work product level. Implement CMMI maturity level three on supplier and customer side (or COBIT and ITIL for IT service providers). Monitor and use early defect ratio as a warning sign of insufficient specification and code quality.

(Continued)

Global Software and IT: A Guide to Distributed Development, Projects, and Outsourcing,
First Edition. Christof Ebert.
© 2012 the Institute of Electrical and Electronics Engineers, Inc. Published 2012 by
John Wiley & Sons, Inc.

Risk	Mitigation Actions
Distance and cultural clashes	Train people in all involved organizations on handling cultural diversity. Provide different communication channels and collaboration tools. Use workflow management and online tools. Have periodic workshops with teams and apply online team-building. Organize around teams and give them ownership and responsibility.
High staff turnover	Establish flexible long-term retention models. Make employees an integral part of the company, such as by partial ownership, direct involvement on certain decisions, etc. Periodically conduct employee engagement surveys to take appropriate corrective actions. Monitor critical resources availability and evolution and implement succession plans. Learn to deal with staff turnover by means of pooled buffers.
Poor supplier services	Agree and apply supplier management and escalation processes. Use flexible prizing schemes depending on uncertainties and risks. Preferably establish a fixed price contract scheme to mitigate estimation risks. Evolve towards a partner model with the supplier. Train suppliers on required processes, specifically interfaces, reporting, requirements engineering and configuration management. During the ramp-up period, carefully educate supplier management on escalation procedures and your own required quality level. Rigorously highlight insufficient quality, delays or lack of visibility. Escalate carefully and step-wise and avoid the SLA "hammer".
Instability with overly high change rate	Follow a systematic RE process covering supplier and customer. Establish clear responsibilities and policies for handling change. Review and sign-off of all requirements. Monitor and control the requirements change index.
Insufficient competencies	Establish competence management. Standardize skill and competency requirements and definitions across all distributed locations. Use professional multi-project management and resource planning. Provide all necessary training and monitor effectiveness.

Risk	Mitigation Actions
Wage and cost inflation	Establish a systematic and consistent accounting and reporting based on engineering/service activities. Review efficiency beyond the traditional measurements of estimation accuracy and cost. Distribute work across regions and anticipate wage increases. Evaluate, together with the supplier, his own situation and review mechanisms for mutual win-win. Evaluate your own and suppliers' business models over future years – and look for risks on either side.
Lock-in with supplier	Establish common processes and tools with clear descriptions for ramp-up and operational usage in order to facilitate move of activities. Communicate, document, and distribute critical knowledge. As a service client keep critical engineering knowledge within your own company. Maintain back-up and recovery mechanisms. Carefully protect against supplier lock-in on the basis of contracts, work distribution and dual sourcing. Evaluate together with the supplier his own situation and review mechanisms for mutual win-win situations.
Inadequate IPR management	Systematically train engineering and management on IPR. Establish and rigorously apply a strong policy on IPR protection. Encourage innovation on all sites and promote patents.

Glossary and Abbreviations

The Glossary has been compiled based on entries from various international standards, such as IEEE Std 610 (Standard Glossary of Software Engineering Terminology) [IEEE90], ISO 15504 (Information technology. Software process assessment. Vocabulary) [ISO04], the SWEBOK (Software Engineering Body of Knowledge) [SWEBOK11], the CMMI for Development [SEI11], ITIL and COBIT standards [COBIT05, ITIL07], and the PMBOK (Project Management Body of Knowledge) [PMI01]. Entries are adjusted to serve the needs of this particular book. This terminology is consistently used across all publications, lectures, and keynotes of the author. The author acknowledges the usage of these standards and takes all responsibility for deviating adjustments within the text below.

Acceptance Criteria The criteria that a system or component must satisfy in order to be accepted by a user, customer, or other authorized entity.

Acceptance Test Test activities for sample checks to verify that a system (or product, solution) has the right quality for deployment and usage. The acceptance test is often done by the customer.

Acquisition The process of obtaining products (goods and services) through contract.

Acquisition Strategy The specific approach to acquiring human resources to serve on a project, products, and services. It considers supply sources, acquisition methods, requirements specification types, contract or agreement types, and the related acquisition risk.

Activity An element of work performed during the course of a project. An activity normally has an expected duration, expected cost, and expected resource requirements. Activities are often subdivided into tasks.

Agile Development Development paradigm to support efficient software engineering for typically small collocated projects. Captures well-known best practices and bundles them toward a style which avoids what is perceived as "unnecessary." Examples of agile methods include **extreme programming**, **feature driven development**, and **test driven development**.

Allocate Assign **requirements** to a **project**, **process**, or other logical element of the system.

Application Service Provider A company that provides servers and services to host and run applications.

Application Service Provisioning (ASP) ASP or netsourcing is a form of **outsourcing** where computer-based services are outsourced to a third-party service provider. The **application service provider** provides these services to customers over a network. ASP is a form of **Information Technology Outsourcing** for operationally provisioning software and IT functionality. Software offered using an ASP model is called on-demand software or software as a service (SaaS). Examples are customer relationship management or sales

Global Software and IT: A Guide to Distributed Development, Projects, and Outsourcing,
First Edition. Christof Ebert.
© 2012 the Institute of Electrical and Electronics Engineers, Inc. Published 2012 by
John Wiley & Sons, Inc.

(e.g., salesforce.com), but also, increasingly, desktop applications. ASP is limited and of risk (performance, security, availability) because access to a particular application program is through a standard protocol such as HTTP. The market is divided as follows: Functional ASP delivers a single application, such as timesheet services; a vertical ASP delivers a solution for a specific customer type, such as a chimney sweepers; an enterprise ASP delivers broad solutions, such as finance solutions.

Appraisal Examination (sometimes called assessment) of one or more processes by a trained team of professionals using an appraisal reference model as the basis for determining at a minimum strengths and weaknesses. Mostly used in context of **CMMI** (Capability Maturity Model Integration). See also **SCAMPI**.

AS Aerospace Standard

ASP See **Application Service Provisioning**.

Audit Systematic, independent, and documented process for obtaining evidence and evaluating it objectively to determine the extent to which audit criteria are fulfilled.

Balanced Scorecard (BSC) A set of well-defined performance measurement balanced to capture different dimensions, such as finance, customers, innovation, and people. Compared to one-dimensional sets of measurements, a BSC allows comparing multiple dimensions at the same time, thus reducing the risk of local optimization (e.g., short-term financial gains at the cost of long-term survival).

Baseline See **Configuration Baseline**.

Benchmarking (1) The continuous process of measuring products, services, and practices against competitors or those companies recognized as industry leaders. (2) An improvement paradigm with a structured and systematic learning from the best in class. Benchmarking is difficult to implement without highly effective and fast industry networks and is therefore offered as a consulting product (contact C. Ebert for details).

Benefits Perceived positive impact of a product or service. Within the **business case** it is the income within a period. Benefits impact **value**.

Best Practice This concept (or recipe for success, success method, state of the practice) describes the use of best practices, technical systems, and business processes in an enterprise. Best practice is typically described by standards and can be relevant in liability issues when a company needs to prove that it applies the state of the practice.

Body Shopping Specific **outsourcing** service used to allocate external resources ad hoc to a task, work package or project to get immediate results. Increases flexibility but at the cost of fragmentation and overheads. Normally done **onshore** by dedicated consulting companies (e.g., timesharing companies) or offshore by offshore suppliers. In Europe it is often restricted by labor laws.

BPO See **Business Process Outsourcing**.

BSC See **Balanced Scorecard.**

BTO See **Business Transformation Outsourcing**.

Business Case Consolidated information summarizing and explaining a business proposal from different perspectives (cost, benefit, and so on) for a decision maker. Often used for assessing the value of a **product** or requirements of a **project**. As opposed to a mere profit-loss calculation, the business case is a "case" which is owned by the **product manager** and used for achieving the objectives.

Business Process   A partially ordered set of enterprise activities that can be executed to realize a given objective of an enterprise or a part of an enterprise to achieve some desired end result.

Business Process Outsourcing (BPO)   A form of **outsourcing** where a business process (or business function) is contracted to a third-party service provider. BPO involves outsourcing of operations and responsibilities of that process or function. Examples are business processes such as supply chain, maintenance, welcome desk, financial services, or human resources. Historically, Coca Cola was the first to use BPO for outsourcing parts of their supply chain.

Business Requirement   See **Market Requirement; Requirements Specification**.

Business Transformation Outsourcing   Outsourcing model that covers both classic services (e.g., IT infrastructure management, software development) but also the reengineering and improvement of the related business processes. The goal is to flexibly adjust an enterprise to changing market demands. Example: outsourcing of product development and production.

Capability Maturity Model Integration   See **CMMI**.

CDE   See **Collaborative Development Environment**.

Certification   Acknowledgment based on a formal demonstration that a system, process, or person complies with specified objectives or requirements. Example: ISO 9001 certification, CPRE certification.

Change   A change (or transition, transformation) is the managed move of individuals, teams, and organizations from a current state to a desired future state. Examples: Introduction of a new culture, strategy implementation, process change, merger, acquisition, cost reduction, outsourcing.

Change Agent   An individual or group that has sponsorship and is responsible for implementing or facilitating change. An example of a change agent is the systems engineering process group. Contrast with change advocate.

Change Control Board (CCB)   A formally constituted group of **stakeholders** responsible for evaluating, approving, or rejecting changes to a **configuration baseline**.

Change Management   The systematic process to implement a change in a controlled manner. It comprises the objectives, processes and actions that are used to successfully implement the change. Typically, organizational change includes the transformation and development of the hierarchical organization and the process organization.

Change Request   Formalized **requirement** to expand or reduce the project scope, modify policies, processes, plans, or procedures, modify costs or budgets, or revise schedules. A change request often ripples into many items of a **configuration baseline**.

CMMI   Capability Maturity Model Integration. The model contains the essential elements of effective **processes** for one or more disciplines. It also describes an evolutionary improvement path from ad hoc, immature processes, to disciplined, mature processes with improved **quality** and **effectiveness**. The CMMI is fully based on ISO 15504. The CMMI have been used successfully for many years for evaluating and improving engineering processes in the IT, software, and systems industries. Created and owned by the **Software Engineering Institute**.

COBIT   Control Objectives for Information and Related Technology is a set of **best practices** and **governance** criteria for IT management created by the Information Systems Audit and Control Association and the IT Governance Institute in 1996. COBIT provides managers, auditors, and IT users with a set of generally accepted measures, indicators, processes and best practices for appropriate IT governance and control in a company. It uses three dimensions, namely, IT processes, IT resources, and business requirements.

Collaborative Development Environment (CDE)   A CDE provides a project workspace with a standardized tool set for global software teams. CDEs combine different tools, and thus, offer a frictionless development environment for **outsourcing** and **offshoring**.

Collocation   An organizational placement strategy where the project team members are physically located close to one another in order to improve communication, working relationships, and productivity.

Commitment   An agreement that is freely assumed, visible, and expected to be kept by all parties.

Competence   From Latin *competere* (being able to do something), the ability of a person to do a specific task.

Component   A constituent part, element, or piece of a complex whole. Product components are parts of the product and help to structure the development and manufacturing processes. They are integrated to "build" the product. There may be multiple levels of product components.

Concurrent Engineering   An approach to project staffing that, in its most general form, calls for implementers to be involved in the design phase.

Configuration Baseline   The configuration information formally designated at a specific time during a **product's**, product component's, or work product's life. Configuration baselines, plus approved changes from those baselines, constitute the current configuration information.

Configuration Management   A discipline applying technical and administrative direction and surveillance to (1) identify and document the functional and physical characteristics of a **configuration baseline** and its items, (2) control changes to those characteristics, (3) record and report change processing and implementation status, and (4) verify compliance with specified requirements.

Conformity   Fulfilling a **requirement**.

Constraint   A constraint is a **requirement** that constrains the way a system can be realized. Constraints extend the functional requirements and the **quality requirements**. Examples: cost, business processes, laws. See also **requirement**, requirements analysis, **requirements engineering**.

Contract   A mutually binding agreement, which obligates the **supplier** to provide the specified product, and obligates the buyer to take it and to pay for it.

Corrective Action   Action taken to eliminate the cause of a detected nonconformity or other undesirable situation

Cost   Expenses for engineering, producing, selling, and so on, of a **product** or **service**. For software systems these are mostly labor cost plus marketing and sales expenses. Costs are typically expensed in the year they are incurred with direct impact on cash and profitability. For long-term investments they can be capitalized with positive impact on cash but not on profit.

Cost Budgeting   Allocating the cost estimates to individual project components.

Cost Control   Controlling expenses and changes to the allocated project budget. See **Earned Value Management**.

Cost Estimation   See **Estimate**.

Cost of Non-Quality (CNQ)   The cost incurred of not having the right level of quality at a given moment. The cost of non-quality includes activities, from that moment onward, related to insufficient quality, such as rework, inventory cost, scrap, or quality control.

Cost of Quality   The cost incurred to ensure quality. The cost of quality includes quality planning, quality control, quality assurance, and rework.

Cost Performance Index (CPI)   A measurement of cost efficiency on a project. It is the ratio of **earned value** (EV) to actual costs (AC). CPI = EV / AC. A value equal to or greater than one indicates a favorable condition (actual cost lower than planned) and a value less than one indicates an unfavorable condition (cost overrun). See also **Earned Value Management**.

Cost Variance (CV)   A measurement of cost performance on a project. It is the algebraic difference between **earned value** (EV) and actual cost (AC). CV = EV − AC. A positive value indicates a favorable condition and a negative value indicates an unfavorable condition. See also **Earned Value Management**.

CPI   See **Cost Performance Index**.

Critical Path   In a project network diagram, the series of activities which determines the earliest completion of the project.

Customer   Organization or person receiving a **solution**, **service**, or **product**. Specified precisely by the contract between **supplier** and **customer**. The customer is not always the **user**.

Customer Requirements Specification   See **Requirements specification**.

Customer Satisfaction   The **customer's** opinion of the degree to which a transaction has met the customer's needs and expectations

Data Dictionary   Description of data elements with structure, syntax, value ranges, dependencies, and a brief content description.

Defect   An imperfection or deficiency in a system or component where that component does not meet its requirements or specifications which could yield a **failure**. Causal relationship distinguishes the failure caused by a defect which itself is caused by a human error.

Design to Cost   A **quality requirement** that directs a solution optimized to low **cost**. The entire **life-cycle** is considered depending which type of cost is put into focus (e.g., cost of production, cost of ownership, reduced pricing to the customer, and so on).

Development   See **R&D**.

Development Project   A project in which something new or enhanced (e.g., software technology, changed functionalities) is developed as a **product** for a **market** or a **customer**.

Document   Information and its tangible transport medium. Documents describe **work products**.

Due Diligence   Systematic evaluation of a company before working together or before an acquisition or merger. The evaluation includes a systematic analysis of strengths and weaknesses. See also **SWOT analysis**.

Earned Value Management   Managing a project based on the value of the results achieved to date in a project while comparing with the projected budget and the planned schedule progress at a given date. Progress **measurement** which relates already consumed resources and achieved results at a given point in time with the respective planned values for the same date.

Ebert's Law on Productivity   Productivity is improved by reducing accidents (e.g., improve engineering and management discipline, processes, and tools) and controlling essence (e.g., understand the real needs are and implement those in the product). Abbreviated as RACE (Reduce Accidents, Control Essence).

Eclipse   Open source framework for software development. With its open plug-in structure based on the Eclipse Rich Client Platform (RCP) that allows data exchange both on access and semantic levels, Eclipse is used in many different engineering tasks. Example: A small supplier offers a tool that easily interacts with a rich basis of other tools.

Eco System   A term from biology for a system of different species that mutually support each other. Example: Supplier A offers a service for a product of supplier B on which B depends. Both suppliers support each other.

Effectiveness   From Latin *effectivus* (creating impact), the relationship between achieved objectives to defined objectives. Effectiveness means "doing the right things." Effectiveness looks only if defined objectives are reached and not how they are reached.

Efficiency   (1) Economic efficiency (from Latin *efficere*, "achieving") is the relationship between the result achieved (**effectiveness**) and the resources used to achieve this result. Efficiency means "doing things right." An efficient behavior like an effective behavior delivers results, but keeps the necessary effort to a minimum. See also **productivity**. (2) A **measurement**. The set of attributes that bear on the relationship between the level of performance of the software and the amount of resources used under stated conditions.

Effort   The number of labor units required to complete an activity or other project element. Usually expressed as person hours, person weeks, or person years. Not to be confused with duration.

Effort Estimation   An assessment of the likely effort, cost or duration of a **project** or task at the time before or during project execution. Should always include some indication of accuracy (e.g., ± x%). See also **estimate**.

ELOC   Executable **LOC**, Effective **LOC**. The amount of executable software code which excludes comments, and so on.

Embedded Software   A software system which is embedded in a larger system, the main purpose of which is not computation (e.g., software for automatic fuel injection in a car). Most embedded systems are real-time systems.

Embedded System   A special-purpose computer system built into a larger system for which the main purpose is not computation. Example: Pacemaker.

Emergency Plan   Description of actions and responsibilities that need to happen if a risk materializes. It is set up for all critical risks as part of **risk management**.

Engineering   (1) The application of science and mathematics by which properties of matter and the sources of energy are made useful to people. (2) An organization in the enterprise that is in charge of product development, applications, or software solutions. Can be software engineering, IT or offshore centers.

Estimate   An estimate is a quantitative assessment of the likely amount or outcome of a future endeavor. It is usually applied to forecast project costs, size, resources, effort, or durations. Given that estimates can, by definition, be imprecise, they should always include some indication of accuracy (e.g., ±x percent). See also **effort estimation**.

Evaluation   A systematic determination of the extent to which an entity meets its specified criteria (e.g., business objectives, quality goals, process needs). See also **validation**; **verification**.

Evolution   The last phase of the **product life-cycle**. Covers all types of maintenance as well as activities that maintain or enhance the value of a **product**.

Extreme Programming   An **agile development** methodology for software development. Underlying principles are to develop only what is needed. It is based on **incremental development**, refactoring, pair programming, no documentation except the code, and so on.

Failure   (1) A departure between observed and expected behavior of a system at runtime. The termination of the ability of an item to perform a required function or its inability to perform within previously specified limits. (2) The effect of a defect in a system on its external behavior. Deficient operational behavior of a system or a component due to a product defect, a user error, or a hardware/software error. See also **defect**.

Feature Driven Development (FDD)   **Agile development** methodology for software engineering. FDD based on **incremental development**. Increments are closely linked to **requirements** (here: features) to assure that each increment delivers tangible value.

Frontloading   Early decision-making in the product life-cycle to reduce overall lead-time and effort.

Full Function Points (FFP)   Extension to Function Points to use this functional size measurement for systems other than software only (e.g., embedded systems).

Function Point Analysis (FPA)   Quantitative method to estimate function points by evaluating the software requirements or design on the number of inputs, outputs, queries, procedural complexity, and environmental factors. The derived function points can be related to effort or duration of a project.

Function Points (FP)   See FPA.

Functional Requirement   A function of a system that is offered by a system or a system component. It describes in the language of the system what the system will do. Example: Calculation of output parameters from input parameters by applying a specified algorithm. See also **requirements**; **requirements analysis**; **requirements engineering**.

General Public License (GPL)   The most widely used open source license type. Right to source code for any binary that is GPL licensed. Right to modify source code and redistribute source and modifications. Licensee must be prepared to distribute source for any distributed binaries derived from GPL code. Licensee must manage licenses for all imported code. Note that an application on top of the Linux kernel does not become GPL.

Global Software Engineering (GSE)   Software engineering in globally distributed sites. Different business models and work breakdown schemes are used, such as **outsourcing**, **offshoring**, **rightshoring**.

Governance   Leadership principle and its operational implementation in the enterprise to ensure that agreements are kept.

GSD   Global Software Development. See **Global Software Engineering**.

GSE   See **Global Software Engineering**.

Guanxi   Chinese for network of personal relationships and their active use on a wide scale of decision-making and mutual support.

Guideline   Operational explanation how a process or tool are used in a specified situation.

Hard Skills   Knowledge on facts, methods, and technologies. Also called know-how or know-what.

HCL   High Cost Location.

History Database   See **Measurement Repository**.

IDE   Integrated Development Environment. Tool suite used to develop application software. It typically supports design, coding, and verification. Additional tools support **requirements management** or test and are integrated to the IDE by its vendors.

IEC   International Electrotechnical Commission

IEEE   Institute for Electrical and Electronics Engineers, the largest global interest group for engineers of different branches and for computer scientists.

INCOSE   International Council on Systems Engineering, an organization that is very active in systems engineering.

Increment   Internal delivery of a **product**. Often increments are planned as steps within a project to deliver the most relevant (valuable) functionality first. Increments and iterations are used to divide complex projects, and thus, mitigate the associated risks. Incremental steps are planned from the beginning to allow stepwise stabilization and measurable value of the project as it progresses. See also **earned value**.

Incremental Development   Project is developed and stabilized stepwise in executable and usable **increments**.

Indicator   From Latin *indicare* (pointing to), an indirect measurement used to estimate or predict another measurement which is not (yet) directly measurable. An indicator points to a trend, a deviation, or some behavior which is otherwise not tangible. Example: The structural design complexity is an indicator for the test effort.

Information Technology (IT)   Denomination for all information, communication, and data processing technologies, covering industries, markets, and software or hardware systems and components.

Information Technology Outsourcing (ITO)   A form of **outsourcing** where software and It related services are outsourced to a third-party service provider. ITO is a form of **business process outsourcing** for software and information technology activities. Historically, EDS was the first ITO supplier. Examples of this are outsourcing of software maintenance or IT provisioning services.

Inspection   Conformity evaluation by observation and judgment accompanied as appropriate by measurement, testing, or gauging. Part of **verification**.

Integration Test   The progressive linking and testing of software components in order to ensure their proper functioning in the complete system. See also **verification**.

ISO   International Standards Organization, a UN-sponsored organization to achieve and enforce globally effective **standards**.

ISO/TS   ISO Technical Standard.

IT   See **Information Technology**.

IT Portfolio   IT assets (static and dynamic) and their relationship to enterprise strategy. See also **portfolio management**.

ITIL   The IT Infrastructure Library is a guidance and set of requirements toward organizations of processes that are necessary for operating an IT infrastructure within an enterprise.

The original British ITIL Standard BS 15000 is, today, a globally used de-facto standard and is maintained as ISO / IEC 20000. The ISO / IEC 20000 IT Service Management serves as a measurable quality standard for IT service management. For that matter the necessary minimum requirements and processes are specified that an organization must establish and manage to be able to provide IT services in a defined quality.

ITO   See **Information Technology Outsourcing**.

IV&V   Independent verification and validation. A software or system (component) is verified by an organization which is neither economically nor organizationally linked with the organization responsible for development. See also **validation**; **verification**.

Joint Application Design   Method for developing systems with different **stakeholders** participating. It allows you to identify critical and important **requirements** early. It is utilized heavily in **agile development**.

Key Account Manager (KAM)   A sales person responsible for a key customer ("key account") which he or she supports and represents in internal decision-making processes. Key accounts are critical to business because they contribute (or should contribute) to a large share of all revenues or profits.

Key Performance Indicator (KPI)   A quantitative **measurement** or **indicator** used in performance management to agree an objective and measure progress during the reporting period and is often linked to bonus payment. See also **balanced scorecard**.

KLOC   Kilo (thousand) **LOC**.

Knowledge Management   The process that deals with systematically eliciting, structuring, and facilitating the efficient retrieval and effective use of knowledge, both tacit and explicit, and stretching from know-how to know-what to know-why.

KPI   See **Key Performance Indicator**.

KStmt   Kilo (thousand) statements. See also **KLOC**.

LCL   Low cost location.

Life-Cycle   (1) The system or **product** evolution initiated by a user need or by a perceived customer need through the disposal of consumer products and their life-cycle process products and by-products from inception until retirement. (2) A framework containing the processes, activities, and tasks involved in the development, operation, and maintenance of a software product, spanning the life of the system from the definition of its requirements to the termination of its use. See also **product life-cycle**; **product life-cycle management**.

Life-Cycle Cost   The total investment in product development, test, manufacturing, distribution, operation, refining, and disposal. This investment is typically allocated across the anticipated number of units to be produced over the entire **product life-cycle**, thus providing a per-unit view of life-cycle cost. See also **business case**.

LOC   Lines of code, the most popular size measurement for software. There are different algorithms for calculating LOC (e.g., executable code, total written lines of source code). LOC is the basis for **effort estimation** and defect forecasting. Also used in hardware and firmware development.

Maintainability   The set of attributes that bears on the effort needed to make specified modifications.

Maintenance   The **product life-cycle** phase of modifying a product or component after delivery to correct defects, adapt to a changed environment, improve performance or other attributes, or perform line and depot maintenance of hardware components. That is, it includes maintenance that may be corrective, adaptive, or perfective.

Maintenance Project   Dedicated **project** to provide changes to an existing **product** for correcting **defects** and for introducing new or changed functionality. See also **maintenance**.

Management System   System that describes how to establish and achieve management objectives, **processes**, consistent process practice, and governance.

Market   A group of people or organizations with an unresolved need and sufficient resources to apply to the satisfaction of that need.

Marketing   The different tasks, functions, and processes that evaluate and improve the enterprise and its **market** position (e.g., advertisement, pricing, **product** vision). Marketing is the whole business seen from the point of view of its final result, that is, from the **customer's** point of view. Concern and responsibility for marketing must, therefore, permeate all areas of the enterprise.

Maturity Level   A well-defined evolutionary plateau toward achieving a mature **process**. Used for evaluating process maturity and for process improvement (**appraisal**) of both own processes and those of a supplier. The five maturity levels in the **CMMI** are labeled initial, repeatable, defined, managed, and optimizing.

Maturity Model   Model which maps **process** capability in defined categories, and thus permits a reliable and repeatable process evaluation. A maturity model provides requirements and expectations to processes but doesn't prescribe processes. It is thus no **product life-cycle** model. Typically used for process assessments and for process improvement (**appraisal**) of both home processes and those of a supplier. See also **CMMI**.

MBO   Management by objective, a goal-oriented management method setting concrete objectives which are followed through. See also **key performance indicator**.

Measurement   (1) A formal, precise, reproducible, objective mapping of a number or symbol to an empirical entity for characterizing a specific attribute. (2) Mathematically: A mapping M of an empirical system C and its relations R to a numerical system N. (3) The use (e.g., extraction, evaluation, analysis, presentation, and corrective actions) of a measurement. Examples: **Product** measurements (e.g., defects, duration, deviation from plan, performance) or **process** measurements (e.g., cost of defect correction, **efficiency**, **effectiveness**).

Measurement Repository   Repository (or storage) used to collect and make available **measurement** data. Such repository contains or references actual measurement data and related information needed to understand, analyze, and utilize (e.g., for estimations or statistical management) the measurement data.

Migration Project   The managed replacement of a system with another system.

MIL   Military standard.

Milestone   A significant event in the project, usually completion of a major deliverable. Used to structure a **life-cycle**.

MIS   Management Information System, a database system for collecting, aggregating, reporting, and analyzing various project and enterprise figures. There are different tools to be used.

Model Driven Development   Product life-cycle model for development of software and systems. (Software) systems are described with a set of related models. The models build a continuous hierarchy of abstractions. The level of abstraction is continuously decreasing from the business process to the system definition, the design, and finally, the implementation. Changes are incorporated first to the model and, afterward, in its implementation to ensure consistency across all models at all times.

MTTF   Mean time to failure, a reliability **measurement** showing the time between two failures.

MTTR   Mean time to repair, a reliability **measurement** showing the time a system is, on average, not working (due to defects or maintenance).

Multi-Project Management   The optimal allocation of resources to different projects. Being different from **portfolio management**, multi-project management looks for only the best possible execution of the respective projects.

Nearshore Outsourcing   The outsourcing supplier resides in a site geographically close to the main site. This reduces impacts of time zones, distance, and cultural variety. See also **offshoring**; **outsourcing**.

Netsourcing   See **Application Service Provisioning**.

Nonfunctional Requirements   See **Quality Requirements**.

Offshore Outsourcing   Large geographical distance between acquirer and supplier (e.g., Europe to India). See also **offshoring**; **outsourcing**.

Offshoring   Executing a business activity beyond sales and marketing outside the home country of an enterprise. Enterprises typically either have their offshoring branches in low-cost countries or they ask specialized companies abroad to execute the respective activity. Offshoring should, therefore, not be confused with **outsourcing**. Offshoring within the home company is called captive offshoring. See also **nearshore outsourcing**.

Onshore Outsourcing   The supplier comes from same country as the acquirer. See also **offshoring**; **outsourcing**.

Outsourcing   A result-oriented relationship with a supplier who executes business activities for an enterprise which was traditionally executed inside the enterprise. Outsourcing is site-independent. The supplier can reside in direct neighborhood of the enterprise or offshore (outsourced **offshoring**).

Peer Review   Internal review activity in which experts on the same organizational hierarchy level as the author verify a work product. See also **verification**.

PEP   See **Product Engineering Process**.

Performance   A quantitative measurement of a product, process, person, or project characterizing a physical or functional attribute relating to achieving a target or executing a mission or function. Performance attributes include quantity (how many or how much), quality (how well), coverage (how much area, how far), timeliness (how responsive, how frequent), and readiness (availability, mean time between failures). See also **efficiency**.

PERT   Program Evaluation and Review Technique, a project management method developed during the 1950s in the United States to integrate planning and monitoring specifically for projects with subcontractors. It includes statistical treatment to the possible time durations and uncertainties, and thus, achieves better accuracy than simple one-value based techniques.

Plan   A documented series of tasks required meeting an objective, typically including the associated schedule, budget, resources, organizational description, and work breakdown structure.

Planned Value   The authorized budget assigned to the scheduled work to be accomplished for a schedule activity or work breakdown structure component. Also referred to as the budgeted cost of work scheduled (BCWS). See also **Earned Value Management**.

PLC   See **product life-cycle**.

PLM   See **product life-cycle management**.

PMBOK   See **project management body of knowledge**.

PMI   Project Management Institute, a globally active organization that trains and certifies project managers independent from the application domain.

Portfolio   The sum of all assets and their relationship to the enterprise strategy and its market position. See also **portfolio management**.

Portfolio Management   A dynamic decision process aimed at having the right product mix and performing the right projects to implement a given strategy. It evaluates all projects in their entirety with respect to their overall contribution to business success and answers the question: Do we have the right projects? It selects projects and allocates limited resources in order to meet business needs.

Present value   The current value of all future expense and income considering a realistic interest rate with the today's ("present") date as a common reference point.

Price   The amount a **customer** is charged for one or more instances or the usage of the **product**. For internal products (e.g., IT services) there is typically an internal pricing scheme based transaction cost and external market prices.

Priority   The degree of importance of a **requirement**, event, task, or **project**.

Process   Set of activities, which uses resources to transform inputs into outputs. A sequence of steps performed for a given purpose. Example: The **product life-cycle**.

Process Capability   (1) The range of expected results that can be achieved by following a process. (2) The ability of an organization to develop and deliver products or services according to defined processes.

Process Description   A documented expression of a set of activities performed to achieve a given purpose. A process description provides an operational definition of the major components of a process. The description specifies, in a complete, precise, and verifiable manner, the requirements, design, behavior, or other characteristics of a process. It may also include procedures for determining whether these provisions have been satisfied. Process descriptions can be found at the activity, project, or organizational level.

Product   From Latin *produco* (to create, deliver), an economic good (or output) which is created in a process that transforms product factors (or inputs) to an output. When sold, it is characterized by attributes that are valuable to its users. It is a deliverable which creates a value and an experience for its users. A product can be a combination of systems, solutions, materials, and services delivered internally (e.g., in-house IT solution) or externally (e.g., SW application) as is or as a component for another product (e.g., IP stack).

Product Engineering Process (PEP)   The process which describes specific to a company the concept, development, and manufacturing of a **product**. See also **product life-cycle**.

Product Life-Cycle (PLC)   The sum of all activities needed to define, develop, implement, build, operate, service, and phase out a **product** or **solution** and its related variants. It is subdivided into phases that are separated by dedicated milestones, called decision gates. With the focus on disciplined gate reviews, the PLC fosters **risk management** and providing auditable decision-making information (e.g., complying with product liability needs, or Sarbanes-Oxley Act section 404).

Product Life-cycle Management (PLM) The **business process** for guiding **products** and **solutions** from inception through retirement. PLM comprises all processes and requires stakeholders to manage and effectively execute the PLC, including business and technology strategy, product and field marketing, and portfolio management and product development. By providing aligned and collaborating processes and tools, PLM facilitates the discipline to implement strategy, planning, and management, and thus ensures execution through each phase of the life-cycle. PLM facilitates an enterprise's ability to monitor activities, analyze challenges and bottlenecks, make decisions, and execute decisions. By lining up goals and processes, it fosters sustainable performance improvements. See also **product life-cycle model**.

Product Line A group of **products** sharing a common, managed set of features that satisfy needs of a selected **market** or mission. A product within a product line shares the common basis and exhibits a defined variability to address specific market needs. Such a product line is a platform with platform elements (P1-Pn) and features (F1-Fm), which are selected within a defined scope for the instantiation of a concrete product.

Product Management The discipline and business process which governs a **product** (including solution or service) from its inception to the market/customer delivery and service in order to generate biggest possible value to the business.

Productivity Defined as output over input. Output is the value delivered. Input covers all resources (e.g., effort) spent to generate the output, the influence of environmental factors (e.g., complexity, quality, time, process capability, team distribution, interrupts, feature churn, tools, and language). Productivity combines efficiency and effectiveness from a value-oriented perspective: Productivity is about generating value with the lowest resource consumption.

Program A set of related **projects**.

Program Management Achieving a shared objective with a set of related **projects**. Historically related to a set of projects for a single customer.

Project A temporary endeavor undertaken to create a unique product or service with people. In software engineering different project types are distinguished (e.g., product development, IT infrastructure, outsourcing, software maintenance, service creation).

Project Controlling Comparing actual performance with planned performance, analyzing variances, assessing trends to effect process improvements, evaluating possible alternatives, and recommending appropriate corrective action as needed. Example: **earned value**.

Project Life-Cycle The set of sequential project phases determined by the control needs of the organizations involved in the **project**. Typically, the project life-cycle can be broken down into at least four phases: initiation, concept/planning, execution, and closure. The project life-cycle and the **product life-cycle** are interdependent, i.e., a product life-cycle can consist of several projects and a project can comprise several **products**.

Project Management The goal-oriented and systematic application of knowledge, skills, tools, and techniques to project activities in order to meet or exceed stakeholder needs and expectations from a **project**.

Project Management Body of Knowledge (PMBOK) A repository presenting a baseline of **project management** knowledge. Serves as a de facto industry and educational standard and is used for certification. Originated and maintained by the **PMI**.

Project Plan A formal, approved document used to guide both project execution and project control. The primary uses of the project plan are to document planning assumptions and decisions, to facilitate communication among **stakeholders**, and to document approved scope, cost, and schedule baselines.

Quality (1) The ability of a set of inherent characteristics of a product, service, product component, or process to fulfill requirements of customers. (2) The degree to which a set of inherent characteristics fulfills requirements.

Quality Assurance (QA) The part of **quality management** covering the planned and systematic means for assuring management that defined standards, practices, procedures, and methods of the process are applied.

Quality Control (QC) The part of **quality management** covering the operational techniques and activities that are used to fulfill requirements for quality (e.g., **inspections**, tests).

Quality Management (QM) The sum of all planned systematic activities and processes for creating, controlling, and assuring quality. See also **quality assurance**; **quality control**.

Quality Management System (QMS) A system to establish a quality policy and quality objectives and to strive to achieve those objectives. See also **management system**.

Quality Measurements Coordinated activities to measure and direct an organization or process toward achieving **quality**. Direct quality **measurements** evaluate specific quality objectives (e.g., defect density, reliability). Indirect quality measurements are indicators for a direct quality measurement before it can be measured (e.g., code complexity for maintainability).

Quality Objective Specific objectives, which, if met, provide a level of confidence that the **quality** of a **product** or **work product** is satisfactory. See also **quality requirement.**

Quality of Service (QoS) A **measurement** that describes quality features of a delivered service. Example: Reaction time of a supplier for a specific defect class.

Quality Requirement A qualitative property that a system or individual **component** of the system must exhibit. They extend the **functional requirements**. Examples: maintainability, security, reliability. Sometimes called non-functional requirements. See also **requirement**; **requirements analysis**; **requirements engineering**.

Quality Requirements Engineering (QRE) The disciplined and systematic approach to elicit, specify, analyze, prioritize, commit, verify, validate, assure, and manage **quality requirements** throughout the life-cycle.

R&D Research and development that typically comprises of any engineering activity in the **product life-cycle**. R&D is not the product management, marketing, or operations activities to produce or deliver the product.

Request for Information (RFI) Initial request to potential **suppliers** by the customer. It introduces the customer, his needs and the requested service or product. The objective is to get initial information about the supplier. The RFI is typically distributed as a questionnaire. Based on the replies, a shortlist of potential suppliers for the **request for proposal** is issued.

Request for Proposal (RFP) Request to potential **suppliers** by the customer. It introduces the requirements of the requested service or product. The objective is to get a solution or project proposal with cost and time horizons from the supplier. Based on the replies, a shortlist of potential suppliers for the **request for quotation** is issued.

Request for Quotation (RFQ)   Request to potential **suppliers** by the customer. It specifies all requirements. The RFI is typically distributed as a questionnaire. The objective is to get a valid offer from the supplier. Based on the replies, the supplier is selected.

Requirement   (1) A condition or capability needed to solve a problem or achieve an objective. (2) A condition or capability that must be met or possessed by a system or system component to satisfy a contract, standard, specification, or other formally imposed document. (3) A documented representation of a condition or capability as in definition (1) or (2). Three different views on requirements are distinguished: **market** requirements, **product** requirements, and **component** requirements. Three different types of requirements are distinguished: functional requirements, **quality requirements**, and **constraints**. Requirements are part of contracts, orders, project plans, test strategies, and so on. They serve as a base for defining, estimating, planning, executing, and monitoring projects. See also **requirements engineering**.

Requirements Engineering (RE)   (1) The disciplined and systematic approach (i.e., "engineering") to elicit, specify, analyze, commit, validate, and manage requirements to transform real-world needs and goals into a product. (2) Activity within systems and software engineering. The goal of RE is to develop good—not perfect—requirements and to manage them during development with respect to risks and quality. Systematic RE is what makes the difference between a winning product and a set of features.

Requirements Specification   A document that summarizes all **requirements** of the product to be developed. Describes what shall be done and why. Owned by the client and relevant for the contract. A requirements specification is not a **solution** description and must not mix the requirement (what is to be done?) with the solution (how is it implemented?).

Resource   Impacting or used input of a **process**. Examples: human resources, equipment, services, supplies, commodities, materiel, budgets, or funds.

Return on Investment (ROI)   (1) A **measurement** of how effectively an organization is using its capital to generate profits. In accounting it is the annual income (profit) divided by the sum of shareholder's equity and long-term debt. (2) The tangible outcome or profitability of an investment measured in business measurements (e.g., money). Defined as the ratio of returns (result from an investment) to the directly related effort (investment).

Review   Performed on a **work product**, following defined procedures, typically by peers of the product's producer for the purpose of identifying defects and improvements. See also **validation**; **verification**.

Rightshoring   Allocating engineering task to the optimum site in a worldwide scenario. Assuring that the work is performed where it has the most benefits for the enterprise. Blend of **outsourcing**, **offshoring**, and **nearshore outsourcing**.

Risk   An uncertain event or condition that, if it occurs, has a positive or negative effect. It is a function of the probability of occurrence of a given threat and the potential adverse consequences of that threat's occurrence. See also **risk management**.

Risk Management   The systematic application of management policies, procedures, and practices to the tasks of identifying, analyzing, evaluating, treating, and monitoring **risk**. Risk management evaluates the effects of today's decisions on the future. It is used in project management, product management, and portfolio management.

Risk Mitigation   Part of **risk management**, taking steps to lessen a **risk** by lowering the probability of a risk event's occurrence or reducing its effect should it occur. There are four techniques for risk mitigation: avoiding, delimiting, handling, ignoring.

Schedule Performance Index (SPI)   A measurement of schedule efficiency on a project. It is the ratio of **earned value** (EV) to **planned value** (PV). SPI = EV / PV. An SPI equal to or greater than one indicates a favorable condition (earlier delivery than planned) and a value of less than one indicates an unfavorable condition (delay). See also **Earned Value Management**.

Schedule Variance (SV)   A measurement of schedule performance on a project. It is the algebraic difference between the **earned value** (EV) and the planned value (PV). SV = EV − PV. See also **Earned Value Management**.

Scrum   From rugby terminology, a method for **project management** and for **agile development**. It means that a team or (sub) project organizes their work themselves. The team takes full ownership for delivering allocated work packages within the externally defined scope. The delivery and planning is based on the so-called product backlog, which prioritizes requirements and synchronizes the team's activities with external stakeholders. A daily scrum meeting with ca. 15 minutes duration ensures daily planning and technical agreements, and thus fosters commitment of each team member.

Security   Security (or information security) is the sum of all attributes of a system which contribute toward ensuring that it can neither be accidentally nor deliberately be attacked or manipulated. Information security implies that the product will not do anything with the processed or managed information which is not explicitly intended by its specification.

Service   Intangible, temporary **product** that is the result of at least one activity performed at the interface between the **supplier** and **customer** and that does not imply a change of ownership.

Service Level Agreement (SLA)   A **requirements specification** and contracted agreement to specify services and their service level. The SLA defines the expected quality of a service and describes how it will be measured (e.g., cost, defects, flexibility to changes). Its limits are part of a contract and serve continuous quality improvement. A SLA has four elements: the service specification, the measurement description, the objective, and the pricing scheme which relates degree of fulfillment of the objective to the price to be paid.

Service-Oriented Architecture   IT infrastructure oriented at demanded business processes. The system architecture offers application and usage-specific services and functions as IT services. Driven by usage demands and rapid adaptation to requirements and changes within the business environment. See also **Service Level Agreement**.

Six Sigma   A process improvement paradigm using statistical process control that governs processes with sufficient accuracy and control to stay with its standard deviation of outputs (sigma) within a range allowing that six times that standard deviation just reaches the allowed control interval.

SLA   See **Service Level Agreement**.

SMART   Acronym describing the desired attributes of objectives or goals, which should be Specific (precise, clearly focused), Measurable (tangible, with an underlying definition), Attractive (to the person who has this objective), Realistic (achievable in the given scope, applicable to a concrete environment), and Timely (currently necessary, showing results in a short time frame).

Soft Skills   Social competences, to facilitate working with other people and organizing one's own life. Includes self-marketing, self-management, communication, and leadership.

Software Engineering (1) The application of a systematic, disciplined, quantifiable approach to the development, operation, and maintenance of software; that is, the application of **engineering** to software. (2) The study of approaches for (1).

Software Engineering Body of Knowledge (SWEBOK) A repository presenting a baseline of software engineering knowledge. Used for developing curricula and certifications.

Software Sourcing A form of **sourcing** where software components are sourced from an external supplier. It includes finding, evaluating, contractually engaging, and managing suppliers of goods and services. Software sourcing includes different types of goods, components, and license models. This starts with commercial off the shelf (COTS), includes a variety of tailored components and solutions, and ends with the different community and open source distribution and access models.

Solution A system tailored to serve a specific business or customer need. Solutions are typically customer-specific and unique and include a combination of different **products**, **processes**, and **resources**.

Solution Model Result of the **requirements analysis**. One or more solutions are modeled and described based on a given set of requirements and environmental conditions. See also **requirements specification**; **solution specification**.

Solution Specification The **specification** of the **solution** which covers the **requirements** of the **product**. Describes how the solution will be done. Owned by the supplier and forms the basis for all subsequent engineering steps. It includes at least a system model and a system specification as an answer to given requirements. The requirements specification and solution specification are controlled and baselined.

Sourcing A business process summarizing all procurement practices. Sourcing includes finding, evaluating, contractually engaging, and managing suppliers of goods and services.

Specification Precise description of an activity or a work product which serves as basis or input for further activities or work products. A specification can comprise **requirements** to a product and how they will be solved. Different parts of a specification (e.g., what is to be done, how it will be done) must not be mixed.

Stakeholder A person or organization, such as customers, sponsors, performing organizations, or the public, actively involved in the project or whose interests may be positively or negatively affected by execution or completion of the project. The stakeholder may also exert influence over the project and its deliverables.

Standard A guideline that reflects agreements on **products** or **processes**. Standards are set by nationally or internationally recognized industrial, professional, trade or governmental bodies. They can also evolve and be accepted de facto by industry or society.

State of the Practice See **Best Practice**.

Statement of Work (SOW) Part of the project contract that describes the general **requirements** of the product or service.

Strategic Outsourcing A form of **outsourcing** with long-term and sustainable focus. A business process is moved to an external supplier in order to focus on resources on the core business. Within engineering projects this can be a process (e.g., maintenance, test) or a system (e.g., legacy product). Strategic outsourcing changes the entire value chain.

Success Method See **Best Practice**.

Supplier   A provider of goods or services to a customer. There are different supplier types: (1) parts and materials, (2) components, subsystems, modules, engineering services, and (3) systems, business processes. The positioning within a supplier network (or supplier pyramid) shows the relevance of the supplier to its customer and is often numbered (OEM, Tier-1, Tier-2, . . . Tier-N suppliers).

SV   See **Schedule Variance**.

SWEBOK   See **Software Engineering Body of Knowledge**.

SWOT Analysis   Analysis of Strengths, Weaknesses, Opportunities, and Threats to understand one's own profile in a market and to identify potential attack or defense plans toward successful strategy execution.

System   An integrated composite consisting of one or more **products**, **processes**, and **resources** and that provides a capability to satisfy a stated need or objective.

Tactical Outsourcing   Form of **outsourcing** with short-term ("just in time") focus. Suppliers are selected on a case-by-case basis for activities within projects. Suppliers who are most suitable for the concrete task at hand are selected. Tactical outsourcing is used to improve operational efficiency. It is similar to subcontract management.

Test   An activity in which a system or component is executed under specified conditions, the results are observed or recorded, and an evaluation is made of some aspect of the system or component. Part of **quality control**. See also **validation; verification**.

Test-Driven Development   An **agile development** approach for software development where tests are designed before the development of the respective **component**. This ensures coverage of relevant functionality, which can be regression tested in case of changes and updates.

Tool   Instrumented and (semi-)automated support for practically applying methods, concepts, and notations in engineering tasks.

Traceability   Tangible relationship between two or more logical entities, e.g., **work products**, by means of recorded identification. The goal of traceability is to assure clean **change** control and provide better quality of work products, such as better consistency. Example: Traceability from customer requirements and test cases. Traceability distinguishes horizontal and vertical traceability.

Unit test   A test of individual programs or modules in order to remove design or programming errors. See also **verification**.

Use Case   (1) Concept to describe a system based on usage of system resources by its environment. Characterized by an objective-driven set of interactions within and at the borders of that system. (2) Notation from UML for describing a scenario (usage approach, operational scenario) from the perspective of its user. A use case enhances requirements, it is not a substitute. See also **requirement**.

User   Person or organization that will use the system during later operation to achieve a goal. The user is not necessarily the **customer** (e.g., a software application is bought by the procurement organization and used by the engineering team).

Validation   Confirmation by examination and provision of objective evidence that the particular **requirements** for a specific intended use are fulfilled ("doing the right thing"). Part of **quality control**. See also **validation**.

Verification   Confirmation at the end of a process by examination and provision of objective evidence that specified requirements to the process have been fulfilled ("doing things right"). Part of **quality control**. See also **verification**.

Virtual Team   A group of persons with a shared objective who fulfill their roles with little or no time spent meeting face-to-face. Virtual teams can be comprised of persons separated by great distances (e.g., offshoring) or separated by organizational limits (e.g., different suppliers). Various forms of technology are used to facilitate communication among team members.

WBS   Work Breakdown Structure, the hierarchical refinement of a project into work packages.

Wiki   A collaborative work environment in the internet or intranet whose contents can be accessed and changed by its users. The name is derived from wikiwiki, the Hawaiian word for "fast." There many Wiki-based tools to easily implement collaborative workflows (e.g., requirements specification, test management).

Win-Win Method   A negotiation strategy to reach the maximum result from diverging opinions of the various stakeholders. The goal is to achieve that all parties leave the concluded negotiation with the perception that they have gained something.

Work Package   A deliverable at the lowest level of the work breakdown structure. A work package may be divided into activities.

Work Product   An artifact associated with the execution of a process (e.g., requirements specification, test case).

Bibliography

[Adler91] ADLER, N.J.: International Dimensions of Organizational Behavior (2nd ed.). Boston: Kent Publishing, 1991.

[Agerfalk06] AGERFALK, P.J., and B. FITZGERALD. Flexible and distributed software processes: Old petunias in new bowls? Communications of the ACM, Vol. 49, No. 10, pp. 26–34, 2006.

[Alberts08] ALBERTS, C, T. AUDREY, and L. MARINO. Mission Diagnostic Protocol, Version 1.0: a risk-based approach for assessing the potential for success. SEI Technical Report CMU/SEI-2008-TR-005, March 2008.

[Allen84] ALLEN, T. Managing the Flow of Technology: Technology Transfer and the Dissemination of Technological Information within the R&D Organization. MIT Press, Cambridge, MA, 1984.

[Aspray06] ASPRAY, W., F. MAYADAS, and M.Y. VARDI, eds. Globalization and Offshoring of Software: A Report of the ACM Job Migration Task Force, Association for Computing Machinery, 2006. Available at http://www.acm.org/globalizationreport/. Accessed January 6, 2011.

[Avram07] AVRAM, G. Of deadlocks and peopleware: collaborative work practices in global software development. In International Conference on Global Software Engineering, 2007, pp. 91–102.

[Avritzer08b] AVRITZER, A., Y. CAI, and D. PAULISH. Coordination Implications of software architecture in a global software development project. In Proceedings of WICSA 2008, 2008.

[Avritzer08a] AVRITZER, A., et al. Experiences with agile practices in the global studio project. In IEEE International Conference on Global Software Engineering, 2008, pp. 77–86.

[Berenbach09] BERENBACH, B., D. PAULISH, J. KAZMEIER, and A. RUDORFER. Software and Systems Requirements Engineering. McGraw-Hill, New York, 2009.

[BCG09] BHATTACHARYA, A., and H. ZABLIT. Taking R&D Global: The Boston Consulting Group. August 2009. Available at http://www.bcg.com/documents/file25452.pdf. Accessed January 6, 2011.

[Birk03] BIRK, A., et al. Product line engineering: the state of the practice. IEEE Software, Vol. 20, No. 6, pp. 52–60, 2003.

[Bloom56] BLOOM, B.S., ed. Taxonomy of Educational Objectives: The Classification of Educational Goals. Susan Fauer Company, 1956, pp. 201–207.

[Boden09] BODEN, A., and G. AVRAM. Bridging knowledge distribution: the role of knowledge brokers in distributed software development teams. In Proceedings of the 2009 ICSE Workshop on Cooperative and Human Aspects on Software Engineering, 2009.

[Booch03] BOOCH, G., and A.W. BROWN. Collaborative development environments.

Global Software and IT: A Guide to Distributed Development, Projects, and Outsourcing, First Edition. Christof Ebert.
© 2012 the Institute of Electrical and Electronics Engineers, Inc. Published 2012 by John Wiley & Sons, Inc.

In Advances in Computers, Vol. 59, Academic Press, 2003.

[Calefato09] CALEFATO, F., D. GENDARMI, and F. LANUBILE. Embedding social networking information into jazz to foster group awareness within distributed teams. In Proceedings of the 2nd International Workshop on Social Software Engineering and Applications (SoSEA'09), 2009, pp. 23–28.

[Carmel01] CARMEL, E., and R. AGARWAL. Tactical approaches for alleviating distance in global software development. IEEE Software, Vol. 18, No. 2, pp. 22–29, 2001.

[Carmel99] CARMEL, E. Global Software Teams. Prentice Hall, Upper Saddle River, NJ, 1999.

[Cataldo06] CATALDO, M., et al. Siemens Global Studio Project: experiences adopting an integrated GSD infrastructure. In IEEE International Conference on Global Software Engineering, 2006.

[Cataldo06] CATALDO, M., P.A. WAGSTROM, J.D. HERBSLEB, and K.M. CARLEY. Identification of coordination requirements: Implications for the design of collaboration and awareness tools. In Proceedings of Computer-Supported Cooperative Work, November 4–8, 2006.

[Cheng04] CHENG, L., C. de SOUZA, S. HUPFER, J. PATTERSON, and S. ROSS. Building Collaboration into IDEs. ACM Queue, Vol. 1, No. 9, 2004.

[SEI11] SEI: CMMI: Guidelines for Process Integration and Product Improvement, 3rd ed. Addison-Wesley, Boston, 2011. Available at: http://www.sei.cmu.edu/cmmi/tools/cmmiv1-3/. Accessed January 6, 2011.

[Clements03] CLEMENTS, P., F. BACHMANN, L. BASS, D. GARLAN, J. IVERS, R. LITTLE, R. NORD, and J. STAFFORD. Documenting Software Architectures Views and Beyond, Addison Wesley, 2003.

[COBIT05] IT Governance Institute. CobiT 4.0. IT Governance Institute, Rolling Meadows, IL, 2005. Available at http://www.isaca.org/Content/NavigationMenu/Members_and_Leaders/COBIT6/Obtain_COBIT/Obtain_COBIT.htm. Accessed January 6, 2011.

[Conway68] CONWAY, M. E. How do committees invent? Datamation, Vol. 14, No. 4, pp. 28–31, 1968.

[Corbett04] CORBETT, M.F. The Outsourcing Revolution: Why It Makes Sense and How to Do It Right. Kaplan Business, New York, 2004.

[Cramton05] CRAMTON, C.D., and S.S. WEBBER. Relationships among geographic dispersion, team processes, and effectiveness in software development work teams. Journal of Business Research, Vol. 58, pp. 758–765, 2005.

[Curtis88] CURTIS, B., H. KRASNER, and N. ISCOE. A field study of the software design process for large systems. Comm. ACM, Vol. 31, No. 11, pp. 1268–1287, 1988.

[Damian03a] DAMIAN, D., F. LANUBILE, and H.L. OPPENHEIMER. Addressing the challenges of software industry globalization: the workshop on global software development. In Proceedings of the 25th International Conference on Software Engineering, IEEE Computer Society, Los Alamitos, 2003, pp. 793–794.

[Damian03b] DAMIAN, D., and D. ZOWGHI. Requirements engineering challenges in multi-site software development organizations. Requirements Engineering Journal, vol. 8, pp. 149–160, 2003.

[Damian06] DAMIAN, D., and J. CHISAN. An empirical study of the complex relationships between requirements engineering processes and other processes that lead to payoffs in productivity, quality, and risk management. IEEE Transactions on Software Engineering, Vol. 32, No. 7, pp. 433–453, 2006.

[Damian07] DAMIAN, D., L. G. IZQUIERDO, J. SINGER and I. KWAN. Awareness in the wild: why communication breakdowns occur. In Proc. of Int'l Conf. on Global Software Engineering, pp. 81–90, Washington, DC, USA, 2007.

[Damian08] DAMIAN, D., F. LANUBILE, and T. MALLARDO. On the need for mixed media in distributed requirements negotiations. IEEE Transactions on Software Engineering, Vol. 34, No. 1, 116–132, 2008.

[DeMarco99] DEMARCO, T., and T. LISTER. Peopleware, 2nd ed. Dorset House, New York, 1999.

[Desikan06] DESIKAN, S., and G. RAMESH. Software Testing: Principles and Practices. Pearson Education, 2006.

[Desouza06] DESOUZA, K.C., Y. AWAZU, and P. BALOH. Managing knowledge in global software development efforts: issues and practices. IEEE Software, Vol. 23, No. 5, pp. 30–37, 2006.

[Duke07] Duke University and Booz Allen Hamilton. Next-Generation Offshoring: The Globalization of Innovation. Available at https://offshoring. fuqua.duke.edu/report.jsp, 2007.

[Ebert01a] EBERT, C., and P. DENEVE. Surviving global software development. IEEE Software, Vol. 18, No. 2, pp. 62–69, 2001.

[Ebert01b] EBERT, C. Improving validation activities in a global software development. In Proceedings of the International Conference on Software Engineering 2001. IEEE Computer Society Press, Los Alamitos, CA, 2001.

[Ebert03] EBERT, C., J. DEMAN, and F. SCHELENZ. e-R&D: effectively managing and using R&D knowledge. In Managing Software Engineering Knowledge. Ed. A. AURUM et al. Springer, Berlin, 2003, pp. 339–359.

[Ebert06] EBERT, C. Global Software Engineering. IEEE Ready Note (e-Book), IEEE Computer Society, Los Alamitos, 2006.

[Ebert07a] EBERT, C., and R. DUMKE. Software Measurement. Springer, Heidelberg, New York, 2007.

[Ebert07b] EBERT, C. Open Source Drives Innovation. IEEE Software, Vol. 24, No. 3, pp. 105–109, 2007. Available at http:// csdl.computer.org/dl/mags/so/2007/03/ s3105.pdf.

[Ebert08] EBERT, C., B.K. MURTHY, and N.N. JHA. Managing risks in global software engineering: principles and practices. In IEEE International Conference on Global Software Engineering, 2008, pp. 131–140.

[Ebert10] EBERT, C., F. LANUBILE, R. PRIKLADNICKI, and A. VIZCAINO. Collaborative tools and PLM in distributed software engineering. In IEEE International Conference on Global Software Engineering, 2010.

[EconomistIntelligence11] Doing eBusiness in . . . country ranking on eBusiness readiness. 2011. Available at http:// globaltechforum.eiu.com/index.asp? layout=channelid_6&channelid=6&title= Global+Technology. Accessed January 6, 2011.

[Egloff06] EGLOFF, S., and N. FUCHS. Best Practices in Culture Management. Report of Swisscom IT Services. Zurich, Switzerland, 2006.

[Ehrlich06] EHRLICH, K., and K. CHANG. Leveraging expertise in global software teams: going outside boundaries. In Proceedings of the International Conference on Global Software Engineering, Florianopolis, Brazil, 2006, pp. 149–158.

[Ellis91] ELLIS, C.A., S.J. GIBBS, and G. REIN. Groupware: some issues and experiences. Communications of the ACM, Vol. 34, No. 1, pp. 39–58, 1991.

[Erickson00] ERICKSON, T., and W.A. KELLOGG. Social translucence: an approach to designing systems that support social processes. ACM Transactions on Computer-Human Interaction, Vol. 7, No. 1, 59–83, 2000.

[Fagan76] FAGAN, M.E. Design and code inspections to reduce errors in program development. IBM Systems Journal, Vol. 15, No. 3, 1976.

[Forrester04] Forrester Research Inc. Applying Open Source Processes in Corporate Development Organizations. White Paper, May 20, 2004.

[Fowler06] FOWLER, M., and M. FOEMMEL. Continuous Integration. 2006. Available at http://martinfowler.com/articles/continuousIntegration.html.

[Frost07] FROST, R. Jazz and the Eclipse way of collaboration. IEEE Software, Vol. 24, No. 6, 114–117, 2007.

[Gotel08] GOTEL, O., V. KULKARNI, C. SCHARFF, and L. NEAK. Integration starts on day one in global software development projects. In IEEE International Conference on Global Software Engineering, 2008, pp. 244–248.

[Graves98] GRAVES, T.L., and A. MOCKUS. Inferring change effort from configuration management data. In Metrics 98: Fifth International Symposium on Software Metrics, Bethesda, MD, November 1998, pp. 267–273.

[Gregori09] GREGORI, R. Leading Virtual Teams. Bosch Intern C/HDC3, March 2, 2005.

[Grinter99] GRINTER, R.E., et al. The Geography of Coordination: Dealing with Distance in R&D Work. Proceedings of GROUP'99. ACM Press, New York, 1999, pp. 306–315.

[Gutwin04] GUTWIN, C., R. PENNER, and K. SCHNEIDER. Group awareness in distributed software development. In Proceedings of ACM Conference on Computer-Supported Cooperative Work. New York, 2004, pp. 72–81.

[Herbsleb00] HERBSLEB, J.D., et al. Distance, dependencies, and delay in a global collaboration. In Proceedings of the ACM Conference on Computer-Supported Cooperative Work. ACM Press, New York, 2000, pp. 319–328.

[Herbsleb01] HERBSLEB, J.D., and D. MOITRA. Global software development. IEEE Software, Vol. 18, No. 2, 16–20, 2001.

[Herbsleb03] HERBSLEB, J.D., and A. MOCKUS. An empirical study of speed and communication in globally distributed software development. IEEE Transactions on Software Engineering, Vol. 29, no. 3, pp. 481–494, 2003.

[Herbsleb05] HERBSLEB, J., D. PAULISH, and M. BASS. Global software development at Siemens: experience from nine projects. In Proceedings of the International Conference on Software Engineering, 2005, pp. 524–533.

[Herbsleb99] HERBSLEB, J.D., and R.E. GRINTER. Splitting the organization and integrating the code: Conway's law revisited. In Proceedings on International Conference on Software Engineering. IEEE Computer Society Press, Los Alamitos, CA, 1999.

[Hillegersberg07] HILLEGERSBERG, J.V., and M. HERRERA. Tool support for distributed software development: the past, present, and future of gaps between user requirements and tool functionalities. In Tools for Managing Globally Distributed Software Development (TOMAG 2007). Munich, Germany, 2007.

[Hirschheim06] HIRSCHHEIM, R., A. HEINZL, and J. DIBBERN. Information Systems Outsourcing. Springer, New York, 2006.

[House04] HOUSE, R.J., P.J. HANGES, M. JAVIDAN, P.W. DORFMAN, and V. GUPTA. Culture, Leadership and Organizations: The Globe Study of 62 Societies. Sage Publications, Thousand Oaks, CA, 2004.

[Hsieh99] HSIEH, T.Y., et al. Are You Taking Your Expatriate Seriously? McKinsey Quarterly, 1999.

[Hupfer04] HUPFER, S., L. CHENG, S. ROSS, and J. PATTERSON. Introducing collaboration into an application development environment. In Proceedings of the ACM Conference on Computer Supported Cooperative Work, ACM, New York, 2004, pp. 21–24.

[Hussey08] HUSSEY, J.M., and S.E. HALL. Managing Global Development Risk. Auerbach Publications, FL, 2008.

[IAOP09] Michael Corbett and Associates. The [annual] Strategic Outsourcing Study. 2009. Available at http://www.outsourcingprofessional.org/firmbuilder/. Accessed January 6, 2011.

[IDC07] IDC: The Early Termination of Outsourcing Contracts, 2007. Available at http://www.idc.com/getdoc.jsp?containerId=CA11SO7. Accessed January 6, 2011.

[IEEE90] IEEE Standard 610.12–1990: IEEE Standard Glossary of Software Engineering Terminology. IEEE, New York, 1990.

[IEEE98a] IEEE Standard 830–1998: IEEE Recommended Practice for Software Requirements Specifications. IEEE, New York, 1998.

[IEEE98b] IEEE Standard 1233–1998: IEEE Guide for Developing System Requirement Specifications. IEEE, New York, 1998.

[Illes-Seifert07] ILLES-SEIFERT, T., A. HERRMANN, M. GEISSER, and T. HILDENBRAND. The Challenges of Distributed Software Engineering and Requirements Engineering: Results of an Online Survey. In Proceedings of GREW'07, 2007, pp. 55–66.

[ISO04] ISO/IEC TR 15504–9:2004. Information Technology. Software Process Assessment. Vocabulary. ISO/IEC JTC1/SC7 Secretariat, Canada, 2004.

[ITIL07] Office of Government Commerce: ITIL. Several Books on Continual Service Improvement, Service Design, Service Operation, Service Strategy and Service Transition. London: Office of Government Commerce, 2007.

[Jones07] JONES, C. Estimating Software Costs. McGraw Hill, 2007.

[Karlsson00] KARLSSON, E.A., et al. Daily build and feature development in large distributed projects. In Proceedings of the International Conference on Software Engineering. IEEE Computer Society Press, Los Alamitos, CA, 2000, pp. 649–658.

[Karolak02] KAROLAK, D.W. Software Engineering Risk Management, with SERIM Learner First Software Package, Set. Wiley-IEEE Computer Society Press, 2002.

[Karolak98] KAROLAK, D.W. Global Software Development. IEEE Computer Society Press, Los Alamitos, CA, 1998.

[Kirkpatrick83] KIRKPATRICK, S., C.D. GELLAT, Jr., and M.P. VECCHI. Optimization by simulated annealing. Science, Vol. 220, pp. 671–680, 1983.

[Kitchenham04] KITCHENHAM, B.A., T. DYBA, and M. JORGENSEN: Evidence-based Software Engineering. Proceedings. 26th International Conference on Software Engineering, 2004.

[Krishna04] KRISHNA, S., S. SAHAY, and G. WALSHAM. Managing cross-cultural issues in global software outsourcing. Communications of the ACM, Vol. 47, No. 4, pp. 62–66, 2004.

[Kuipers03] KUIPERS, T., and A. van DEURSEN. Source-based software risk assessment. In International Conference on Software Maintenance, Washington, DC, 2003.

[Kuipers07] KUIPERS, T., J. VISSER, and G. DE VRIES. Monitoring the Quality of Outsourced Software. In Tools for Managing Globally Distributed Software Development (TOMAG 2007), Munich, Germany, 2007.

[Lacity09] LACITY, M.C., S.A. KHAN, and L.P. WILLCOCKS. A review of the IT outsourcing literature: Insights for practice. Journal of Strategic Information Systems, Vol. 18, pp. 130–146, 2009.

[Lanubile03] LANUBILE, F., T. MALLARDO, and F. CALEFATO. Tool support for geographically dispersed inspection teams. Software Process: Improvement and Practice, Vol. 8, No. 4, pp. 217–231, 2003.

[Lawrence01] LAWRENCE, B., K. WIEGERS, and C. EBERT. The top risks of requirements engineering. IEEE Software, Vol. 18, No. 6, pp. 62–63, 2001.

[Louridas06] LOURIDAS, P. Using wikis in software development. IEEE Software, Vol. 23, No. 2, pp. 88–91, 2006.

[Lyu95] LYU, M.R. Handbook of Software Reliability Engineering. McGraw-Hill, New York, 1995.

[McConnell03] MCCONNELL, S. Professional Software Development. Addison-Wesley, Boston, 2003.

[McConnell98] MCCONNELL, S. Software Project Survival Guide. Microsoft Press, Redmont, 1998.

[McKinsey08] GOEL, A., N. MOUSSAVI, and V.N. SRIVATSAN: Time to rethink offshoring? McKinsey Quarterly, Sept. 2008.

[Metropolis53] METROPOLIS, N., A. ROSENBLUTH, M. ROSENBLUTH, A. TELLER, and E. TELLER. Equation of state calculations by fast computing machines. Journal of Chemical Physics, Vol. 21, pp. 1087–1092, 1953.

[Midha97] MIDHA, A.K. Software configuration management for the 21st century. Bell Labs Technical Journal, Vol. 2, No. 1, Winter 1997.

[Mikulovic06] MIKULOVIC, V., M. HEISS, and J.D. HERBSLEB. Practices and supporting structures for mature inquiry culture in distributed software development projects. In International Conference on Global Software Engineering, 2006.

[Mockus01] MOCKUS, A., and D.M. WEISS. Globalization by chunking: a quantitative approach. IEEE Software, Vol. 18, No. 2, pp. 30–37, 2001.

[Murugesan07] MURUGESAN, S. Understanding web 2.0. IT Professional, Vol. 9, No. 4, pp. 34–41, 2007.

[NASSCOM06]: NASSCOM, BOOZ, Allen & Hamilton: Globalization of Engineering Services, The next frontier for India, August 2006. Available at: http://www.globalservicesmedia.com/News/Home/Nasscom-Sets-$40-Billion-Target-for-India-in-Engineering-Outsourcing-by-2020/21/27/0/general 20070521579. Accessed January 6, 2011.

[Nguyen08] Nguyen, T., T. Wolf, and D. Damian. Global Software Development and Delay: Does Distance Still Matter? In IEEE International Conference on Global Software Engineering, 2008, pp. 45–54.

[O'Hara94] O'HARA-DEVEREAUX, M., and H. JOHANSEN. Global Work: Bridging Distance, Culture and Time. Jossey_Bass, San Francisco, CA, 1994.

[OI05] Offshore Insights: Captive offshore development centres: how do we obtain the desired value? In Offshore Insights Market Report Series, Vol. 3, No. 3, March 2005.

[Olson00] OLSON, G.M., and J.S. OLSON. Distance matters. Human-Computer Interaction, Vol. 15, pp. 139–178, 2000.

[O'Sullivan09] O'SULLIVAN, B. Making sense of revision-control systems. Communications of the ACM, Vol. 52, No. 9, pp. 56–62, 2009.

[Palmisano09] PALMISANO, S.J. The Globally Integrated Enterprise. Available at http://www.ibm.com/ibm/governmentalprograms/samforeignaffairs.pdf. Accessed January 6, 2011.

[Parnas72] PARNAS, D.L. On the criteria to be used in decomposing systems into modules. Communica-tions of the ACM, Vol. 15, No. 12, pp. 1053–1058, 1972.

[Parnas85] PARNAS, D.L., P.C. CLEMENTS, and D.M. WEISS. The modular structure of complex systems. IEEE Transactions on Software Engineering, SE-11, pp. 259–266, March 1985.

[Paulish02] PAULISH, D. Architecture-Centric Software Project Management: A Practical Guide, Addison-Wesley, Boston, 2002.

[Perry98] PERRY, D.E., et al. Parallel changes in large scale software development: an observational case study. In Proceedings of International Conference on Software Engineering. IEEE Computer Society Press, Los Alamitos, CA, 1998, pp. 251–260.

[Phalnikar09] PHALNIKAR, R., V.S. DESHPANDE, and S.D. JOSHI. Applying agile principles for distributed software development. In International Conference on Advanced Computer Control, 2009, pp. 535–539.

[PMI01] A Guide to the Project Management Body of Knowledge. Project Management Institute, 2001.

[Prikladnicki08] PRIKLADNICKI, R., M. CRISTAL, D. WILDT: Usage of scrum practices within a global company. In Proceedings of the IEEE International Conference on Global Software Engineering, pp. 222–226, IEEE, Washington, DC, 2008.

[Ramesh06] RAMESH, G., and R. BHATTIPROLU. Software Maintenance–Effective Practices for Geographically Distributed Teams. Tata McGraw Hill, 2006.

[Ramesh09] RAMESH, G. Managing Global Software Projects: How to Lead Geographically Distributed Teams, Manage Processes and Use Quality Models. Tata McGraw Hill, 2009.

[Ramesh10] RAMESH, G., and M. RAMESH. The ACE of Soft Skills: Attitude, Communication and Etiquette for Survival and Success. Pearson Education, 2010.

[Rivard08] RIVARD, S., and B.A. AUBERT. Information Technology Outsourcing. ME Sharpe, New York, 2008.

[Rottmann06] ROTTMANN, J., and M. LACITY. Proven practices for effectively offshoring IT work. Sloan Management Review, Vol. 47, No. 3, pp. 56–63, 2006.

[Royce98] ROYCE, W. Software Project Management. Addison-Wesley, Reading, MA, 1998.

[Rus02] RUS, I., and M. LINDVALL. Knowledge management in software engineering. IEEE Software, Vol. 19, No. 3, pp. 26–38, 2002.

[Sangwan07] SANGWAN, R., M. BASS, N. MULLICK, D. PAULISH, and J. KAZMEIER. Global Software Development Handbook. Auerbach, 2007.

[Schwaber01] SCHWABER, K., and M. BEEDLE. Agile Software Development with Scrum. Prentice Hall, 2001.

[Schwaber04] SCHWABER, K. Agile Project Management with Scrum. Microsoft Press, Redmond, WA, 2004.

[Sengupta06] SENGUPTA, B., S. CHANDRA, and V. SINHA. A research agenda for distributed software development. In International Conference on Software Engineering, 2006, pp. 731–740.

[Silva06] SILVA, EE. de S., et al. Modeling, analysis, measurement and experimentation with the Tan gram-II Integrated Environment. In International Conference on Performance Evaluation Methodologies and Tools, Vol. 180, 2006, pp. 1–10.

[Sinha06] SINHA, V., B. SENGUPTA, and S. CHANDRA, Enabling collaboration in distributed requirements management. IEEE Software, Vol. 23, No. 5, pp. 52–61, 2006.

[Sureshchandra08] SURESHCHANDRA, K., and J. SHRINIVASAVADHANI. Adopting Agile in Distributed Development. In IEEE International Conference on Global Software Engineering, 2008, pp. 217–221.

[SWEBOK11] Guide to the Software Engineering Body of Knowledge (SWEBOK). Prospective Standard ISO TR 19759, 2011. Available at http://www.swebok.org. Accessed January 6, 2011.

[USA07] U.S. Committee on Science and Technology. Hearing Charter: The Globalization of R&D and Innovation, June 12, 2007.

[Whitehead07] WHITEHEAD, J. Collaboration in software engineering: a roadmap. In International Conference on Software Engineering. IEEE Computer Society, Washington, DC, 2007, pp. 214–225.

[Worldbank11] World Bank: Doing Business 2011—Making a Difference for Entrepreneurs. Available at http://www.doingbusiness.org/reports/doing-business/doing-business-2011. Accessed January 6, 2011.

[Zencke04] ZENCKE, P. Communication in Software Development. Unpublished conference report. SAP AG, Germany, 2004. Available at http://science.house.gov/Publications/hearings_markups_details.aspx?NewsID=1926 http://www.idc.com/getdoc.jsp?containerId=CA11SO7. Accessed January 6, 2011.

[Zhou10] ZHOU, M., and A. MOCKUS. Developer fluency: achieving true mastery in software projects. In ACM SIGSOFT/FSE, Santa Fe, NM, November 7–11, 2010. Available at http://mockus.org/papers/fluency.pdf.

FURTHER INFORMATION

Global Software and IT

ASPRAY, W., F. MAYADAS, and M.Y. VARDI, eds. Globalization and Offshoring of Software: A Report of the ACM Job Migration Task Force, Association for Computing Machinery, 2006, (http://www.acm.org/globalizationreport/). *Description*: This report summarizes recent trends in migration of software related roles and functions with increasing globalization. Aside from looking into specific profiles and regional trends (mostly with a U.S. perspective, though), it also indicates that global software engineering and IT creates new jobs onshore, something that several studies already highlighted.

IEEE Software, Vol. 18, No. 2, April/May 2001, and Vol. 23, No. 4, September/October 2006. *Description*: IEEE Software (http://www.computer.org/portal/site/software/) is the global journal for the leading software practitioner, available in print and online. It publishes many articles on global software engineering and best practices. The two mentioned issues from 2001 and 2006 are collections of several articles on best practices in global software engineering.

RIVARD, S., and B. A. AUBERT. Information Technology Outsourcing. ME Sharpe, New York, 2008. *Description*: Reference book on IT outsourcing. Many concrete case studies are described in readable and clear language. It specifically covers the broad topic of supplier agreement management, negotiations, risk management, and so on. Unfortunately, software product development falls short in this book. There are two case studies from IT outsourcing from the United Kingdom and South Africa.

SANGWAN, R., M. BASS, N. MULLICK, D. PAULISH, and J. KAZMEIER. Global Software Development Handbook, Auerbach, 2007. *Description*: As the title suggests, this book is a good reference to global software development and global software engineering. It provides useful insights in team building, code structure, distributed validation, and architecture.

THONDAVADI, N., and G. ALBERT. Offshore Outsourcing: Path to New Efficiencies in IT and Business Processes. Authorhouse, 2004. *Description*: This book looks primarily to the business case of global software engineering and IT. Different IT offshoring formats are described with clear focus on activities in India (where the authors draw their experiences). The profound introduction of a GE manager from India underlines the huge potential of global development and IT offshoring.

TIWANA, A. Beyond the black box: knowledge overlaps in software outsourcing. IEEE Software, Vol. 21, No. 5, pp. 51–58, 2004. *Description*: A very practical article looking toward how to evaluate outsourcing scenarios. The underlying studies stem from interviews with IT project managers. The embedded checklists for supplier selection and supplier management are very helpful if you embark on outsourcing.

General Offshoring, Rightshoring, and Outsourcing

BHATTACHARYA, A., and H. ZABLIT. Taking R&D Global. The Boston Consulting Group. August 2009. Available at http://www.bcg.com/documents/file25452.pdf. Description: Overview on global R&D strategies and how they are implemented. This article is easy to read and provides some useful examples from different industries. It is not software- or IT-related.

CORBETT, M. F. The Outsourcing Revolution: Why It Makes Sense and How to Do It Right. Dearborn Trade, 2004. Description: The reference book for outsourcing. It covers the entire bandwidth of outsourcing domains (i.e., not only IT or software), specifically business process outsourcing, and offers a balanced view of what to expect and how to calculate cost. Many concrete hints and guidelines help in operationally managing and succeeding in outsourcing.

ROUX, D. and J. R. WENTWORTH. Laborgistics: A New Strategy for Management. Economica, 2004. Description: This book portrays outsourcing and offshoring differently from most other literature and, certainly, published opinions. The authors envisage the future of outsourcing (again not dedicated to IT and software domains) as a continuously renewing combination and integration of people and technology. Starting from partnerships and alliances, a whole set of new formats of collaboration and industry relationships beyond outsourcing is described.

Locations and Countries

http://www.cia.gov/cia/publications/factbook/geos/xx.html. Description: The CIA fact book with continuously updated information on each country of the world. The first entry point if you are researching a country.

http://www.doingbusiness.org/reports/doing-business/doing-business-2011. Description: The World Bank provides on an annual report on doing business in countries, regions, and cities around the world. The report provides the latest evolutions, some business indicators, and much information on the sub-national level.

http://www.wto.org/english/docs_e/docs_e.htm. Description: The annual world trade report of the World Trade Organization (WTO). This summary increasingly looks at outsourcing and the numbers behind it.

http://globaltechforum.eiu.com/index.asp?layout=channelid_6&channelid=6&title=Global+Technology. Description: Doing eBusiness in… provides world-wide country descriptions and a ranking on their eBusiness readiness.

HOUSE, R. J., P. J. HANGES, M. JAVIDAN, P. W. DORFMAN, and V. GUPTA. Culture, Leadership and Organizations: The Globe Study of 62 Societies. Sage Publications, Thousand Oaks, CA, 2004. Description: This report has looked over many years into 62 societies or what we often call "cultures" across the world and investigated the beliefs, values, and major paradigms driving those societies. It is a great work to get insight into why certain societies behave as they do and how to cope with opposed society explanatory factors, such as time or trust.

International Conferences

The IEEE-sponsored International Conference on Global Software Engineering is fully devoted toward improving the state of practice in global software engineering and IT by bringing together researchers and practitioners from universities and industries. It is organized on an annual basis. Details: http://www.icgse.org

The Outsourcing World Summit is the annual event of the International Association of Outsourcing Professionals. This conference is based on a simple premise: that outsourcing can be successful only when all participants—customers, providers, and consultants alike—come together to break through the myths, misunderstandings, and occasional missteps that come with change of this magnitude. Details: http://www.outsourcing professional.org

Internet Resources and Newsletters

Articles, literature, and news on outsourcing:
http://www.outsourcing-journal.com/
http://www.outsourcing-books.com/

Newsletters with outsourcing events and news specifically for IT and global software engineering:
http://www.globalservicesmedia.com/News
http://www.outsourcing-alert.com
http://www.outsourcing-news.com
http://www.blogsource.org/
http://www.offshore-outsourcing.com/
http://www.outsourcing-events.com

News, events, and information on organizational change management:
http://www.vector.com/change

Index

Global Software and IT: A Guide to Distributed Development, Projects, and Outsourcing, First Edition. Christof Ebert.
© 2012 the Institute of Electrical and Electronics Engineers, Inc. Published 2012 by John Wiley & Sons, Inc.

Printed and bound by CPI Group (UK) Ltd, Croydon, CR0 4YY

27/10/2024

14580257-0005